PENGUIN
ARKANA

THE SACRED ...

Diana Brueton studied Art at the University of Essex and the Birmingham School of Art. She has worked as a teacher and for the BBC and is the author of *Many Moons*, a study of the myths and lore surrounding the moon. As well as being features editor for *Kindred Spirit* magazine she is a registered art therapist working for the NHS and for the Bristol Cancer Help Centre.

Anand Chetan read English at Selwyn College, Cambridge. He has travelled extensively and lived for several years in the Osho International Commune. He is a furniture maker with a workshop on Dartmoor.

The Sacred Yew

ANAND CHETAN AND
DIANA BRUETON

ARKANA
PENGUIN BOOKS

ARKANA

Published by the Penguin Group
Penguin Books Ltd, 27 Wrights Lane, London w8 5tz, England
Penguin Books USA Inc., 375 Hudson Street, New York, New York 10014, USA
Penguin Books Australia Ltd, Ringwood, Victoria, Australia
Penguin Books Canada Ltd, 10 Alcorn Avenue, Toronto, Ontario, Canada m4v 3b2
Penguin Books (NZ) Ltd, 182–190 Wairau Road, Auckland 10, New Zealand

Penguin Books Ltd, Registered Offices: Harmondsworth, Middlesex, England

First published 1994
3 5 7 9 10 8 6 4 2

Set in 10/13 pt Monophoto Janson
Filmset by Datix International Limited, Bungay, Suffolk
Printed in England by Clays Ltd, St Ives plc

Contents

Illustrations

Picture Credits

1. Photo: Paul Freestone. 2. Courtesy of the Harlington and Hayes Local History Society. 3. Victorian print. 4. *The Saturday Magazine*, 1837. 5. Seventeenth-century woodcut from 'Le Songe de Poliphile' by Beroalde de Verville. 6. Photo: Paul Freestone. 7. Photo: Allen Meredith. 8. Photo: courtesy of The Conservation Foundation. 9. Reproduced from *The Yew-Trees of Great Britain and Ireland*, John Lowe, 1897. 10. Engraving, published 1788. 11. 'Arboretum et Fructicetum Britannicum', J. C. Loudon. 12. *The Gardener's Chronicle*, February 17 1877. 13. Reproduced from Lowe, op. cit. 14. Photo: J. Edward Milner/ACACIA. 15. 1832, private publication. 16. *The Myth of the Goddess*, Anne Baring and Jules Cashford, p. 212. 17. Drawing by H. W. Burgess. 18. Photo: J. Edward Milner/ACACIA. 19. Map by Nigel Andrews of Capricorn Design. 20. Drawing of carved head in the stave church at Hegge, Norway, by Diana Brueton. 21. From *Northern Antiquities*, M. Mallet, 1888. 22. Drawing of section of carved stone from Holy Island, Northumberland, by Diana Brueton. 23. Photo: courtesy of The Conservation Foundation. 24. Baring and Cashford, op. cit., p. 223. 25. *The Mabin of the Mabinogion*, M. O. Morgan, frontispiece. 26. Ibid., p. 71. 27. Baring and Cashford, op. cit., p. 497. 28. Photo: Paul Greenwood. 29. *Brailey's History of Surrey*, E. W. Brailey, 1846. 30. Photo of Green Man at Lydia Bridge, South Brent, Devon, by Anand Chetan. 31. Drawing of section of the Gosforth Cross by Diana Brueton. 32. Photo: Diana Brueton. 33. Old English woodcut. 34. German woodcut. 35. Print made by R. E. Hollingsbee from original glass plate negative.

Foreword

What magic is there in the ancient yew trees! What is it in them that fires our vision and fills the soul with mystery, touching ageless history?

We associate our yew trees with our churchyards. There we constantly find them gracing the church and spreading their great arms among the graves. And many people may tacitly assume that the 'old folk' planted yews in churchyards. But no! The great yew trees can be 2,000 years old, or 3,000, or, in some cases, they may reach 4,000 years or more, and our churches were mostly built less than 1,000 years ago. The yews came first, planted on sacred sites known to the Druids. The later church builders were sensitive to the holy places and knew where to build their churches. So let us awaken to the wonder of the yews, planted long before the churches were built, and linked with ancient pre-Christian ritual and mystery.

What a marvel is the ancient yew! It is claimed that the great yew could be absolutely immortal. Grasp what it is doing. The central complex of bole and trunk often seems like a number of trees flowing into each other to make an entity of incredible strength. Then the branches around the central trunk dip down and reroot themselves so that, as a virtually new tree, they may send out further branches. Thus, theoretically at least, the process can go on till the ringed complex covers a great area.

Our imagination is fired by this tree. Once we have 'seen' a yew tree, then it becomes fascinating to study the complex bole and see how the streams of energy flow along its ribs. Our imaginative vision can merge with the wondrous structure. Theoretically, the yew tree could be ageless and never die, the central trunk like a compact pillar of immense strength.

Alas that through ignorance and indifference many great trees in our churchyards have been destroyed as inconvenient. But they are sacred trees, and it is vital that we recover this knowledge. Preserving the great yews is a duty that we owe to our forebears, to the history of our countryside and to those who come after us.

Allen Meredith has done tremendous work in arousing interest in the preservation of these magnificent trees. His tireless campaign is awakening many people, and once the vision has touched us and our eyes have been opened to the significance of these wonderful trees, then we must realize that this heritage has got to be saved.

What is vital is to awaken consciousness of this phenomenon and love for 'creatures' of beauty. The surviving trees must be classified and guarded against damage, and any destruction of ancient yews must be made illegal.

The saving of the yews will fire imagination and enthusiasm and so awaken many people to the excitement of working creatively with living nature. Allen Meredith has launched more than an interest. It is a veritable crusade to save the yew trees.

Sir George Trevelyan

Acknowledgements

The authors and Allen Meredith would like to thank the many parishioners, churchwardens and vicars who have sent information about the ancient yew at their particular church, and the very many people who have corresponded with Allen about particular trees over the years.

Special thanks are also due to the following, who have generously given their time and support:

Bill Bowen
Reg Wheeler
Libby Ketchum at the Conservation Foundation
Dorothy Smith
Sir George Trevelyan
The staff at *Country Living* magazine
Andy Morton
The National Library of Wales, Aberystwyth, whose staff have been very helpful; similarly the Bodleian Library, Oxford, and other county librarians and archivists
John Andrew
Percy Morgan
Jan Fry
Brian Meredith
Rod Wilson, photographer
Annie and Spot
Katie and Edwin
Jerry Elloy of the Church Commissioners

ACKNOWLEDGEMENTS

John and Mary Brueton
Oliver Rackham, Corpus Christi College, Cambridge
P. R. Kitson, University of Birmingham
Russell Ball, Tree Officer
Gunnar Hannson
Philip T. Sherwood (Hayes and Harlington Local History Society)

Allen would especially like to record his thanks to David Bellamy and Robert Hardy, who he says 'listened to the story I had to tell', and to Alan Mitchell, 'who persevered with me in the beginning'.

Authors' Note

Allen Meredith's work has had extensive coverage in the media over recent years, including on BBC TV's *Country File* and Channel 4's *Spirit of the Trees*. This book is the result of a lengthy collaboration with Allen and is based largely on his research and on conversations with him. He has been closely involved with every stage of its writing.

Introduction
A Man for All Seasons –
A Heritage for All Reasons

This book is about a tree and a man.

The tree, or rather trees, in question are yews, *Taxus baccata*, and some have been growing where they stand for at least 5,000 years. The man, Allen Meredith, has given much of his life, come rain or shine, to increase the knowledge of his species about the yew.

'Dedication' is a word which springs to mind, but in the case of Allen it would be the wrong one to use, for the word has connotations of duty or even penance. Allen's life has become a joyous pilgrimage into the facts which surround the yew. This tree is the Tree of Death, being poisonous and standing as so many of them do at the gate of the churchyard; but it is also the Tree of Life, for if allowed to grow it appears to be almost immortal and is now known to contain the power to help or at least stave off the effects of cancer.

Sir James George Frazer's *Golden Bough*, first published in 1922, reminds us of the legend of the Lake of Nemi in Italy. Sanctuary of Diana Nemorensis, or Diana of the Wood, it was home to a priest-king who enjoyed the favours of the Lady and the bounty of her lake and forest; an enviable and precarious position, for anyone who murdered him took on his cloak of office.

As people moved across and around Europe in the wake of the melting ice sheets of the last glaciation, they moved through or came upon landscapes covered with deciduous trees. Forests of lime, hornbeam, beech, oak, elm, alder and ash stood in their way, obscured their view ahead and provided them with all they required.

The technology of polished stone was the first that allowed them to fell the forest giants, feeding the nutrient-rich leaves to their stock and eventually clearing the way for pastures and for crops.

One tree had always stood out in all this, with its coral-red fruits in summer and its dark green leaves in winter: the yew. Though used for longbows, its regenerative powers and the poisonous nature of its leaves and seeds denied its use for other things. So, many were spared the axe and grew to gnarled old age – patriarchs of a fast disappearing forest, things of wonder, mystery and imagination. They became special meeting places where decisions were taken, secrets shared, a place of reverence and worship, for the sacred tree could kill or cure.

This book reveals for the first time the secrets of that tree which still welcomes the dead at many a lych-gate and now, thanks to modern science, offers hope to many who could die young from cancer.

This feast of knowledge is thanks to the tenacity of Allen Meredith, who has given his life to interpret what *Taxus baccata* is telling him.

Read this book with care and then join the work not only to save the ancient yews of Europe but what is left of the old-growth forests of the world. For without the blessings of Diana Nemorensis the world upon which we all depend will surely die.

Thank you for caring.

David Bellamy
Bedburn, 1994

CHAPTER I

The Tree of Life

Let this Tree of Life be the tree of hope for all of us.

ALLEN MEREDITH

To write a book about a single species of tree is an unusual enough undertaking to require some explanation. As far as the yew tree is concerned, it has been attempted before, once in America, and in Britain three times in the last 100 years. Although this book will survey ground covered in those other works, its main source and inspiration come from a very different quarter: the visions, dreams and psychic intuition of one very remarkable man, Allen Meredith. For the last two decades he has devoted his time and his energy to a cause that he holds dearer than anything else: the location and preservation of the few hundred remaining ancient yew trees. This book is a celebration of a magnificent tree and a record of the researches and discoveries of those years.

From the mid-1970s onward Allen became both preoccupied by the significance of the yew tree and appalled at its plight. Before the Second World War there were about 1,000 sites with yews aged over 1,000 years in Britain;[1] by the mid-1970s this number had shrunk by about half. Information from a series of dreams flooded into his consciousness, until Allen realized that he needed help in publicizing the yew's great significance. He decided to approach people who might help with this daunting task. One of them was the botanist and conservationist David Bellamy, who appreciated the importance of Allen's work and generously arranged for his own organization, the Conservation Foundation, to provide support. He also warned Allen that if his work was to gain the acceptance which alone would produce practical help for the trees, research and data would be needed to convince the sceptical. Allen's work was also given great support by Robert Hardy, the actor and expert on the longbow. Allen says: 'I turned up on his doorstep, dishevelled from camping out, and he listened to what I had to say about the yew trees.'

Allen's research falls into two parts. First there is the fieldwork and the subsequent scientific conclusions drawn from it. Secondly there are customs and traditions associated with the tree, and myths and religious practices stemming from it, which are evidence of the yew's earlier importance. Allen believes this information contains evidence of a truth completely lost in the modern world, perhaps only preserved in a degenerate and incomplete form by later prehistoric peoples such as the Celts. It is nevertheless a truth of critical importance to us at the present time. The yew tree has a unique spiritual significance; Allen calls it the watcher, the guardian of the planet.

Obviously this is not a truth that we expect to be cheerfully accepted straight away, but we feel it is important to put our cards on the table. When Allen talks of the yew tree as the Tree of Life or the Tree of the Cross, many people feel they have heard something close to the mark, however much their rational mind recoils at the idea. From time to time this book will dwell in the uncomfortable space between those two poles. This is necessary because Allen, unavoidably, finds himself there much of the time. The driving force of his work is the truth of his inner world. It fuels his research, his battles with planning authorities and his attempts to bring awareness to communities that within their midst is a yew tree, the oldest living thing on the planet and a link with their own origins.

So this is a book primarily about a sacred tree. It does consider botany and the various ways in which a yew is rather unusual. It is not easy, for instance, to study the life cycle when a single tree flourishing today may have been a sapling in prehistory. Natural history, however, is really a side issue. And, although the yew has played a major part in the great formal gardens of Europe and in landscape design, there is little of this, or of topiary, here.

Allen Meredith with the yew at Totteridge

During the seventeenth and eighteenth centuries there was a bizarre obsession with pruning and clipping the yew into all manner of fantastic shapes and designs. John Evelyn, the diarist, who also wrote *Sylva – a Discourse on Trees*, claimed 'without vanitie' the credit for introducing yew 'into fashion whether in hedges, or pyramids, cones, spires, bowls or what other shapes'. 'I do againe,' he said, 'name the yew for hedges, preferably for beauty and a stiff defence, to any plant that I have ever seen.' (Evelyn's own yew hedge was sorely tested as 'a stiff defence' by one of his own house guests. He lived at Deptford not far from the Royal Dockyards and for this reason entertained Peter the Great of Russia, who came to Britain to find out how to set up his own navy. Peter liked to amuse himself by sitting in a wheelbarrow and having his servant push him at full tilt through Evelyn's hedges. Presumably the diarist could only look on in anguish.)

The poet Alexander Pope had some fun producing a mock-catalogue for the fashionable nurseryman:

An eminent town gardener has arrived at such perfection, that he cuts family pieces of men, women, or children, in trees. Adam and Eve in yew, Adam a little shattered by the fall of the tree of knowledge in the great storm. Eve and the Serpent very flourishing. Saint George in box, his arm scarce long enough, but will be in a condition to stick the dragon by next April. A green dragon of the same with a tail of ground ivy for the present. (NB – These two not to be sold separately.) Divers eminent modern poets in bays, somewhat blighted, to be disposed of a penny-worth. A quickset hog, shot up into a porcupine, by its being forgot a week in rainy weather.[2]

Topiary does provide some insights into the relationship between humanity and nature in the eighteenth century, but ultimately it says more about the species that inflicted the indignities than about the one that endured them. Even the churchyard yew was not immune to these creative attacks, and the tree at Harlington in Middlesex suffered more than most, spending a century looking rather like a dumb-waiter. By the mid-nineteenth century this tree had been allowed to return to normal, and it is flourishing now despite severe storm damage in 1959.

In a strictly botanical sense the yew is an unusual tree and a very old species. Unlike most conifers it is dioecious – that is, there are male trees and female trees. Normally conifers are monoecious; the male stamen and the female ovule are on the same tree. The male yew tree has tiny cones which in spring bear the pollen. The slightest breeze produces clouds of pollen, so much in fact that, despite the relative scarcity of the tree, its atmospheric pollen count is among the highest in the United Kingdom. The flower eventually fertilized by this pollen is a small fleshy disc with a single ovule in the centre; from this grows the familiar red, berry-like aril that contains the seed. Birds feed on the berries and spread the seeds.

In the northern temperate zone, yew is found from Ireland to the Caucasus, in northern Iran, the mountains of North Africa and the Himalayas. In Britain it is one of the few truly native trees – that is, one of the thirty-five or so species that re-established themselves as the glaciers of the last Ice Age retreated and before the sea-level rose and breached the land bridge that joined Britain to continental Europe. All the other species growing naturally in Britain now, about 600 of them, have been introduced since then by human activity. Along with the yew the only other conifers in that group of native trees are the juniper and Scots pine. In Ireland the only native conifers are the yew and the juniper.

Conifers were the first trees, emerging during the Carboniferous period 350 million years ago, at least 100 million years before the angiosperm plants such as beech and oak appeared. The earliest record of the yew is a fossil of *Paleotaxus rediviva*, 200 million years old. *Taxus jurassica* fossils, about 140 million years old, contain the recognizable characteristics of the modern *Taxus baccata*. *Taxus grandis*, almost a million years old, is virtually indistinguishable from the modern tree.

As a species, then, yew is immensely old and successful. It was also probably a far more dominant species before the last Ice Age than it has been since. Peat bogs have provided ample evidence to suggest this, both in pollen counts and in fossilized yew trunks. A large part of the yew's success must lie in its extraordinary ability to regenerate itself. Left undisturbed for millennia, the branches root in the earth, producing widening circles of new trees and forming what must have appeared to early peoples as vast natural cathedrals – the sacred groves. Remaining green throughout the long winter, these sanctuaries were both the place for and the object of the earliest human impulses to worship. Allen believes that when our prehistoric ancestors built sacred sites such as Stonehenge and the nearby Woodhenge, constructed from concentric circles of posts, the circular design was determined at least in part by a desire to re-create the yew grove.

The longbow, too, has only a brief mention in this book. There are enough glowing accounts of that period of English history elsewhere. Allen is not much interested in an academic point such as whether the churchyard yew was planted to provide wood for longbows used at Agincourt. He is far more interested in the plight of yew woods like the one at Whatley in Somerset, where the trees certainly were pollarded for bow staves centuries ago but are now covered by a thick coat of limestone dust from the nearby quarry that threatens their survival.

One man's private vision of a sacred tree would be of little import by itself if Allen had not succeeded in convincing the mainstream of scientific opinion of the truth of one particular claim. Until recently the accepted scientific wisdom on the age of yew trees was that they lived to a maximum of around 800 years. Allen, working alone, and with no scientific training, has now proved to the satisfaction of leading botanists that many yews are thousands of years old. The story of this piece of scientific investigation is told in a later chapter, and like all good detective work it involved a lot of legwork, too. Allen has visited hundreds of trees, a good number by bicycle.

He has also been chipping away at another seemingly unassailable 'fact', this time a historical one. Along with 1066 and the Battle of Hastings, the other item everybody remembers from medieval history is that the Magna Carta was signed at Runnymede. 'Not so,' declares Allen. He says the ceremony must have taken place beneath the ancient yew at Ankerwyke, a small island in the river Thames

Engrav'd by James Wigley in Peppings Court Fleet-Street, LONDON.

The Harlington yew fared worse than most during the
eighteenth-century topiary craze

Taxus baccata

a short distance from the designated site at Runnymede now dignified as the birthplace of liberty and civil rights. Not that he particularly wants the tourist buses that now flock to the mock-Greek temple on Cooper's Hill to be redirected to this still remote and tranquil island.

The yew at Ankerwyke is now threatened by nearby development schemes. Allen knows as well as anybody that in such circumstances even a Tree Preservation Order is a worthless piece of paper; the cost of paying the fine is simply built into the contractor's price for clearing the site. The best protection for his beloved tree is if its place in national history is acknowledged. Allen argues his case tenaciously, and the evidence will be considered later in depth, but he is probably right. King John was a feudal baron under threat in a society where older symbols would still have held powerful sway. It is very likely that he would have encamped under a tree which was, even then, immensely old and which would have bestowed on him an aura of authority. In tribal society the tree was *axis mundi*: the centre of the tribe's territory and a source of temporal power and spiritual authority. This belief was also part of a cosmology found throughout ancient cultures; the tree at the centre was the hub of the wheel of the earth, spreading its roots into the underworld and its branches into the heavens, and linking all three planes of existence together.

Allen's work with trees began in the mid-1970s, when he was to be found tramping the country lanes of Oxfordshire, pushing acorns into the soil of the hedgerows as he went. Then, as now, a private passion grew into a public crusade. Over a three-year period forty local schools joined the campaign, and Allen paid a firm to make metal badges to distribute to the children who helped him. He had left school at fifteen with no qualifications and then joined the Royal Green Jackets. He served with the United Nations in Cyprus. When he returned to civilian life he considered a career in professional football and had a trial with Oxford United. He later spent time 'living wild' in a wood, and he now sees this period as part of the preparation for his work, which grew out of the series of dreams that occurred over months, halted, then began again and have continued intermittently ever since.

There is one other very early incident in his life that may have contributed to the course it has taken. At the age of six weeks he underwent surgery for a digestive problem and 'died'. The surgeon pronounced him dead and left the operating theatre, but later the family priest detected signs of life, and he was revived. In adults the near-death experience seems to bring about a radical change of balance and perspective in the individual's life, but of course there is no way of knowing how it affects an infant.

Before the dreams Allen had no interest in yews. 'To me,' he says, 'like everyone else, the yew was just a bush in a churchyard. I think I realized that the dreams were some kind of message. All I know is that there was obviously something I had to do. I still have to do it.' The dreams began to alert him to the fact that the ancient yews were dying from neglect and indifference, because no one was aware of their great age. Astonishingly the dreams also brought warnings that the survival of the ancient trees is linked to our own survival. Allen says:

The yew tree is the most sacred thing on this earth, here for some very special reason. If we don't recognize why the yew is here, then I don't think we will survive. What I dreaded was going off this planet without telling people about yew trees: that they are the most important species on earth – including human beings.

The yew tree is part and parcel of each one of us. We evolved from the yew in a sense. It is obviously a divinity; the neolithic people would have seen that. Generation after generation has seen these things living on; that is why the ancient yew tree is so important.

While Allen is also concerned with more general environmental issues, his whole effort and work are to preserve and raise awareness of the ancient yews. If one of these trees is lost, something is gone from the planet which cannot be replaced by just planting a sapling. A being and a focus of ancient wisdom have gone too, and the human race and the planet are more than just diminished by the loss – they are endangered. According to Allen: 'There are holy trees, sacred trees, still existing all over the world, but not that many. The most sacred of all trees, the holy of holies, were called in ancient language the *deva daru*.' In the Himalayas this tree may originally have been the deodar – God's tree, the lost origin of countless myths and the true Tree of Life. 'As all life is precious, all life starts from the source,' Allen says. 'The Tree of Life is our guardian and may be our only hope. There are very few *deva darus* left in the world. I know of one very special one which may become a symbol of hope to come – if we recognize this tree.'

CHAPTER 2

'The Man Who Has Almost Become a Yew Tree'

Everybody must discover the yew for themselves.

ALLEN MEREDITH

Researching yew trees sounds like the stuff of down-to-earth, pains-taking scientific investigation. It necessitates dating them, tracing their history and extracting data. The gradual gathering of information on yew trees has certainly had its share of such work; but for Allen this has been very much the second step in the way he has come to understand their importance. What he knows about yews, and what he has spent years validating, has come to him through dreams, intuition and what he calls just 'knowing'. This is hardly the stuff of which science is made, yet frequently his 'knowing' has subsequently been proved correct.

In 1974 Allen chanced to visit Broadwell in Gloucestershire, to give a talk to some children about bird-watching, and during the visit the yew tree in the churchyard was pointed out to him. He was told that the tree was 200 years old. Allen instantly 'knew' that this was not right, and that the tree was very much older. This knowledge, he says, came completely out of the blue.

He would probably have forgotten all about this experience but for a series of dreams which began about a year after the visit to Broadwell. These dreams gradually led him to understand the significance of the yew.

In one of the first dreams, Allen saw a group of people sitting in a circle. They wore long gowns with hoods which hid their faces. He was not admitted into the circle, but as he approached it he was told to look for the 'Tree of the Cross'. He says: 'Somebody indicated a cross to me, and a tree. Somehow I knew it was a yew tree, although I don't know how. It was called by another name which I don't remember, but I knew it was yew.' In another dream from around the same time, he saw the witch-like face of an old woman, and knew that it was death. He dreamt that he was repeating over and over again to the hag a series of words which meant 'Go away, I don't believe in you. I don't believe in death.' He was still shouting the strange words as he awoke. He felt that this dream, too, was connected with yew: 'The yew tree doesn't believe in death, in the sense that it is a continuation, it can exist for ever.'

Many other such dreams followed. In the one which most impressed him he was given a word, and, he says: 'That one word was the whole reason why I'm doing this work. That word remains unspoken. It's up to individuals to discover the word themselves.'

These powerful dreams spilled over into Allen's waking life, and indeed propelled it into a completely new course. He felt compelled to look for the 'Tree of the Cross' which he had been told of in the first dream. For a long time he thought he was looking for something like a tree in the shape of a cross, perhaps with cross-shaped branches. 'I was clumsily trying to interpret what the dream was saying. We humans tend to see things in black and white.' He felt he had to gather information on yew trees, but at this stage it was purely to deepen his own understanding rather than to spread it to other people. Allen was deeply concerned with protecting the yews right from the start, but at first he thought that the trees would be more endangered if other people knew of their significance. 'I didn't want to tell anyone about their great age, or reveal the information,' he says, 'in order to protect them.'

During the 1970s Allen started his work of compiling a list of the most ancient yews. He initially based this on the work of Vaughan Cornish, whose book *The Churchyard Yew and Immortality*, published in 1946, gave him a lead. He wrote hundreds of letters to anyone who he thought might be able to give him up-to-date information about particular trees, and travelled the country by bike to visit tree

This 1837 engraving of the yew at Dibden shows it smothered by ivy. The tree was blown down soon after

after tree that he had read or heard about. Through doing this he began to realize that many of the trees he hoped to find had vanished. Some had been blown down in storms, but they had mostly been felled, out of ignorance; people seeing the hollow trunks and apparently lifeless wood had assumed they were dead and cut them down for the sake of safety. It is likely that the vast majority of these trees were needlessly felled. The need to preserve the remaining trees, which Allen had felt since the beginning, became increasingly apparent. We now know that of approximately 1,000 sites where ancient yews grew which still existed between the wars, only about 500 such sites remain intact today.

Allen had also known, since at least his visit to Broadwell, that the yews were far more ancient than people were remotely aware of. At this time it was generally accepted by the academic world that there were no British trees which could live more than a few hundred years, certainly not into the thousands. W.J. Bean's *Trees and Shrubs Hardy in the British Isles*, for instance, which has long been the acknowledged text on such matters, says that the yew's maximum life-span is 800 years. The 1983 *Encyclopaedia Britannica* also dismisses any idea that the yew could live for thousands of years by saying that the notion was 'based on the fusion of close-growing trunks, none of which is more than 250 years old'. It is therefore hardly surprising that he initially met with a good deal of scepticism: 'When I mentioned to people that trees like this were a thousand years old or more, no one really wanted to know.'

Allen spent an enormous amount of time checking the information that had come to him through dreams and intuition. He studied intensively, using reference libraries to check the most diverse sources, ranging from Victorian botanists to biblical scholars. He unearthed church records and estate inventories, and sent letters to find more information from record offices, archives, libraries and museums. In so doing he realized more fully the depth of misunderstanding about the trees. For instance, archaeologists whom he approached at one of the country's leading museums were totally dismissive of his suggestion that yews still standing might have been there since Saxon times. He recalls:

I was banging my head against a brick wall wherever I went. I knew that what I was saying was the truth, but people wouldn't listen. They'd ask how I knew, and I'd say, 'I just know.' They won't listen unless you can provide the supporting evidence. You have to understand that, not being academic or qualified in any way, I couldn't make my judgements that way. Also, being fairly ignorant, I couldn't translate a lot of the things that were coming to me – and I still can't.

Allen's research, which still continues, has therefore been carried out not to satisfy himself about the truth of what he has come to know, but to give his argument the weight it needs to be accepted by scientists and scholars. 'I knew people wouldn't believe it all,' he says. Gaining people's acceptance of the yews' great age has been important simply in order to gain recognition, and hence much-needed protection, for them.

He gradually began to see that he would have to start making his work public:

When I first began I felt it was right not to tell anyone where the yew trees were, that it was enough just that I knew myself. Over a few years it dawned on me that I might be gone off the earth without having told anyone. So in the early 1980s I did tell one or two people. I felt pretty bad about it, and wondered if it was the right way to go. I wanted to stop everything connected with the yews. I felt as if my life was threatened because I'd been revealing things. I don't feel that now; I've accepted my fate. I knew what had to be done and have accepted it as the right way to go. My main aim is to get ancient yews protected.

In 1980 Allen saw a letter in a magazine from Alan Mitchell, one of the country's leading tree experts, and got in touch with him. Now in his seventies, Alan Mitchell used to work for the Forestry Commission. His passion for trees developed from boyhood, when he would note the measurements of trees alongside engine numbers and bird-spotting notes in a notebook as he sat on the bus. Some years later he found himself again spotting interesting trees, and his notes grew into the Tree Register of the British Isles, now a registered charity. It contains records of 93,000 trees of 1,730 species and 1,200 varieties. Alan Mitchell was initially highly sceptical of Allen's findings, but was persuaded by the evidence which Allen was able to present to him. He now supports Allen's ideas about yews' great age: 'We've now more or less agreed that these trees can be more than 4,000 years old. In fact, there appears to be no theoretical end to this tree, no reason for it to die.' Alan Mitchell's support has been invaluable in corroborating Allen's work and in challenging 'accepted knowledge'. Allen has also received great help and encouragement from other yew enthusiasts, such as Bill Bowen of Bath University.

If Allen was to be able to bring yew trees to the public's attention, and to get his understanding of what he had learned generally accepted, he needed just this kind of backing. He decided to write to David Bellamy, setting out his findings, and in 1983 he approached the botanist after a lecture. David Bellamy says: 'I immediately realized that Allen Meredith knew what he was talking about.' He, too, believed that this was an important cause which could not be ignored: 'We are destroying our heritage. A yew tree is just as important as Durham Cathedral, and a hell of a sight older.'

It was David Bellamy in particular who encouraged Allen to do as much research as he could to back up his case, and also he who dubbed Allen 'the man who has almost become a yew tree'. He told Allen that, while he believed him, a lot of people would not, and he should do much more work to prove his case. According to Allen:

My initial attitude was, well, that's their problem, I know I'm right, I'm content with that. But David Bellamy also said, 'Don't you think other people should be given a chance to know?' So that's why I did something which was alien to my character, which is to study or research, going through books and records. I didn't want to do it, but it needed doing and getting across. I felt people needed to be given a chance to discover for themselves whether it's true or a load of rubbish. I only know from what's been given to me on a personal basis.

Allen also elicited the help of Robert Hardy, who as well as being one of Britain's leading actors is an expert on the yew longbow and military history. His book on the history of the longbow prompted Allen's approach to him. 'This extraordinary man got in touch and pointed out that the yew is the oldest living thing in the country,' comments Robert Hardy. 'I decided to lend what help I could. These trees need tender loving care.' Robert Hardy's support has helped bring the yew trees to the attention of a great many people.

The work really moved into the public arena in 1988, when David Bellamy presented Allen's work to the Conservation Foundation in London. A campaign started to take shape, and *Country Living* magazine published an article in its first issue, asking for people to send in details of ancient yews. The public response was enormous; the article had tapped into a rich vein of local knowledge, half-

remembered stories and people's deep curiosity about these enig-
matic trees. The media have since then been increasingly interested
in yew trees and the campaign. Every mention in newspapers or on
television or the radio brings letters to the Conservation Foundation
detailing more trees, or making comments such as these:

Yews are probably the most magical and mystical tree in these islands, and
certainly the oldest.

I have always felt something really mysterious and secret about yew trees,
since a child.

I find yew trees weird, to say the least . . . the yew would seem to be God above
trees, dark and aloof, 'other' to us, not of our cycle, or rather transcending it. It
is an ever-present watcher. I think of the ancient yew of Fortingall, there when
the megaliths were planted, the later Roman forts, the much later church, and
it knowing all the time, being aware of something we can only feel.

In 1990 the Conservation Foundation compiled a data base of
yews. It lists all the ancient yews which are known of at present, and
is being updated all the time as more trees and more information
become known. The significance of yew trees was publicly under-
lined when in 1992 the Conservation Foundation chose to launch its
'green Magna Carta' underneath a yew, the ancient yew tree at
Ankerwyke. The new Magna Carta aims to give the right of survival
to all flora and fauna on the earth and to protect all wild spaces.

Allen has sometimes found the intensity of his work hard to bear,
and has on occasion thought of giving it up. He has twice even tried
abandoning it. The first time was in 1984, when for a while he gave
all his notes away for someone else to take care of. The second
attempt, in 1985, ultimately led him deeper into the work. He
decided to spend some time living wild in a wood in a Welsh valley,
where he built himself a shelter and lived for three months, initially
surviving on whatever food he could find, such as crab apples and
sloes. He did this, he explains, because he needed to forget about the
yew trees and spend some time away from any pressures. However,
the experience did not turn out quite as he expected:

When I first went to the valley I took a small tent with me. It was getting dark when I pitched it, and I didn't see what was around me. I wanted to get away from the yew trees and everything. When I woke up in the morning there was a yew tree just a few yards away from the tent. I hadn't seen it when I set the tent up, and there it was looking at me! That changed things again; I accepted then that this was the way it was meant to be.

During this time in Wales it became clear to Allen that the Tree of the Cross which he had spent so long looking for was in fact the yew tree itself. Again, this realization came to him through a moment of recognition, rather than through academic research. He was talking about the cross with a friend when, as he says:

I realized in that instant. That was it! That was what the dream was telling me: it's not the cross, it's the tree itself. The yew tree is the cross, and the cross is the yew tree. It's very important, because the cross symbolizes immortality. The yew represents the beginning of life and the end of life, and the continuation. It represents the Resurrection because it can live for ever. The idea of the cross came from the yew tree. It's so obvious. The idea of Christianity emerged from the yew tree.

Proving the age of yews was just the first stage of what Allen really wished to show. He wanted to demonstrate that the yew has been of major spiritual significance to humanity from the earliest of times, and that it is only in the most recent times that we have, at our peril, fallen out of touch with it. To people who doubt that the yew was once so important spiritually, he says: 'Read all the ancient writings.' Certainly his evidence for dating yews, which is outlined later, is now widely accepted.

Allen's main message is that the World Tree, or the Tree of Life, is actually the yew. He explains:

I think people are becoming aware of the Tree of Life again. Over time it became looked on as a myth, a symbolic thing like Yggdrasil, but it is an actual living tree. The yew tree was the first tree on earth, it predated humans by millions of years. The tree is part of us; we grew from the tree; it was our food, our water, our shelter, our home, our medicine. The trees, the guardians of the planet, are still here, though they number very few and despite our destruction, giving human life hope. It is we who have grown away from the tree, from the ancient wisdom, but the tree is still here. Protect it, care for it, as it has cared for us.

Evolution of woman from a tree. Seventeenth-century woodcut

CHAPTER 3

Regeneration

Root and branch shall change places, and the newness of the thing shall pass as a miracle.

PROPHECIES OF MERLIN

Allen's contentions about the significance of the yew and the important role it has played in spirituality, religion and mythology rest on claims of the tree's longevity. It has been said that there is no reason why the yew should ever die, barring acts of God or man. Why, though, should the yew be more likely to grow to a great age than other kinds of tree? The answer lies in the way it grows and reproduces itself. It can do this through its fruit, but as it ages it also develops the power of regeneration. What appears to be a hollow, decaying wreck of a tree may be in the process of putting forth new life, for it is just when it reaches this state that a yew can support and renew itself by a variety of methods.

One way in which this happens is that an aerial root grows down from a branch, or put another way, a branch slowly grows towards the ground and finally embeds itself there, then grows into a new tree. This takes place over centuries, and, so long as there is no human interference, new trees will grow around the original one. They will form a complete grove. This, says Allen, is why when people used to talk about a grove they were actually talking about one tree, not a mass of separate ones. 'There's the tree in the centre, then the circle of trees, but they're really all one and the same tree. And this process can continue and continue.' Sadly there do not seem to be any fully established examples left on the planet today, but there are plenty of references to them, and the beginnings of yew groves can be seen in places such as Great Yews, Druid's Grove and Newlands Corner.

An important distinction needs to be drawn between churchyard and 'wild' yews. Unfortunately only a very few ancient yews now survive in the wild. One reason for there being so few examples of yews spreading via groves is that the vast majority of surviving yews which would be old enough to start this process are in churchyards, where they are likely to have been considerably interfered with over time. Many have had branches chopped off here and there, for reasons of safety or just for the sake of tidiness, and this will have prevented their spread. While the aerial root may eventually grow into a new tree, its basic function is to support the spreading limbs and the original trunk.

There are times when the human desire for tidiness in the churchyard is little short of vandalism. It is possible to walk around some churchyard yews and count up to a dozen sawn-off branches where the yew has made repeated efforts to root itself. Without these additional natural supports the tree is far more vulnerable to losing its crown or larger limbs, or even to being uprooted, in high winds. Ironically people will in time feel the need to attempt a poor imitation of this by calling a tree surgeon to fit chains and braces. The yew at South Brent in Devon, for example, has had several large branches chopped off which might well have eventually embedded themselves in the ground. This has no doubt been done out of the best of intentions, to stop them from growing into the nearby graves.

Growth by spreading outwards to form a grove is not the yew's only method of regeneration. Over the centuries the tree's root system will gradually pull the tree outwards; the heart-wood is then exposed to the elements and is likely to rot away. This happens to most yews whose girth is over about 30 feet in circumference, and it is rare to find one much larger which has not split in this way. This is not the end of the tree's life, however. In fact, becoming hollow may be part of its survival tactics. Being hollow may make it more flexible and better able to resist high winds. Some people have even gone so far as to suggest that the yew, and other trees such as the oak which also become hollow, may be 'hurrying to become hollow'.

The hollow trunk can also serve another purpose. Just as a branch may put down an aerial root at some distance from the trunk, so an aerial root may appear within the hollow trunk, thus regenerating the tree from the inside out. The formation of an aerial root inside the trunk is considered unusual by many tree 'authorities', but a quick count of trees which are known to be engaged in this process shows that it is not so rare. Examples of aerial roots within hollow trunks include yews at Snoddington Manor, Stanmer, West Tisted, Llanarth, Llanthewy Rytherch, Acton Scott, Bettws Newydd, Kemble, Linton, Lytchett Matravers, Mamhilad, Mid Lavant, Portbury, Druid's Grove and Ankerwyke. These are just the trees which have very obvious signs of such growth; it is likely that other trees are at least beginning the process.

The yew at Linton in Hereford and Worcester, for example, with its central growth, is a dramatic sight. The internal stem is now about 7 feet in circumference, giving a strong feeling of a tree within a tree. This young offspring tree could itself be about 300 years old.

This, then, is another way in which a yew could be immortal. The Revd Bree, who contributed to Loudon's great botanical work *Arboretum et Fructicetum Britannicum* in 1842, commented: 'A yew tree ... could remain there for as long as the world continued.'

A further way in which the yew can ensure its continuation and regrowth is by encasing its old 'dead' wood in a sheath of new growth. This is more difficult to see than an aerial root, but close inspection of gnarled, hollow trunks will reveal wood of different textures and colours. The new wood grows over and around the old. The yew at Holne in Devon is typical of this process. Yews at Hambledon churchyard in Surrey show the same tendency; all the trees are very hollow, and they are only held together by the sheer strength of the yew wood combined with added new growth. The

The yew at Linton has a large aerial root growing inside the hollow trunk

oldest of these trees at Hambledon is 35 feet in girth; where the heaviest low branch joins the shell of the trunk there is a much thickened slab of solid wood, which has probably grown to strengthen the trunk and so support the crown.

The rot inside trees like this spreads slowly, and is kept pace with by the new skin of fresh strong wood. It has been estimated that this growth will be slower than that on younger trees, but will still be sufficient to produce a solid inch all round approximately every twenty-five years, and this wood will have tremendous tensile strength.

The yew can, therefore, regenerate itself in many different ways. 'This is what makes it the immortal tree,' says Allen. 'This power of regeneration would have been obvious thousands of years ago to

Yew trees at Langley Park with layered branches

ancient people. They would have realized the significance of the yew in that it can resurrect itself from complete decay – death, to all intents. The tree would be beyond life yet it would have the power to regenerate itself.'

A fine example of a tree which has regenerated itself is at Langley Park in Buckinghamshire. The shattered remains of an ancient yew are surrounded by many other yews. The casual observer might not realize that these younger trees, which a sign proclaims to be 800 years old, grew from the ancient one. 'The tree is obviously of a vast age,' says Allen, 'certainly in excess of 1,000 years, and the other yew trees around it have layered from the parent tree. It is only if you look closely that you can see what is happening.' Branches which have grown down and now touch the ground spread out along the surface, until they find a suitable place to embed themselves and put down roots. Sadly in churchyards this process is never allowed to take place. Branches may travel along the ground for some distance before finding a suitable place to root themselves.

The yew at Astbury, still healthy despite its precarious angle

Many yews look as though they should have been dead long ago, yet they continue to live and to put out new growth. At Astbury in Cheshire the hollow yew tree leans at a precarious angle over the path, as it has done for hundreds of years. The yew at Benington in Hertfordshire actually fell over about 100 years ago, and remains in this position, yet it is still vigorously alive and growing. A tree at Iffley in Oxfordshire, whose girth now measures 25 feet, was graphically described over a century ago, in *Chambers's Journal* (1892):

an ancient tree, whose furrowed half-prostrate trunk seems 'weary worn with care', and as we stand beside its bending form, a feeling of sympathy, akin to that which we extend to a fellow-being stooping low with a load of years, rises within us. This yew is considered by competent judges to be the oldest living tree in Britain, and must have been full-grown long before the first Oxford spire was raised in the vale below.

The Iffley tree is only around 1,500 years old, so while certainly older than the spires of Oxford, it is by no means the oldest tree in Britain. A hundred years after the *Chambers's Journal* entry it is still very healthy.

The 1882 *Journal of Forestry* speaks of how yews at Newlands Corner in Surrey regenerated themselves:

Many of them are remarkable as specimens of the rejuvenescence which the yew is capable of displaying beyond all trees, a power to which its long life may be attributed. Several of the trees have grown younger in appearance during the past thirty years, having more life in them, more young wood and bark, more leaf and branch than they had thirty years ago. I remember one very aged tree whose immense hollow trunk had a fire lighted in it by mischievous persons thirty years since, and for several years it stood a mere shell of wood which hardly seemed able to support the head of branches above. At the present time the charred marks of the fire have disappeared and a fresh growth of bark and wood has more than repaired the damage to the tree, it has very much strengthened its trunk and given to the giant a new lease of life with a fresh crop of branches.

The journal also describes how 'ingenious shepherds' of the Downs used to fashion keepsakes such as nut-crackers, cups or snuff-boxes with their pocket-knives, while tending their flocks in the summer months:

They preferred yew wood which they used to obtain by sawing a slab from the living tree. Many of the giants of Yew-tree Vale [Newlands Corner] had lost portions of their bulging trunks at the hands of shepherds in past years, and at the present time the effort of rejuvenescence has almost closed the wound, by a new growth extending from their edges. In some cases the unhealed part of the trunk still exhibits the marks of the tool upon its surface, and there is evidence that the removal of the slab may have occurred several hundred years ago. The power of renewing the growth of bark and wood is greater in the yew than in the apple or oak.

Yew is, then, capable of living virtually indefinitely. This potential is one thing, but hard factual evidence to show that it does actually do this is another. To find out whether yews do in reality live to a great age it is necessary to date the trees as accurately as possible. There are various methods for dating trees, of which the four main ones are:

- tree ring counts;
- radio-carbon dating;
- girth measurements;
- known planting dates.

The first two of these would appear to offer the most concrete, irrefutable evidence. In fact, when it comes to dating yews they both have their drawbacks.

In theory, counting the rings in a tree's trunk should give a ready reckoning of its age, as each ring represents a year's growth. In yews the growth rings are very close together: ten per inch in young trees, and up to 100 per inch in old ones. This implies that yews of over about 20 feet in girth, with 80 to 100 rings per inch in the outer six inches, could be well over 1,000 years old. Although such tightly compacted rings are hard to count with the naked eye, specialized equipment used by dendrochronologists allows it to be done very accurately.

Ring counting has provided some general evidence for dating yews but is obviously not always practical. No one would wish to chop down or remove part of an ancient tree just to prove its age. Even increment boring, a technique whereby a thin plug of wood is extracted from the tree without doing it any great harm, or doing ring counts on trees which have fallen down naturally, will not necessarily give an accurate age.

The main weakness of both ring counting and carbon dating, which involves the removal of a core sample of wood, lies in the nature of the yew tree itself. Yew tends to have a particularly complex growth process, and rings may not always be annual, as the tree can stop growing altogether for periods of time. One reason for this is that the assumption that each year's growth is marked by a ring in the wood is open to question in the case of the yew. The theory of annual tree rings was put forward by the early-nineteenth-century Swiss botanist Augustin de Candolle, but Loudon questioned whether his findings could be applied to yews. Loudon showed that ring counts taken of the trunks of two yews whose ages were already known were horribly inaccurate; the ring counts gave, respectively, 200 and 650 years too few for the two trees.

Factors such as soil conditions and the tree's stage of life may affect its growth unpredictably, and the way that the yew grows makes it extremely difficult to obtain a piece of wood which is as old as the whole tree. Not only do the trees eventually become hollow, but they also grow in a lopsided way, depending on the slope of the ground, humidity, aspect and shade. The side of the tree which faces the sun will, in Britain, grow much faster, thus producing uneven growth.

It is also difficult to generalize from one tree to another. For instance, a yew which blew down in the 1980s in the northernmost part of Argyll was found to have 310 rings in a mere $5\frac{1}{2}$-inch-radius section. But this northern tree growing on a rocky cliff is unlikely to have been representative of southern yews growing in sheltered conditions.

Even more problematic is the choice of which part of a hollow tree to take for measurement. This is a particular conundrum with the oldest trees, the very ones where carbon dating would be most informative, as the old heart-wood gradually rots away, leaving only the much younger outer 'casing'. It is impossible to obtain an accurate sample from a hollow tree.

Several attempts have been made to carbon-date yew trees. This technique has made it possible to date organic remains very precisely. It analyses the isotopes of atmospheric carbon which are absorbed into the wood as it grows, and which are known to break down at a particular rate. This again sounds as though it should be a foolproof technique, but, mainly for the reasons already outlined, the few times the technique has been applied to yew trees the result has been unsatisfactory. For example, a tree which is known from historical evidence to be at least 1,000 years old was carbon-dated at 187 years. Similarly, carbon dating on a hollow tree at Overton on Dee in Clwyd was said by scientists to reveal an age of between 450 and 600 years, but it was also verbally conceded that the yew could be as old as 1,000 years. In such cases, where the oldest wood no longer exists, the living tree does not readily reveal its age to scientific analysis.

This is not to say that ring counting and radio-carbon dating are useless for dating yews. Rather, this apparently hard scientific evidence must be approached with some caution. Certainly these techniques can at least show the tree's minimum age, and even this can be impressive. For instance, a sample of a hollow yew at Loughton in Shropshire with a girth of 30 feet was carbon-dated and given an age of 550 years. Andrew Morton, who has done considerable research into the yews of Shropshire, then estimated that the tree would have taken 400 years or more to grow to where the sample was taken from.[1] This would then give the tree an age of about 1,000 years, and even this is likely to be an underestimate according to evidence from girth measurements and historical documentation.

As carbon dating and dendrochronology are of little help, there remains the promise of historical evidence. To calculate how long yew trees can live and how old some existing trees are it would help greatly if we knew the tree's rate of growth, and it seems reasonable to expect some sort of correlation between growth rate and the tree's girth. Yew trees do not increase in height after reaching maturity, and often lose their crown in high winds, so their girth is a far more reliable guide to growth than is height. A century ago John Lowe, physician to the Prince of Wales and author of what is still the standard work on yews, reached the same conclusion.

'The Life of a Yew, the Length of an Age'

> The lives of three wattles, the life of a hound;
> The lives of three hounds, the life of a steed;
> The lives of three steeds, the life of a man;
> The lives of three eagles, the life of a yew;
> The life of a yew, the length of an age;
> Seven ages from Creation to Doom.
>
> NENNIUS, *Seven Ages*

'Passing on to the question of growth rate in yew trees,' wrote John Lowe, 'we have two methods by which this can be arrived at: By the measurement of trees of known age. [And] By the measurement of increased girth at a fixed point and at stated periods.'[1]

Lowe set about finding as much information about the trees as he could by sending a questionnaire to every parish church in the land. At this point the clarity of theory tumbles into the pitfalls of practice and interpretation. Lowe was clear that he wanted measurements taken at both ground level and three feet from the ground, to minimize error. The first measurement might be unreliable, as in churchyards the ground level is rising, whereas in other situations soil erosion may expose the swelling roots and give an excessive reading. The second measurement, three feet from the ground, might be misleading due to 'knobs and excrescences' on the trunk and to many trunks being covered with young shoots or ivy. Taking both measurements should, he believed, highlight a distorted reading. Even so, Lowe was relying on hundreds of different people armed with tape measures or pieces of string approaching trees across a lawn or through a field of nettles. They might have had time on their hands and pride in their yew tree, or alternatively it might have been raining or a Saturday when they still had a Victorian sermon to write.

Similar problems colour all the historical evidence. There may be a seventeenth-century planting date precisely recorded in a parish register, but we can never be entirely certain that the tree we measure today is the original one. Even if we are certain that we have the correct site, the possibility remains that the tree may have succumbed at some time and been replaced. Lowe's second method – periodic girth measurement – perhaps involves the most frustrating examples, with some oft-measured ancient trees swelling and deflating disconcertingly over the years. However, Allen has now collected such a quantity of information which shows consistent patterns that it cannot be dismissed on these grounds. Among his seventy-odd pre-nineteenth-century planting dates there may be handful that are unreliable, but it cannot be argued that *all* are – especially when the rate of growth deduced from them is so consistent.

Moving on to the known planting dates, probably the most interesting of the very early ones is the yew at Dryburgh Abbey in Scotland. According to records the monks planted it in 1136. In 1837 the only yew of any size there was measured at 12 ft 1 in and at that time considered too small to be the same tree. In 1890, though, Lowe measured the same tree, rather higher up the bole, and recorded its girth as 11 ft 4 in. By 1988 it had grown to only 12 ft 7 in, an increase of girth of only 6 inches in 150 years, and a rate of growth considerably slower than that achieved in the previous 700 years.

To compare rates of growth the girth measurement in inches is divided by the age in years when the measurement was taken. Hence the simple equation for the reading at Dryburgh:

$$\frac{145 \text{ in}}{701 \ (= \ 1837 \ - \ 1136)}$$

produces an average annual growth of 0.21 of an inch per year. In the last 150 years it has managed an increase of only 0.04 of an inch per year. There seems little doubt that this was the tree the monks planted, and that likelihood is supported by the fact that in 1789 the monks planted another tree which, two hundred years later, has a girth of just 3 ft 8 in, an annual average growth of 0.22 of an inch per year.

Many factors must influence the tree's growth: the fertility and balance of the soil, the level of rainfall and whether the site is sheltered or exposed. Damage to branches may cause variations in the growth of the bole. The genetic pattern must be considered, too; as with all other species, some individuals grow larger and more quickly than others. Of the three trees known to have been planted in about 1349 in the south of England in the wake of the Black Death, the annual average growth rate varies no more than one-tenth of an inch, though over a period of nearly 650 years that produces a considerable difference in girth – over 5 feet. In 1509 two yews were planted at Penkridge Hall in Shropshire, in medieval times a head-quarters of the Knights Templar. The taller tree has the lesser girth by nearly 2 feet, but their annual growth rate varies no more than one-twentieth of an inch per year.

Most authorities expect the rate of growth to decline with age, and a glance at the chronological table shows this to be the case; the younger trees have a higher average girth increase. The trees at Hurstbourne Tarrant in Hampshire provide an interesting illustration of this. At the end of the seventeenth century the parish register records 'the ewtree near to the vicar's garden planted by Sam. Hoskins, vicar, in ye year 1693'. Half a century later there is another entry: 'Memorandum Oct. 10th 1741. There was a yew tree planted in the churchyard pretty near the outward rails. By the order and at the expense of James Wilkins M.A. Vicar of this Parish.' By 1897 the older tree had grown, at an average annual increase of 0.49 of an inch, to 8 ft 4 in, and the second tree, younger by half a century, at the rate of 0.55 of an inch to 7 ft 3 in. By a strange coincidence, when Allen measured both trees in 1981 they had reached the same girth measurement: 9 ft 5 in. The rate of growth in both trees had slowed considerably in the eighty-four years up to Allen's visit, the older tree managing only 0.15 of an inch increase per year and the younger 0.3 of an inch.

Another well-documented tree from the eighteenth century is the one at Woodbury in Devon. Its early history was singular enough to merit a lengthy entry in the parish register:

Memorandum 1775, that a yew or palm tree, grew in ye North side of ye tower, seven foot down from ye top, and was Dug out and Planted, in ye churchyard, ye south side of ye church, in ye same place where was one blown down by ye wind a few years ago. NB The above tree when dug out was 4 feet long and supposed to be nine years growth. Witness our hands this 25th Day of Novr 1775 Jn Snow Hayman, William Channon Churchwardens.

The tree had reached 8 feet by 1983.

It is surprising that the planting dates, coming from so many fallible sources, show such a consistent picture of average growth. As would be expected, the annual growth figure creeps up with the later plantings, but for trees planted in the same period the growth rates are clustered very close together. Of the twenty-seven known trees planted in the eighteenth century, for example, the difference between the slowest and the fastest rate of all but one is less than half an inch per year, and a dozen are within one-tenth of an inch of each other. Seeing that the figures take no account of climate or position, they seem to give a fairly accurate picture.

It might be sensible at this point to pause and draw the most striking conclusion from these figures: the yew, when compared with other species, is a very slow-growing tree. In considering those other species, Alan Mitchell gives, as a very basic rule of thumb, the view that most trees, with a full crown, will increase in girth an inch a year. A tree 8 feet in girth would be around 100 years old, although in close competition with other trees it might take 200 years to reach that girth. If it was partly restricted it could reach this size in about 150 years.

One of the biggest and oldest oaks in the country is the Majesty Oak at Fredville Park in Kent, with a girth in excess of 38 feet. In the first seventy-odd years of this century its girth increased by $4\frac{1}{2}$ feet. Alan Mitchell estimates its age at 380 years, so it probably was not around in 1597 when, a few miles away at Wateringbury, a yew was planted in the churchyard and the event recorded with a dreadful piece of doggerel:

> Friends as you look
> At this yew tree
> Was planted here by me
> On the 2nd of January
> One thousand five hundred
> And ninety-seven
> By Thomas Hood.

Nearly 400 years later the yew has reached a girth of just over 11 feet. In this case, the oak has grown about four times as fast as the yew since the two trees were planted.

In an article in *The Field* magazine Alan Mitchell reviews the longest-lived specimens from other species in the UK.[2] The Bowthorpe Oak in Lincolnshire appears to be the oldest, possibly 600 years. Although the ash grows very fast and dies quickly, he thinks the ash tree at Clapton Court in Somerset might be 500 years old. Beech is similar, 'rarely reaching 300 years and old hulks decay rapidly'. Sessile oaks also grow quickly, and he estimates the one at Cowdray Park in Sussex at around 450 years. His oldest planting date is 1550 for a sweet chestnut at Easter Ross, although he considers the sweet chestnut at Canford School in Dorset probably older. Sycamore and lime, he maintains, 'certainly live for several centuries', and Dr Donald Pigott, Director of Cambridge University's Botanic Garden, believes there are small-leaved limes in the Lake District that are 1,000 years old. Even so, none of these specimens remotely approaches the longevity of the yew. Even the mighty American redwood, *Sequoia giganteum*, growing up to 300 feet high with a girth in excess of 80 feet, is unlikely to match it. Probably the only rival is the ancient bristlecone pine that grows in the semi-arid White Mountains of California and the Great Basin Lake area in Nevada.

As the heart-wood does not rot, the age of these trees can be accurately measured; the oldest still standing is around 4,300 years old.

Mention should be made here of one argument that is sometimes put forward against yews reaching any great age. This is that all yews with large girths are 'multi-stemmed', consisting of several fused saplings. Alan Mitchell says that fusing of trees is so rare that it can be discounted. It would first require a period when the saplings rubbed against each other, wearing away their bark. This would have to be followed by a period of complete stillness for fusion to take place. Nature clearly does not readily provide these conditions. Bill Bowen adds that, even if fusion ever does occur, yews live to such a great age that in a hundred years or so the tree would in any case have become as one, with the same characteristics of growth as a single-stemmed one.

To make the case of the yew's great longevity more fully we must turn to Lowe's second method: the measurement of the girth of a tree at known periods. The planting dates show the slow growth of the youthful tree, and this could be confirmed by increment boring. With the ancient hollow tree there are no such certainties. The yew at Totteridge in Hertfordshire was measured in 1677 at 3 feet from the ground as 26 feet. It was measured twice in the eighteenth century, once in the nineteenth and by Allen twice in the last ten years. It remains at 26 feet. There has been no change in 315 years. It can never be known for how long its girth remained at that figure before 1677. The tree is perfectly healthy in every respect yet appears to have ceased growing.

Another tree where there are a series of measurements taken over more than 300 years is the old churchyard yew at Crowhurst in Sussex. There is a Crowhurst in Surrey, too; it also has a magnificent ancient yew tree, and both will be referred to from time to time. Possibly the first historical reference to the Crowhurst, Sussex, yew is in the Saxon chronicles describing the Battle of Hastings. That section of the south coast has changed dramatically in the last 900 years, and in William the Conqueror's time the Hastings area was a peninsula protected on three sides by water. An inlet to the west, at the site of present-day Bulverhythe, extended almost to Crowhurst.

To the north the estuary of the river Brede extended inland as far as Sedlescombe. William's army waited for Harold in an ideal defensive position, its flanks and rear protected by water, confident that it could only be approached from the north-east. The chroniclers describe the battle: 'Harold gathered a great army and came against them at the ancient apple tree.' Another translation has it: 'Before the Battle of Senlac, King Harold pitches his camp beside the Hoar Apple Tree.'

Now, it is Allen's belief, discussed in more detail later, that the female yew was in past times known as an apple tree, apple being used then as a more general term for red fruit than the specific meaning it has today. The Crowhurst yew is on a hilltop site with commanding views. Even at this period it would have been about a thousand years old, and in autumn – the battle was fought on 14 October – the red berries would have been conspicuous and plentiful. Trees were common landmarks in Saxon times, and the Crowhurst yew with its huge bole and vast evergreen canopy seems a likely candidate. The cultivated apple, by contrast, is rarely ancient, as the wood is very susceptible to insect and fungus attack. As Harold held the manor of Crowhurst, the likelihood is that the hoar apple tree referred to in the chronicles is the yew in Crowhurst churchyard. Local legend has it that William hung a Saxon from the tree for failing to reveal the whereabouts of Harold's army.

The next recording of the tree is dated 1680, when the antiquary and author of *Brief Lives*, John Aubrey, visited the yew and found it 27 feet in girth at 4 feet from the ground. Two nineteenth-century recorders found the tree reduced in girth to 26 ft 7 in in 1879, and it had added only 2 inches by the time Lowe recorded it in 1894. These variations are very frustrating, but in this case the explanation seems clear enough. The Victorians cared for their trees and fussed around them with props, iron hoops and cables that braced heavy branches against the trunk. Left alone, of course, the yew, with its extraordinary regenerative powers, needs none of this, and Allen's advice

The yew at Crowhurst in Sussex, photographed for John Lowe's
Yew-Trees of Great Britain and Ireland of 1897

is almost always to leave the tree alone. However, the Victorians were certainly no more misguided than the modern quackery of the tree surgeons, and their efforts were a good deal less unsightly than the polystyrene foam pumped into the hollow Major Oak in Sherwood Forest. Nevertheless, in 1876 a Mr Papillon bound the trunk with a band of iron. As the tree has two large openings in the bole and is completely hollow, this pressure probably reduced the girth. Mr Papillon must have loved the tree, because he was sensitive enough to feel later that the tree 'appeared uncomfortable' and he had the band loosened. He may be the 'Colonel Papillon' who erected the railings around the tree in 1907. Since that time the girth has increased; Allen found it to be 28 feet in 1982. An increase in girth of one foot in 302 years, though, is small indeed: under four-hundredths of an inch per year.

Another well-documented old yew is the one at Aldworth in Berkshire. A storm in the night in 1976 brought much of the trunk down, but what remains is around 13 feet in girth and has a healthy branch growing from it. Captain Symonds, the royal diarist, visited the tree in 1644 and wrote: 'In the churchyard is an immense yew tree, celebrated far and near for its gigantic dimensions and extreme old age. The trunk of this magnificent old yew, which is said in its prime to have shaded an acre of ground, measures at four feet from the turf, no less than nine yards in circumference.'

Over 100 years later both the *Gentleman's Magazine* and the *History of Compton* described the tree and confirmed the unchanged girth. According to the latter:

It is now going fast to decay, but its branches still ascend to a considerable height, and spread around many yards on every side. Its dimensions and venerable decay, fully corroborate the report that it is coeval with the sacred pile. It does not appear to have increased of late, for, according to Rowe Mores, it measured just over 27 ft in the year 1760.

In 1897 Lowe again recorded the girth at 27 feet and noted that the tree had not grown since 1760. Presumably he was unaware of Symonds's visit. If the girth had not changed in 250 years it must be assumed that the process of decay mentioned in 1760 had continued, for Lowe's correspondent describes the tree as 'now a ruin'. The tree was measured again in both the 1930s and the 1970s and found to be 28 feet. It must be assumed that this sudden increase was due to splitting of the bole that culminated in a major part of the tree crashing down in 1976.

It may be asked why a tree with such a long and well-documented period of decline has not exhibited any of the regenerative processes described earlier. One reason is that the churchyard situation is unconducive to it. Graves are tended, and boughs descending and seeking to root are lopped. Also, hollow trees make an ideal storage place; Lowe records a tree as 'hollow, holding a ton of coal for church purposes'.[3] This must have been commonplace, and nowadays heating oil tanks are often found sited inside the tree. Spades, brooms and churchyard rubbish also end up within the trunk. No new shoots or aerial roots can cope with this. There are nineteenth-century records that describe a tree hollow enough to store a wheelbarrow in. However, such is the tree's capacity to regenerate that today the cavity has disappeared, replaced by a growth of new wood. It may be that the 'demise' of the Aldworth tree in 1976 was simply a more drastic step in the regenerative process.

At Eastham on the Wirral peninsula there is an ancient yew in the churchyard that was first recorded in 1152. At that time the manor of Eastham changed hands and became the property of the abbot and monks of St Werburgh. The villagers of Eastham entreated the new owner 'to have a care of ye olde yew'. In 1898 members of the Royal Archaeological Society visited the village and thought the yew might originally have been planted against the east end of the timber-framed wattle-and-daub church that preceded the Norman building. The tree is hollow with a girth of 21 feet and is flourishing.

The concern of their forebears is still alive among the Eastham villagers today, and a letter to Allen from the church warden, Mr Freeman, stresses: 'Some hundreds of years ago when the tree was handed over to us, an undertaking was given it would be cared for and this has been done up to the present day.' Some years later,

The Selborne yew in 1788, when Gilbert White described it
in his *Natural History of Selborne*

when the Conservation Foundation Yew Tree Campaign was
launched, another proud resident wrote in with details of 'our local,
already famous yew tree'. She, too, was concerned to record how
well the tree had been cared for, mentioning a recent trim by an
arboriculturalist. She also said that Charles Dodgson – better known
as Lewis Carroll, author of *Alice in Wonderland* – took regular walks
out to see the yew when he was canon of Chester Cathedral. The
yew has found its way into the *Guinness Book of Records* as a challenger
for the honour of being the oldest tree in Britain, but in fact it is not
especially old. Allen considers it to be about 1,600 years old, so it
would have been around 760 years when the villagers petitioned the
monks of St Werburgh to take proper care of it.

On 25 January 1990 a terrible gale, equal in intensity to the great
storm of 1987, swept across southern England. At ten past three in the
afternoon it uprooted and flung down the great yew in the church-

yard at Selborne in Hampshire. The tree was 60 feet tall with a massive 25 feet girth of trunk. The crown of the tree was particularly splendid. Bill Bowen believes that the crown was original – that is, it had never lost major branches before, even though the trunk was hollow. Ironically it was this that probably contributed to its downfall, as the sheer weight of foliage formed a fatal barrier to the wind, and the branches had not been able to root themselves into the ground and thus stabilize the tree. The appalled vicar described his church-yard as 'a stormy sea of twisted boughs and dark foliage pierced here and there by a white tombstone like a sinking ship'.

This tree was particularly well documented. It had been measured a dozen times since the mid-eighteenth century, probably because Selborne was the home of Gilbert White, the pioneer naturalist who published his *Natural History of Selborne* in 1789. A stained-glass window inside the church, installed to mark White's bicentenary, shows St Francis preaching to an audience of British birds. The yew tree is clearly depicted in the background. Most of the 150-odd editions of the book published over the years do not include the *Antiquities of Selborne*, which is of more local interest, but it is here that White describes the tree:

In the churchyard of this village is a yew tree whose aspect bespeaks it to be of great age: it seems to have seen several centuries, and is probably coeval with the church, and therefore may be deemed an antiquity: the body is squat, short and thick, and measures twenty-three feet in the girth, supporting an head of suitable extent to its bulk. This is a male tree, which in the spring sheds clouds of dust and fills the atmosphere with its farina.

In 1823 William Cobbett, the radical campaigner for the rural poor, dismounted at Selborne during one of his famous Rural Rides. He found the tree's girth increased by 8 inches since White's time. The vicar in Lowe's day recorded 25 ft 3 in, and Allen in 1981 found it 25 ft 10 in and considered the tree to be around 1,400 years old. In the 200 years from Gilbert White's time it had increased nearly 3 feet at the relatively brisk rate of 0.17 inches per year.

The uprooting of the Selborne tree exposed human remains, and this gave the Hampshire Archaeological Society the opportunity to investigate. As it was planned to re-erect the tree, this required a larger hole, so the excavation was around 10 square yards to a depth of about 2¼ feet. A semicircular patch of undisturbed grey-brown subsoil just off-centre in the trench revealed the site that the yew had occupied in its youth. The earliest burial, dated from pottery sherds as having taken place *c.* 1200–1400, cut into this area. The archaeologists therefore deduced that the burial had taken place when the girth of the tree was about 10 feet. They concluded that 'an age of a thousand years or more therefore seems possible for the Great Yew'; evidence which does not exclude Allen's estimate of 1,400 years.

Indeed, this age would give an annual average girth increase of 0.22 in, which, if anything for a tree of great age, seems rather fast. If the tree were that age, this would give it a planting date of about AD 600. St Birinus began his mission to the West Saxons in 634 and converted King Cynegils the following year. Presumably Christianity reached Selborne relatively soon after. It is Allen's view, in cases like this, that the yew was planted as a symbol of immortality because it was already held in great awe and respect by the local population. The practical business of conversion was rather different from the fond picture that has grown up over the centuries. The arrival of the glad tidings did not magically uproot millennia of religious experience from human consciousness; rather, Christianity was grafted on to, and drew its nourishment from, that older root stock.

Three weeks after the gale the Selborne tree was raised and replanted by a team from a nearby agricultural college. Most of the roots had been severed by the fall, and the entire head of the tree had to be sawn off to facilitate re-erection. Allen was concerned that as many large branches as possible should remain; with no apparent lifeline into the earth, his view was that the branches are 'the tree's main life source and means of continuation'. Early signs were optimistic, and for two years the tree put forth new shoots. These withered, though, in April 1992. Cuttings were taken and have rooted, but Allen believes the great trunk could still spring to life, even after years of being, to all appearances, dead.

At Tandridge in Surrey is an immense tree. Very tall for a yew, it has a girth of 35 feet and a presence that can be felt throughout the churchyard. Allen estimates its age as in excess of 2,500 years. Tandridge provided a very particular piece of dating evidence. The tree is around 25 feet from the church, which has Saxon foundations. In the crypt it is clearly visible that the Saxon builders constructed stone vaulting over the tree's roots. While this shows that the Saxons were respectful of the tree's needs, it convincingly proves that even at that time the tree was fully grown. It was this piece of evidence that finally swayed Alan Mitchell; as he says: 'Roots increase extraordinarily slowly in diameter, and recent studies at Kew show that they taper sharply near the trunk and then extend far, at a nearly uniform size, much smaller than had been thought. Yet 1,000 years ago the Tandridge root was so big it had to be bridged.'

As Allen's data grew, it became clear to him that a pattern was emerging that connected the position of the yew tree in relation to the church with different historical periods. He considers three trees – those at Fortingall, Discoed and Llangernyw – to be over 5,000 years old. These are all male trees sited to the north of the church; to avoid confusion here it is easier to take bearings from the church, although it is clear with pre-Christian sites that the position of the church was carefully chosen with regard to the already existing yew tree.

The yew at Fortingall in Tayside could be the oldest tree in the world and has long been celebrated. Today it appears almost as two separate trees, but both portions are male and from the same root system. Part of the original bole is still visible; a few inches of old trunk protruding through the earth indicate its outline. The larger of the two portions measures 20 ft 6 in in girth and has a great deal of new growth. The other section grows tight against a wall and is estimated at about 18 feet. This was clearly an immense yew which over the centuries has split and separated.

Gilbert White's *Natural History of Selborne* was a compilation of his correspondence with Thomas Pennant and Daines Barrington, both of whom visited the tree at Fortingall. Barrington in his *Philosophical*

The Fortingall yew, possibly the oldest tree in the world

Transactions found it 'not less than 52 ft', while Pennant in his *Tour of Scotland* describes 'the remains of a prodigious yew tree whose ruins measure fifty-six and a half feet in circumference'. He records a conversation with a local resident, Captain Campbell of Glen Lyon, who assured him that as a boy he had often climbed over the connecting part joining the two portions. The *Topographical, Statistical and Historical Gazetteer of Scotland* published in 1841 quotes the then minister of the parish at Fortingall: 'At the commencement of my incumbency 32 years ago there lived in the village of Kirkton a man of the name of Donald Robertson, then upwards of 80 years of age, who declared that when a boy going to school he could hardly enter between the two parts; now a coach and four might pass between them.' It seems, then, that as late as the early eighteenth century the tree was recognizably a vast, though split, whole.

A series of practices and beliefs associated with the Fortingall tree seem to have hastened its deterioration. In 1882 the *Journal of Forestry* recorded:

The great tree in Fortingall churchyard spanned the pathway with its gaping trunk, and the funerals of Highlanders borne to the grave passed through the opening under an archway of overshadowing foliage. It was a common practice for the mourners in funeral processions to gather yew boughs at the gate of the graveyard, and these were borne along and finally held over the coffin and then placed upon it in the grave.

Local legend has it that at Fortingall there was a small Roman camp and that Pontius Pilate was born there, son of a Roman officer, and as a child played beneath the tree, even scratching his initials on it. As the adult Pilate was washing his hands in Jerusalem a good ten years before Claudius's successful invasion of Britain in AD 43, this is best seen as a shrewd piece of marketing by the infant Highlands tourist industry – a test run perhaps for the Loch Ness campaign. It was highly effective, and, particularly in the latter years of the eighteenth century, large quantities of the tree were carried away by souvenir hunters. Dr Patrick Neill, writing in 1833, comments on the 'considerable spoliations that have been committed on the tree' and notes approvingly that 'further depredations have been prevented by means of an iron railing which now surrounds the sacred spot'. The minister at that time attributed the dilapidation of the tree to boys of the village kindling fires at its root.

Altogether the tree endured a century of sustained human vandalism that has robbed us of the sight of it in fuller grandeur. The only recorded tree that could have rivalled it was the 'superannuated eugh' that the seventeenth-century diarist John Evelyn found in Brabourne churchyard in Kent. That measured nearly 60 feet in girth but had vanished, even from local memory, by 1889 when Lowe investigated it.

One legend about Fortingall that may be significant is that it was long regarded as being at the centre of Scotland. A glance at the map does support this, at least as far as the east and west coasts are concerned. This may be significant in viewing the yew at Fortingall as an *axis mundi*. We know from Caesar's account in *The Conquest of Gaul* that the Druids assembled annually in the territory of the Carnautes because this was regarded as the centre of Gaul. Fortingall is an ancient site with a Bronze Age tumulus known as Carn nam

Marbh, the Mound of the Dead. Even as late as the early years of this century a ceremony was being held on this mound on 11 November. A bonfire made up of furze and sticks was lit; people held hands around the blazing fire; and boys ran into the fields with burning faggots. The recent folk memory was that the mound was the site of a plague pit, but it is clearly Bronze Age, and the ceremony has all the essentials of the Celtic Samhain festival.

Samhain, later Hallowe'en, and Christianized as All Saints' or All Souls' Day, was the great festival to mark the beginning of winter. It was also a festival of the dead. The bonfire and the lit brands carried into the fields were a fertility rite impregnating the earth with the seed of the dying sun, so that after a long winter of gestation vegetation would burst forth again in spring. The cattle too were driven through the fires, and people leaped over them. At the time when the life energy of the world was at its lowest ebb, so influences from the otherworld were more powerful, and hence ghosts and evil spirits had to be propitiated. Animals were slaughtered because of lack of winter fodder, and feasting followed. The evergreen yew was a reminder that the current of life, though hidden from view, remained.

Other evidence that points to the pre-Christian past of Fortingall is recorded by Professor Watson, who found a farmhouse opposite the church called Duneaves, meaning 'house of the *nemed*'. *Nemed* or *nemeton* refers to a sacred grove or tree.

At Discoed in Powys most of the trunk of the tree is gone, yet it still measures 37 feet. The churchyard in which it stands is circular, and this in itself is of considerable significance. The circular origins of our churchyards are today mostly lost, but clear examples remain, especially in Wales, and there is also a fine example in Brockenhurst in Hampshire. As the churchyard is the setting for most of our ancient yews, it will help to understand just how that setting has evolved.

It has long been recognized that many of our most ancient parish churches stand on land that is some feet higher than the surrounding area. William Cobbett noticed this on a Rural Ride in the 1820s and assumed it must be due to the great number of interments that have taken place. Oliver Rackham, the modern historian of the British landscape, estimates that the average English country churchyard contains at least 10,000 bodies, so at first consideration the argument has some appeal.[4] Hadrian Allcroft, however, writing before Rackham in the 1920s, considered the matter in more detail than it is necessary to reproduce here, and refuted the theory.[5] A brief calculation with Rackham's 10,000 cadavers should suffice to make his point. Only a reasonably small proportion of them would have been buried in coffins; decayed, they would reduce to around 10 lb in weight individually or about 45 tons in total. One cubic yard of earth weighs about a ton, and an average churchyard covers an area of about 5,000 square yards. To raise that area by three feet would take 5,000 cubic yards of soil, of which our 45 tons of remains, occupying only 45 cubic yards, would be a very small proportion. The mound on which the church stands may well be 5 or 10 feet above the surrounding area, so even if this estimate for the volume of human remains was doubled or quadrupled to accommodate considerations of soil disturbance or whatever other factor, it still remains a poor explanation for the mound. The church itself, while it may have sunk within the crest of the mound, still usually has its floor level some feet above the level of the area outside the churchyard. The only explanation that can be arrived at is that the mounds were raised as burial barrows long before they became Christian graveyards.

The earliest burial sites that are known in Britain are the long barrows erected by the people known to archaeologists as the long-headed Mediterranean people. These barrows were built in the New Stone Age, and while sometimes they were just a simple mound, they usually contained a chamber of wood or stone that enclosed the body. About the time the round-headed Beaker people spread to Britain, probably from the Iberian peninsula in the early Bronze Age, at about 2300 BC, the round barrow appeared. In time the long barrows were no longer constructed, although as with all barrows they continued to be used for secondary interments for centuries afterwards. Although there were various types of round barrow, the circular shape, surrounded with a ditch and bank of earth, remained the constant feature, unchanging for many hundreds of years.

The literature on burial and barrows reveals an immense number of different practices and situations. Often there are surprisingly few bones; sometimes skeletons are disarticulated and the bones arranged in various piles. There are cremations, corpses that have been left on platforms, Parsee fashion, before interment, and some coffin burials within tree trunks. At a later date there were urnfields. Allcroft's conclusion was that 'where everything else is variable there remains constant the predilection for a circular burial place'. The evidence has accumulated over the seventy years since Allcroft's time, but a contemporary archaeologist, Timothy Darvill, examining the subject at length, confirms that 'a major theme to emerge from changes during the later third millennium BC is the development of circular monuments, henges and barrows'.

For Allcroft the sheer difficulty in constructing the superbly symmetrical round barrows in preference to the long mounds that preceded them, coupled to the fact that the custom endured for so long, is evidence of an urgent religious impulse behind their construction. Recent researches into prehistory have thrown much light on what that impulse was. Early people were undoubtedly deeply in tune with the rhythms of the earth and nature, and observed the birth, burgeoning and decay of vegetation with the passing seasons. They perceived the world around them as the mother goddess who had given them birth and would, as part of the cycle of life, receive them back to be reborn, just as the vegetation appears again in spring. What more natural, then, than that they should desire to have their remains interred in the womb-shaped barrow, within the belly of the goddess, to await that time?

It is safe to say that the barrows remaining today can be only an insignificant number of those which must have existed at, say, the arrival of the Romans. Over the centuries those on low ground would have disappeared under the plough, and as Christianity established itself, so the significance of the circular mound would have ebbed away. Even so, within the vicinity of Stonehenge there are over 250 barrows. The Iron Age yields far less burial evidence, but circular cremation urns were often placed under small barrows. Interment in cists – stone chests – was practised, the soil being heaped on top. There were burials in pits, sometimes with rich grave goods, as at Lexden in Essex, where the pit was then covered with a large barrow. By Roman times tombstones appeared on top of barrows, inscribed 'DM' ('Dis manibus' – 'To the spirits of the departed') and 'HSE ...' ('Hic situs est ...' – 'Here lies ...'). Stone sarcophagi and mausoleums appeared, too. Along with cemetery burial, barrows were still in use in pagan Saxon times, and there were often secondary interments in existing barrows.

Allcroft's case is that the arrival of Christianity would not have produced a sudden upheaval in burial practice or an immediate abhorrence for long-established burial sites. The early edicts of the Roman Church emphasized the need merely to sanctify a pagan site rather than uproot it. In AD 530 the Emperor Justinian decreed that the setting up of a cross, the 'truly holy rood', must predate the construction of any church. The early missionaries were concerned mainly with the conversion of kings and chieftains, sometimes achieved by bribery, and the work of instilling Christian doctrine into the mass of the population took decades or centuries. The likely case is that pagan barrows slowly become sanctified and Christian. Prior to the building of a church there may for a long time have been only a cross, or a monk's cell or hermitage, on that site. Until well into medieval times the practice seems to have been that the church was also the dwelling place of the priest; it was indistinguishable from the monastery. Itinerant monks slowly established a tiny cell or hermitage on the site. There are records that many of the early hermitages were in hollow trees that served the monk both as home and shelter and as an early oratory. St Kevin is reputed to have lived alone in a hollow tree for seven years from about AD 510. In the Dee valley near Rhydyglafes a hermit used to live in a hollow yew near a Bronze Age mound.

There is also evidence that yews were planted on the top of

barrows. There is a large barrow called Wormelow's Tump, or St Weonard's Barrow, near Treago, which was recorded by the ninth-century historian Nennius. In 1855 a Thomas Wright recorded 'a decayed yew tree of very considerable antiquity' growing on the mound. All trace of it has now vanished. At Manest Farm in Llanhamlach in Brecon there is a field which is said to be the burial place of St Illtyd, who was in the area around AD 520. It is mentioned several time in *Archaeologia Cambrensis*, which in 1867 reported that 'a large mound stands on the farm, a circle of stones once surrounded this area, though the decayed yew tree still leans over and shades part of the ground'. When Allen visited Manest Farm in 1984 the owner told him that the yew tree had been taken away over fifty years previously.

These are still only glimpses but they do suggest that the yew tree was a feature on the barrow at the beginning of Christianity and probably long before. There are not many trees that grow large enough and survive long enough to become hollow and serve as a dwelling. The oak is a possibility, but the yew is the most likely candidate. As recently as 100 years ago gypsies were living in the hollow churchyard yew at Leeds in Kent. If the early saints lived in hollow yews on ancient burial mounds this may be yet another example of Christianity's conscious integration with the revered totems of the old religion.

A further site which has both an ancient yew and a burial mound is at Cascob in Powys. The church is on a ley-line rediscovered by Alfred Watkins and described in his book *The Old Straight Track*. The church tower is built on the tumulus, and the yew tree, over 25 feet in girth, is west of the church.

At Knowlton in Dorset there is a line of ancient yews alongside Bronze Age circular burial mounds. Within this enclosure there is also a ruined Norman church.

Another curious point needs to be mentioned here. The records of the early church are full of stories of saints planting their staff into the ground and this rooting itself and becoming a tree. St Canna planted his staff at a place called Coychurch; it burst into leaf and had red berries. St Beon's staff rooted into a tree on the Isle of Feringmere, as did St Etheldred's at Stowe in Lincolnshire. St Congar planted his at Congresbury and St Erfyl hers at Llanerfyl; both produced yew trees the remnants of which still exist. St Mochoemog absent-mindedly left his staff in the ground overnight and found it growing in the morning. Likewise the saints Melorus, Treranus and Adhelmus; it is a long list. Probably the best known is Joseph of Arimathea, whom legend has visiting Glastonbury and whose staff grew into the Glastonbury thorn. Similar stories are told about dozens of saints, and while they are clearly an early piece of church propaganda they may have also recorded a ceremony for sanctifying a barrow and rededicating it as a Christian site. The planting of a tree by a holy man or woman had undoubtedly been a sacred act for millennia, and the early missionaries may have found it a ritual that held significance for their congregation.

St Winifrid's church at Gwytherin in Clwyd is a good example of this intermediate period between pagan burial site and Christian churchyard. There are many yews there, including two female trees both over 26 feet in girth which Allen dates at over 2,000 years old. The church and the two ancient trees are on a mound, all aligned on an east–west axis. This is very characteristic of a Celtic site. In the graveyard to the north of the church, and leading directly to the yews, are four standing stones, almost certainly pre-Christian menhirs. The westernmost stone has been Christianized with a Latin inscription added much later, in the fifth or early sixth century AD: 'Vinnemagli fili Sennemagli' ('The stone of Vinnemaglus, son of Sennemaglus'). Both the stones and the yews mark the pagan burial site and are there today, an inextricable part of the Christian graveyard.

As the years passed, the tiny religious cells were replaced with oratories or bedehouses, known in Wales as *bettwys*. The Venerable Bede (*c.* 673–735) recorded going to bless a burial place at the request of a nobleman. In time the first wooden churches followed. From this point on, to complete Allcroft's thesis, the barrow that housed the remains of the first Christians and generations of their pagan forebears began to evolve; over the centuries the church was enlarged, rebuilt and extended, possibly several times, and a tower or spire was added. Allcroft cites the features of graveyards that are immediately recognizable: the sunken path to the door, with the graveyard banked on either side, and the surrounding graveyard wall cut steeply into the bank so that the top of the wall is at the ground level of the graveyard. Changes outside the churchyard, such as fences being replaced, roads straightened and more space being required, would have meant that the original shape of the churchyard was gradually eroded. The original circle at whose centre the church building stood slowly lost its definition, and with the passing centuries of Christianity the significance of the circular form of the burial mound would have faded. The Norman Conquest brought a rectangular churchyard, which Allen has found to be delineated with four yews, one planted at each corner. The practicalities of surveying, landownership and registry would all have been pressures to straighten the boundaries. Slowly in the majority of cases, over the course of a thousand years, the barrow would have wasted, and the circle was lost beyond recognition.

The churchyard at Llanelly in Gwent was clearly circular originally, although it has later rectilinear additions. Here the church, dating from only the twelfth century, is within a circle of ancient yews. Thirteen remain, but the gaps in the circle suggest that there were originally eighteen. The author Vaughan Cornish was told in the 1940s that Penpont, between Brecon and Senny Bridge, has a circle of yews that, while of no great age, replaced a much older circle.

At Llanfihangel-nant-Melan in Powys the church is again ringed by ancient hollow yews. It may be that the circle of yews marked the boundary of the burial mound, or that they are the descendants, layered and rooted from the branches, of an ancient and long-vanished parent that once stood at the summit of the barrow. There is a persistent tradition that at Llanfihangel the church was built within a stone circle, but nothing remains of this except perhaps one large stone, two feet across and four feet in length, that Allen found half-buried at the base of one tree.

All these strands come together at Discoed in Powys. Here there is a circular churchyard, an ancient mound near the church and a tree that Allen considers dates back to the neolithic period. If he is right, then the oldest yews go back to the megalithic culture; they were planted at much the same time, for example, as the extraordinary passage grave at New Grange in Ireland, *c.* 3200 BC, was constructed. Silbury Hill in Wiltshire, the oldest part of the Avebury complex, is about 4,500 years old. Most of the stone circles in Britain, about 900 of them, including Stonehenge, were built between 2600 and 1500 BC, as were the stone rows at Carnac in Brittany. There are at least half a dozen trees existing now that were in their prime at that time and probably a dozen or so more that have been recorded but have now gone.

What we know of that culture is limited, but our understanding of it is growing. It may be that the yews were placed as consciously in the landscape as the huge stones were. Allen believes that the stone circles may have been a representation of the circle of trees of the grove. The archaeologist Sir Arthur Evans believed there had once been a sacred tree at the centre of Stonehenge, and there are several sites where wooden pillars have been planted in circles, such as Woodhenge in Wiltshire and Emain Macha, or Navan Fort, in Ireland, where there was an enormous structure with five pillars of tree trunks and an even larger pillar in the centre.

Over the years Allen has scoured many sources for information, and sometimes old guidebooks and county histories have provided useful clues. In the 1938 edition of *The King's England* he found a description of Ashbrittle in Somerset, which reads: 'In the churchyard an ancient hollow yew grows on a tumulus more ancient still.'[6] This of course was irresistible, and as soon as possible he went there. He found an ancient trunk which over centuries has separated into six portions. There is a central stem, solid and healthy in the middle of the hollow shell, 10 ft 5 in in girth and probably not much older than 400 years. The six outer stems are all quite decayed and slope outwards at the same angle; a casual observer might imagine them to be individual trees, as some have girths of up to 16 feet. Allen is sure they are portions of an original single trunk that probably, when intact, measured around 38 feet. A sketch of the churchyard drawn in 1848 clearly shows both the inner stem and that separation of the trunk had already taken place. Archaeological evidence about the mound is scanty, but it seems certainly Bronze Age. It is oval, around 60 yards in circumference at ground level, aligned east to west, and the tree is in the centre. Locally it is said to be the last resting place of a pre-Roman chief.

In the Ashbrittle churchyard a skeleton was discovered buried on a north–south axis and deemed to be neolithic. Allen spoke to local people, and particularly to Jack Smith and his wife. Mr Smith has worked in the churchyard for many years. The area is rich in local legend, and the church is believed to have been built on a Druid circle. It is said that in the Roman period battles took place in the valley below Ashbrittle, and Roman soldiers had their heads cut off and were buried fifty at a time. That piece of local lore is curious, as it bears witness to a practice of the Celts that is not general knowledge: their reverence for, and fondness for collecting, severed heads. Allen also heard that around 1980 some headless skeletons were uncovered near the yew and quickly reinterred at the church-warden's insistence. This is so neat that it may be embroidery on the established legend, but it is certainly recent enough to be checked. Bill Bowen has also visited Ashbrittle, and he was told that the church was built on seven skulls and that bones found near the mound were stained red, which attests to pagan practice. Another story has it that the yew tree was struck by lightning about 350 years ago.

Fortingall, Discoed and Llangernyw, then, are all massive trees with girths of 34 feet and upwards, male and situated to the north of the church site. This north siting also applies to three of the four trees that Allen considers to be at least 4,000 years old: those at Bettws Newydd in Gwent, Tisbury on the Wiltshire/Dorset border and Linton in Hereford and Worcester. The fourth tree, at Crowhurst in Surrey, has an east–north-east position. Again these are all trees with girths in excess of 31 feet. Hence Allen arrived at the conclusion

The tree at Bettws Newydd has hardly changed since this engraving of 1877

that the northern position was useful evidence, suggestive of a tree dating back to the neolithic period. He is not dogmatic about it; of the twenty-odd yews he has studied on the north side of the burial ground, he considers only three to be neolithic, but he does feel that the north side is the original position of the yew and that it was deliberately planted there, as one of the strongest protections against evil, to guard the souls of the departed. The belief may have been that the souls resided in the tree itself.

In 1926 Mr R.N. Worth, who had investigated long barrows for some years, wrote: 'Interments are conspicuous by their absence on the north side of certain prehistoric long barrows.' It has been a long-held tradition that the north side is the 'dark side', the abode of Satan, the place of demons and evil spirits. It is only in recent centuries that burials have been sited on the north side of church-yards; certainly up to the rise of Puritanism the south side was the

A Victorian gentleman inside the Tisbury yew. The gaping trunk
is now bricked up

customary place, with the north being reserved for a host of social
activities such as fairs, ball games and dancing. In the north wall of
some old churches there was a so-called 'devil door'; there is one at
Chipstead in Surrey, for instance, which interestingly also had a
north-sited ancient yew. At Ashampstead in Berkshire the church
builders in Norman times incorporated an old yew stump into the
north wall.

There is much evidence in folklore of yew as a protective
talisman; even in modern Germany the proverb 'Vor den Eiben
kann kein Zauber bleiben' ('No magic can survive in the presence of
the yews') is still heard. This belief may well have its roots in the
association of the yew with Samhain, the time when evil influences
from the otherworld were abroad.

As well as position, the sex of the tree may also be significant.
Certainly the three oldest trees are male, as are the ones at Bettws

Crowhurst, Surrey. The door was hung during the nineteenth century

Newydd and Crowhurst, but this is obviously too small a sample to draw conclusions from.

Incidentally, the trees at Bettws Newydd and Linton, as well as being among the very oldest in the country, provide two of the finest examples of the regenerative process. The tree at Bettws Newydd has changed little from a sketch of it that appeared in the *Gardener's Chronicle* in February 1877. The accompanying report describes a 'columnar stem of great size, which serves to support and feed the battered and time-riven old shell'. As the sketch shows, the trunk of the tree is not easy to measure, but in 1983 the internal stem was 6 ft 8 in, and the one at Linton is of similar size.

Allen's observation is that trees sited to the east and west of the church are likely to indicate a planting date in the Celtic period. The alignment with the rising and setting sun would have been significant for pagan Celtic society, and trees may have been sited to the east and west of the barrow. The early church would have grown up between them, or perhaps the traditions of sun worship in the old religion still influenced Celtic Christianity. The modern Druid Phillip Carr Gomm describes the west as 'the place of entrance, of beginnings – the receptive, feminine west that faces the east of the dawn ray'. The east is 'the place of the Druid, for it is from the east that the sun rises, from which illumination comes'. At Dartington in Devon the tree has seen both the coming and the passing of the church; it stands to the west of the tower which is all that now remains of the original church; the Victorians built a new one nearer the village.

Of the 400-or-so trees in the Gazetteer (see page 262) only around seventy are aligned east–west along the axis of the nave. A far greater number, more than 150, are to the south and south-west. These are usually Saxon sites; the tree to the south is usually female, while the tree to the south-west is male. A fine example of this is the two trees in the churchyard of St Peter and St Paul at Cudham in Kent. The female tree is hollow and slightly larger, with a girth of 28 ft 8 in. The male tree is forty paces away to the west. In his typewritten notes Allen has recorded a quotation from the *Gentleman's*

Magazine for 1804: 'on the south side of Cudham Church, Kent, are two very large old yew trees, one of them with a door would form a good gypsy's cabin'. Clearly the female tree was hollow even then. Just beneath this Allen has added a handwritten note: 'Charles Darwin lived here for some years.' Momentarily this seemed quite a new side to the life of the eminent Victorian, but it was soon clear that Allen was referring to Cudham itself, not the yew.

Curiously Allen is insistent that the Cudham trees are 1,800 years old, which would give them a planting date in the middle of the period of Roman occupation. This is not as contradictory as it first seems. There were Anglo-Saxons living in Britain at that time, probably mostly serving in the Roman army. 'The distribution of the earliest Anglo-Saxon cemeteries,' according to the *Kingfisher Historical Atlas*, 'makes more sense as the disposition of mercenaries accompanied by their families than as territories seized by sea invaders.' They are located at defensive positions along the east coast and may have served garrisons stationed there. Saxon pirates raided the coast sporadically. Cudham is only a few miles from the Thames estuary. Probably more Saxon mercenaries were recruited soon after the last Roman troops were withdrawn in AD 408. They may well have provided a bridgehead for the later large-scale fifth- and sixth-century Saxon invasions.

Allen believes that his theory of the position of yews could have uses for archaeologists in pinpointing churches that have gone. At Middleton Scriven in Shropshire, for example, standing alone in a field on the opposite side of the road to the present church, there are two ancient yew trees. One male and one female, they both have girths in excess of 25 feet. Their presence, marooned some distance from the existing church, suggests an earlier Saxon building, the exact position of which could be easily found by triangulating a position from the two trees. In fact, local legend at Middleton Scriven has it that there *was* an earlier wooden church that was burnt down.

One more Saxon site needs to be considered here, even though it has neither church nor yew tree. Taplow Court in Buckinghamshire was the Sutton Hoo of its day when it was investigated by Victorian archaeologists in 1883. A large barrow, 15 feet high, stood 30 yards west of the site of a ruined church. Here, indisputably, is a pagan mound within a Christian churchyard, because when the barrow was opened it was found to be the grave of a Saxon warrior, buried with his gold buckles, jewelled studs, drinking horn and arms. These date his burial to about A D 600.

The Taplow Court excavation revealed that the area had been occupied both by British and by Roman British settlements. Secondary interments were also found. Excavations in the church area revealed that the tower had been erected over an ancient fosse or defensive ditch. Originally the site must have been a British settlement defended by earthworks. Pagan Saxons occupied the site and buried a chief there. Slowly the area became Christianized; other bodies were added to the barrow and surrounding ground, so that the church had to be built, when the time arrived, some 30 yards away. What is less well known is that on top of the barrow was an ancient yew. The archaeological report records that it was not less than 21 feet in circumference. Such was the hurry to plunder the contents that had lain undisturbed for over a thousand years that the excavators did not take the trouble to underpin the tree properly; it sank into the barrow, took the form-work with it and injured one of the archaeologists in its path. For a yew of that size the most likely origin is that it was planted by the Saxons when they interred their dead chief.

Allen is the first to admit that the dating of yew trees is a clumsy affair, and his position theory is no hard-and-fast rule but simply another factor to be considered along with the size and condition of the tree. His theory of the position of the tree does influence his view of the yew at Ulcombe in Kent. The tree has a huge bole, 37 ft 6 in at 3 feet from the ground. It is male and to the south-west of the church. There is also a hollow female tree to the south which is only 26 feet in girth. For Allen this is a typical Saxon site. He believes that the smaller, hollow tree is the older of the two, but that neither of them is of really great age; he considers that the larger tree may be 1,200 years old. The churchwarden's accounts for Ulcombe record that in 1722 a Goody Rogers was paid two pence for watering the yew, and a further two pence for similar work the following year. Allen is clearly influenced by the siting of the trees to think a Saxon planting the most likely, particularly as Ulcombe is in the heart of the area colonized by the early Saxon migrants, and the name itself is suggestive of a link with the Norse god Ullr, who was strongly connected with yew trees. He lived in a yew dale and was the god of archers.

For Alan Mitchell, however, a scientist with a lifetime spent in forestry, the massive bole of the male tree at Ulcombe is the more compelling evidence. He considers it 'at least 3,000 years old and probably the oldest tree in the country'. While Allen and Alan Mitchell now agree that yews can live to these immense ages, their methods, and sometimes as in this case their views on individual trees, can differ. Allen's formidable accumulation of historical evidence has highlighted the yew's slow growth and capacity to remain dormant for centuries. As scientist Mitchell generously acknowledges: 'Meredith was absolutely right about their age.' But he remains a scientist when asked about Allen's intuitive or psychic approach: 'I'm interested in the nuts and bolts of it. Meredith dances out of sight with all that stuff.'

CHAPTER 5

Why Are Yews in Churchyards?

Whether the planting of Yews in churchyards hold not its original ancient funerall rites, or as an embleme of resurrection from its perpetual verdure, may admit conjecture.

SIR THOMAS BROWNE, 1658

The question is often asked: why are yews in churchyards? While this may be no more than idle curiosity, it has produced, as the folklorist Jennifer Chandler discovered, some enduring and doggedly held fallacies.[1] She was asked to comment on this question on the BBC Radio 4 programme *Enquire Within* in January 1991 and re-hearsed the popular theories about yews providing bows, preventing cattle from being poisoned and protecting the church. She dismissed these, as her view is that they are no more than 'pieces of antiquarian speculation from the seventeenth and eighteenth centuries which have been accepted into "lore"'. She called them 'old men's fancies' rather than 'old wives' tales' and maintained that their scholarly plausibility, along with the fact that this information is usually learned from respected adults in childhood, explain why these fallacies are still current.

Jennifer Chandler then went on to explain what she felt to be the orthodox view: that the true explanation of the churchyard yew probably lay not in social but in ecclesiastical history. To her surprise, after the programme she received many letters from people who ignored what she had said and simply restated one or other of the popular explanations of the churchyard yew as *fact*, as *common knowledge*, as something they 'had always understood'. Those letters also showed a range of interpretation of the same 'fact': yews were planted in churchyards 'to provide bow-wood' but also 'to prevent people cutting bows'; churchyard yews 'prevented cattle being poisoned' and also 'prevented consecrated ground being desecrated by cattle'.

Bearing in mind, then, the obduracy of hearsay once it has become part of 'common knowledge', these popular opinions as to why the yew grew in churchyards can be looked at in greater detail. They are neatly summarized in an unpublished poem written by the Revd J.G. Copleston, vicar of Offwell in Devon, in the first half of the nineteenth century.[2] His poem also provides evidence that supports Allen's views on the tree's ability to regenerate and is worth looking at in detail. Entitled 'The Decayed but Reviving Churchyard Yew', it is, despite its poetic diction, a deeply felt celebration of the tree in his own churchyard.

In 1832 building work began on Copleston's new vestry, an extension to the chancel, and he felt obliged to be present to ensure that the roots of his beloved tree remained undamaged during the digging of the foundations. During this period of enforced idleness he produced the poem, which neatly relates the early Victorian accepted wisdom as to why yews grow in churchyards:

> Whate'er thy claim to stand in holy ground
> Whether funereal deem'd, and cypress like
> Thou greet'st the mourner well; or else in joy
> The palm tree's substitute, thou gave thy boughs
> A paschal token of Messiah's reign:
> As now my villagers his birth attest
> By festal decorations plucked from thee;
> Or whether green longevity, the winds
> Defying, immortality fore-shews
> And fits thee to adorn the house of God;
> (For who believes the idle tale profane,
> That here thou stood'st in days of piety
> The archer's ready aid for warlike deeds,

THE

DECAYED BUT REVIVING

Churchyard Yew,

OFFWELL, DEVON.

" Yet is thy root sincere, sound as the rock,
A quarry of stout spurs, and knotted fangs,
Which, crook'd into a thousand whimsies, clasp
The stubborn soil and hold thee still erect."——Cowper.

" And this our life, remov'd from public haunt,
Finds tongues in trees, books in the running brooks,
Sermons in stones, and good in every thing."——Shakespeare.

—»»●●●●««—

1832.

Within the sanctuary of the Prince of Peace?)
Whate'er thy right, I recognize it just
And ancient; while each recollection pure
And pleasing, shall to me thy form endear.

The first possibility that Copleston considers is the yew as a symbol of mourning, and he connects it with cypress because that was the tree of mourning in ancient Greece and Rome. Our main experience of yew today is the churchyard yew, either in reality or through literature where 'gloom' and 'dark' are the adjectives usually associated with it. Hence our consciousness is very conditioned to seeing yew as 'funereal'. This impression changes with a visit to one of the few yew groves in open country, such as Kingley Vale or Druid's Grove, where the trees exist within their own silence and power.

Copleston's next possibility is the exact opposite to this. For many hundreds of years in the English Church the yew served as a substitute for the palm and therefore as an emblem of celebration used on Palm Sunday. As far as is known, this customary use of yew has died out in Britain, but the *Encyclopaedia Britannica* of Copleston's day saw this as the most probable reason for yews in churchyards, pointing out that in Catholic countries palms were carried on Palm Sundays and in Britain yew was substituted for the palm.

In 1483 William Caxton published *Directions for Keeping Feasts throughout the Year*, in which is written: 'Wherefore holy Chirche thys daye makyth solemne processyon in mynde of the processyon that Chryst made thys daye. But for encheson [the reason] that we have not olyve that berith greene leafe, algates [always] therefore we take Ewe instede of Palm and Olyve and beren about in processyon and so is this daye callyd Palme Sundaye.'

At Wells Cathedral there is a square within the cloisters with a central yew tree surrounded by gravestones; the area is known as the Palm Churchyard. In east Kent particularly it seems 'yew' and 'palm' were synonymous; Samuel Pegge in *An Alphabet of Kenticisms* published

Frontispiece of the poem by the vicar of Offwell, 1832

in 1735 stated that many of the older generation call yew 'palm', though knowing it is yew. At Stowting in Kent there is a Tudor cottage known as Palm Tree Cottage; local tradition has it that the processional route to the church passed the cottage and its owner distributed yew branches.

It is possible that the custom declined after the Reformation, when there was a lively debate as to whether it was superstitious, and therefore popish. Henry VIII, in a proclamation of 1536, declared in favour of the practice: 'bearing of palms reneweth the memorie of the receivinge of Christe in lyke manner into Jerusalem before his deathe'. Twelve years later, though, Henry's son Edward VI banned the practice as Catholic superstition, and the term 'Palm Sunday' was excluded from the Book of Common Prayer in 1552.

By then the custom was probably already enshrined in place names such as Plymtree in Devon. The *Topographer* of 1790–91 records, quoting an earlier sixteenth-century source: 'Plymtree (perchance Palm-tree) of a fayr Yew tree used to be carried by some instead of Palms, and such a tree is there now, curiously cutt and keept, like a pyramis but circular and in grandation, near the River Clyft.' There is a yew tree in the churchyard at Plymtree with a girth of over 21 feet, suggesting that it dates back to at least Saxon times. Happily it has now recovered from the topiary craze.

It is well known that medieval pilgrims returning from the Holy Land carried or wore a palm branch. There are stories that tell of small yew saplings being brought back to Britain during the Crusades; a bishop brought several back from the Garden of Gethsemane, one of which was planted at Rycote Manor in Oxfordshire. Allen believes there were yews growing in Lebanon and Gethsemane in the Middle Ages, even though this is on the southernmost limit of the tree's natural range. Evidence collected by Polish scientists shows that this natural range has been shrinking over recent centuries. In any event, there certainly is a yew tree with a girth of over 24 feet at Rycote Manor today.

Palm Sunday is a very ancient church festival, traceable at least as far back as the fifth century, so it is probable that yew was used for this purpose from the very beginnings of church history in Britain.

This view is supported by the fact that the yew was undoubtedly sacred to the Celts and that the policy of the early church was to Christianize pagan practices rather than attempting to combat and destroy them. A letter from Pope Gregory to St Augustine in Britain dated 12 July AD 594 bids him

not to destroy pagan temples, but rather to replace the idols with the relics of saints; to sprinkle the old precincts with holy water and rededicate them, because people come more readily to the places where they have been accustomed to pray. At festivals the people shall be allowed to build their booths of green leaves and to slay their bulls.

The connection of yew and palm is linked to the yew's extraordinary ability to renew itself from within its own apparently complete decay. That the yew survived not only winter but also its own death must have been awe-inspiring to prehistoric people, and the Revd Copleston, witnessing the same process happening to his own tree, was stunned and delighted. Both his father and grandfather had been vicars at Offwell before him, so we can assume that knowledge of the tree's history had been handed down to him. He dates the age of the tree as being similar to that of the church tower:

> Thy stem, coeval with the plinth, I ween
> That lifts my flinty tower above the sod.

As the church is late Norman, this gives an estimated planting date, in Copleston's reckoning, of *c.* 1300, so the tree would have been about 500 years old in 1832.

Copleston describes the presence of the tree through centuries of village life, including the Civil War period when the vicar was imprisoned and the church desecrated by the Roundheads. During the early eighteenth century the tree commenced a long, slow process of decay, and Copleston cannot resist the temptation to link the tree's decline to the state of Anglicanism at that period. The eighteenth century saw a prospering clergy, having a living derived from several parishes; however, this meant that many parishioners had no spiritual care. The process of redressing this, initiated by the

Oxford Movement, was beginning at the time Copleston was writing:

> Thine own decay dates piety's relapse.
> A century thy vigour had declin'd,
> And with it Christian zeal. Yet thou giv'st hope
> Dear venerated tree, when pleas'd I doat
> Upon thy recent growth. I hail thee still
> An emblem, in thy scath'd and leafless head
> Of man's mortality; I hail thee more
> As pointing, in thy renovated boughs
> And new clad shell, to man's awaited change
> From vile to glorious. Thou wast shrunken, dead,
> But art alive again.

Such was the parlous state of the tree that the villagers planted a sapling as a replacement in 1808. The older tree continued to decline until 1825, when the archdeacon ordered the churchyard to be tidied up. The north side, as Copleston carefully puts it, was 'lowered but not levelled', and the soil which was removed was deposited around the tree. This was enough to trigger the tree's regeneration, so that every subsequent summer it produced an increasing 'ampler garb of greenest foliage', and the 'tide of sap fresh flowing made thee twofold, young and old'. Both trees continue to flourish today in Copleston's churchyard.

It may be that the interchangeable use of 'yew' and 'palm' up until fairly recent times is not explained purely by the practical convenience of yew as a substitute for the palm of the Bible; the two trees could have been seen, at various times, as immortal. In his *Natural History*, Pliny (*c.* AD 23–79) recorded a connection between the palm and the legend of the phoenix, the mythical bird that burnt itself to death on a pyre every 500 years and then was reborn from its own ashes.

Concerning the palm we have heard a wonderful story too, to the effect that it dies and comes to life again in a similar manner to the phoenix, which is generally thought to have borrowed its name from the palm tree.[3]

God and goddess with tree of life. Sumerian seal *c.* 2,500 BC

There is little doubt that the palm was revered throughout the ancient world. The New Testament records Christ being greeted by palm-waving crowds on his last entry into Jerusalem and centuries earlier it was written in Psalms 93 v. 12 that 'the righteous shall flourish like the palm tree'. In Egypt the palm was sacred to the great goddess, mother of the sun god.[4] The link with immortality is found again in the Egyptian word for palm, bai, which also served as their word for the soul.[5] In Apuleius' description of a great procession in honour of the goddess Isis, the god Anubis marches carrying palms. His priests at his temple at Hermopolis stuck palm fronds in their sandals as a sign of their devotion to him. The Greeks mistook the palm fronds for feathers and so Hermes, the Greek deity closest to Anubis, had winged feet. In Greece, too, the goddess Leto gave birth to Apollo and Diana while reclining against a palm (Euripides, *Ione* v. 920). This honouring of the palm dated back at least as far as the earliest Middle Eastern civilizations in Mesopotamia. There the Tree of Life was a dominant deity and in some representations of it, found on Sumerian seals cast around 2500 BC, the tree is clearly a palm. It is hardly surprising, given that very few species of tree could survive the desert climate of much of the Middle East, that the palm was revered as the Tree of Life and linked with the goddess. Yet it is a curious tree to be literally regarded as immortal in the way Pliny suggests. Its trunk is a mixture of fibre and pith that can hardly be described as wood. The large bud at the top of the trunk, vital for the tree's survival, is an important food source for animals, so the palm is always vulnerable to foraging before it attains real height. It is certainly not long-lived.

Further north, in mountainous Anatolia and Syria, it was an evergreen tree, almost certainly the yew, that was being worshipped by contemporaneous cultures such as the Hittites. The yew, able to rejuvenate itself, not only from old age, but from fire and lightning damage as well, is a uniquely appropriate tree to be connected with the source of the phoenix legend. It is quite possible that legends originating with the yew attached themselves to other trees when tribes migrated beyond the yew's geographic range. The Hittite word for yew was 'eya' and altars were sited beneath the yew. Sheepskins and the fruits of the harvest were hung from the tree, which was regarded as a living cornucopia. One Hittite inscription states: 'As the eya tree is ever verdant and does not shed its leaves, even so may King and Queen be thriving.' One authority on the Hittite language considers that 'eya' derives directly from the Sanskrit word 'ayu', meaning eternity and life-force.[6]

To return now to the next possible reason in Copleston's summary as to why the yew grows in churchyards: 'my villagers his birth attest. By festal decorations plucked from thee'. To the modern mind this is a surprise, used as we are to holly and mistletoe as the Christmas evergreens. Copleston, however, was writing a decade before Prince Albert introduced the Christmas tree to Britain, and a century before the marketing men at Coca Cola decided that Santa Claus needed a smart relaunch in the company's colours.[7] His red coat trimmed with white fur, the night cap and the thigh boots date no further back than 1931. Our modern Christmas is an extraordinary tangle of myths and customs that have grown around the pre-Christian midwinter festival. The church did not celebrate Christ's birth at all until AD 353, and even then Epiphany, 6 January, was the date chosen. Not until the middle of the fourth century did Pope Julius I decide on 25 December as Christ's birthday.

This date happened to be the winter solstice, when the sun, at its furthest point from the equator, hangs motionless at its closest to the horizon. The sun's proximity to the earth was seen as the moment of union when the earth was impregnated with the sun's energy, ensuring light and fertility for the coming year. It was a seemingly universal festival in the ancient world: the nativity of Tammuz, Osiris, Dionysus, Mithras and others. In Scandinavia the festival was Yule and the occasion of the appearance of Baldur, the god of light and joy. Odin, too, came to earth to bring peace, joy and presents. He rode across the sky on Sleipnir, his eight-legged white horse. The church's tactic was often to associate a saint with a stubborn article of pagan belief, and in due course St Nicholas emerged at Christmas, dispensing gifts and as patron saint of children.

The focal point of the Yule festival was the yule log. This custom was widespread and found not only in Scandinavia and Celtic Britain but in Germany, France, parts of Switzerland and the Slav countries. The custom as it survived in Christian times was to cut the log the previous winter and allow it to season, decorate it with evergreen and kindle it with a fragment of the previous year's log. It was allowed to burn for at least twenty-four hours, but enough had to be left to be lit again at Candlemas on 2 February, and with sufficient left after that to kindle the new log the following Christmas. Candlemas entered the Christian calendar in the sixth century as a celebration of the Purification of the Virgin Mary, but it has pre-Christian origins. The Celtic festival of Brigit, celebrated at the same time of year, was a rite of purification and fertility; it became Christianized as the feast of St Bride.

In the forests of northern Europe it was essential for survival to keep a fire alight throughout winter, and the yule log is akin to many of the vegetation gods who died and were reborn annually. The midwinter celebration must have been marked from the very dawn of history, long before the human conception of gods evolved into the sophisticated dramas and beliefs represented by the Norse myths. The gods of the legends were embryonic in the trees of the forest. It must have been a process developing over an immense period of time; but, Allen believes, a yew cult was one of the first human expressions of religious awe: worship of the flame-like berries on the verdant tree amid the frozen wastes of northern winters was expressed in the burning of the yule log. From those ritual fires grew Yggdrasil, and tales of Ullr the archer god in Ydalir, his yew dale, but the womb which gave them birth was the yew.

It is a vast stretch of time from that period to the devout villagers of Offwell, but in another sense it is only an instant. Their minds may have been concerned with the anticipation and bustle of that immediate Christmas, but their hands performed a ritual that was both current and timeless. The cutting of the evergreen yew in a village in nineteenth-century Devon celebrated Christ's birth, but the same act had always been performed at the winter solstice, celebrating the nativity of other gods, the yule log or the tree itself.

This act can usefully be compared with an everyday event that can regularly be witnessed on Torquay seafront. Here, amid all the other attractions of the English seaside, is a plastic bath embedded in concrete. It is covered over with a grille and wire netting. Placed there by the local Rotary Club, it is a 'wishing well' to raise funds for charities. Unprepossessing though it is, it seems to be highly successful. It exerts on passers-by a magnetic pull that holds them only momentarily, but long enough for them to toss a coin in. No doubt if people were asked about what they had done they would be only briefly nonplussed and then would say they had simply made a donation to a good cause. Perhaps they might say they have acted 'on impulse'. It seems, though, that a memory buried deep in the unconscious is half-stirred, unlike during an encounter with a flag seller with a collection box, when the conscious mind makes a logical choice to give or to avoid. The impulse is not to give, but to throw something into water. The votive offering, cast into a sacred spring or well with ardent hope, was a powerful act in Celtic and pre-Celtic religion. For today's passers-by, in what they imagine is a distracted moment, the faintest ripple of that devotion holds them in a spell.

Something of this sort may have been there with the Offwell

parishioners, with the medieval masons who carved the Green Men who are present in the shadowy corners of our cathedrals and churches (see Chapter 12), and with all who allow the yew tree to speak a little. Allen talks of the yew tree as the guardian, of us and of the planet. It undoubtedly was so, within human consciousness, whether people were huddled by a yule log or in a sacred grove. Now, as our frenzy of destruction of the natural world reaches a crescendo, Allen believes the yew is beginning to make its presence felt once again. Whatever the human race felt and experienced in the sacred groves – the wonder, the oneness, whatever ecstasy or terror – is contained within us. The yew, the oldest and first tree, is the source of the wisdom of that immensely long relationship, in comparison with which the span of the Christian era is brief. As we threaten our very survival, so the conduits to that wisdom are opening. Now, while on the mundane level we must become the tree's guardian, more profoundly our relationship remains precisely the same: only what we knew in the groves can save us now.

The reason that nowadays may be the most commonly proffered for the proliferation of yews in churchyards is that they were there to provide wood for longbows. Copleston is indignant at the very thought of it, and it could be inferred from this that the idea did not have all the authority of 'common knowledge' in his day that it has now. Indeed, G.A. Hansard, who published his *Book of Archery* in 1841, shortly after Copleston wrote his poem, agreed that 'the piety, or, as some men choose to style it, the superstition, of our ancestors would have been decidedly opposed to the application of wood reared within consecrated ground to any such purpose'. This may seem at first sight to have been a peculiarly nineteenth-century inhibition; the medieval churchyard with its fairs and entertainments was a distinctly more lively place than the Victorian one. But it may be supported by the fact that when Henry IV authorized Nicholas Frost, his royal bowyer, to enter private land to cut yew he expressly exempted the estates of the religious orders. It is Hansard's view that planting in churchyards was just not worth the effort: 'Is it not absurd to suppose that men would plant within these contracted bounds, a single tree of such slow growth, that in the space of a century its height and substance are scarcely sufficient to supply half a dozen bowstaves . . ?'

The great age of the English longbow began with the Norman Conquest, but yew was used for weapons, probably continuously, since the very earliest times. The world's oldest known artefact of wood, dating from the Hoxnian interglacial layer, 250,000 BC, is a yew spear, found at Clacton in Essex. Another yew spear, probably flint-tipped, has been found in Lower Saxony. It was retrieved from the Saale-Warthe interglacial layer where it had been deposited at about 200,000 BC. The spear was lodged between the ribs of a straight-tusked elephant, *Hespero-loxodon antiquus*. Possibly the two oldest examples of yew bows are from the Somerset Levels dated about 2700 BC. The neolithic corpse of the 'Iceman' discovered in 1991 on the Italian–Austrian border had with him a yew longbow measuring 6 feet, even though the man himself was only 5 ft 2 in tall. This bow may be even older than the Somerset ones, possibly from about 3500 BC.

Even before 1066, then, yew had been the natural resource for weapons, as well as other implements, for about 4,000 years. At Hastings the Normans used a bow about a metre in length, but by the thirteenth century that had grown to the formidable 6 foot bow. Even the most cursory glance at the military history of the 500 years that followed the Norman invasion shows that the quantity of yew consumed must have been enormous. During the Crusades, Richard I is reported to have halted the charge of the entire Saracen and Turkish army with seventeen knights and 300 archers. Edward I's forces at Falkirk lost only 100 men while their bowmen inflicted losses on the Scots of 12,000. Edward III's victory at the Battle of Crécy in 1346 was achieved despite being outnumbered ten to one. His force of 7,000 archers could release a terrifying assault of over 80,000 arrows a minute. The slaughter was appalling; a contemporary chronicler described the arrows as 'flying in the air as thick as snow, with a terrible noise, much like a tempestuous wind preceding a tempest'. For various reasons, chief among them the fear of providing their own peasantry with such a devastating weapon which they were afraid could be turned on themselves, the French nobility developed no effective reply for the rest of the Hundred Years War. The battle at Poitiers a decade later, John of Gaunt's campaign in Portugal and finally Agincourt in 1415 told the same story.

The longbow remained dominant throughout the campaigns in France in the first half of the fifteenth century and in the Wars of the Roses during the second half of it. The recent raising of the *Mary Rose*, Henry VIII's flagship that sank during a skirmish with the French in the Solent in 1545, enabled 139 longbows and 2,500 arrows to be recovered. This was evidence that the bow was in use in naval warfare as well as on land, both to clear the decks of enemy ships and also to dispatch fire-arrows. Examination of a skeleton retrieved from the wreck proved to be that of an archer. 'Two of the middle vertebrae of the spine were pulled forward and twisted to the left and the lower left arm bone was noticeably enlarged and flattened, the result of prolonged strain,' comments archaeologist Margaret Rule of the Mary Rose Trust.

Faced with this demand for yew, there were various edicts from the thirteenth century onwards attempting to ensure a proper supply and a readiness for civil defence. Edward III, after the success at Crécy, wrote to the sheriffs of London instructing that proclamations be made that 'every one of the said city, strong in body, at leisure times on holidays, use in their recreations bows and arrows'. The same proclamation forbade as leisure-time activities 'the throwing of stones, wood, or iron, hand-ball, foot-ball, bandy-ball, cambuck, or cock-fighting, nor such vain plays, which have no profit in them'. A similar Act was passed in the reign of Richard II at the end of the fourteenth century, specifically relating to servants, and a further one in 1511 enforcing archery practice and the provision of bows for males over seven years old.

By the reign of Edward IV (1461–83) concern was evident about the price, and presumably therefore the supply, of bow staves. A petition from the Commons to the King suggested that, as bow staves had reached an outrageous price, four must be imported with every 'tun-tight of merchandise' brought in by ship. Accordingly an Act of his reign set the price of a bow at three shillings and fourpence. This price was held throughout the reigns of both Henry VII and Henry VIII; it was repealed in 1556 during the reign of Queen Mary and replaced by an order setting the price of a bow of best foreign wood at six shillings and eightpence, for one of inferior sort three shillings and fourpence, and for one made of English yew two shillings. We also know that in 1483 Richard III ordered a general planting of yew and made it compulsory that bow staves were imported with every butt of malmsey.

In 1545 Roger Ascham published *Toxophilus*, a treatise on bows and archery in which he says that 'every bowe is made of the boughe, the plante or the boole of the tree. The boughe commonly is very knotty, and full of prinnes weak of small pithe ... the plante is quicke enough of caste, it will plye and bow far afore it breakes, and the boole is best.' We can infer from this that the 'best foreign wood' must have come from the bole or trunk, meaning that the whole tree was destroyed. The 'two shilling English bows' could only have come from the 'plante', presumably the sapling or the branch. It seems that the supply of English yew of any quality had dried up. Loudon speculates that in the past yew was probably grown close together to produce straight saplings suitable for a bow. In Elizabeth I's reign a statute was passed directing bowyers to stock fifty bows of elm, witch hazel or ash and to have four of these woods to one of yew. Eventually yew bows were prohibited to children except to those of the gentry.

It would seem from all of this that the relatively small amount of yew produced in the churchyards would have made little contribution to the immense amount used during the period. Curiously, in France Charles VII did order yew to be planted in all the churchyards of Normandy, but in Britain there appears to have been no such specific instruction. Certainly most of the bows used in Britain from the mid-fifteenth century, and possibly much earlier, were from imported wood, mainly from Spain and Germany. The best-quality timber came from the trunk of the tree and could only be obtained by felling; there seems to be a fond misconception that the yeoman went to the churchyard, cut a wand with his pocket knife and thereby had a weapon of sufficient power to propel an arrow 250 yards with sufficient force remaining to pass through chain mail. The demise of the longbow came about as much through the exhaustion of the supply of yew as through the advance of firearms; the seventeenth-century musket was wildly inaccurate and time-consuming to load.

Copleston is therefore right that churchyard yews had little to do with longbows; indeed, it is probably the fact that those few hundred trees were on consecrated ground, with many probably already hollow and therefore useless to the bowyer, that saved them. Whatever remained in Europe of the sacred groves of prehistory, and a vital clue to humanity's deeper relationship with the yew, must have been swept away in late medieval Europe to provide bow staves.

Working through Copleston's list of speculations as to why yews grow in churchyards, only 'green longevity' as a symbol of immortality has been omitted; this has already had a chapter to itself. Copleston did not mention the belief that yews were planted in churchyards to deter cattle, but this is another common idea, as Jennifer Chandler mentioned. There is some doubt concerning how toxic yew is to cattle, and therefore how great a deterrent it would have been regarded as. Cole, in *The Art of Simpling*, published in 1656, wrote: 'Master Wells, minister at Adderbury, seeing some Boyes breaking Boughs from the Yew tree in the churchyard, thought himself much injured. To prevent the like Trespasses, he sent one presently to cut downe the tree and to bring it in ... his cowes began to feed upon the Leaves, and two of them within a few hours dyed. A just reward.'

John Evelyn, however, was much surprised that cattle and horses were not poisoned more. He wrote in his great *Sylva – a Discourse on Trees*, published 1664, that 'I marvel there are no more such effects of it, both horses and cattle being free to browse on it, where it naturally grows.' At the end of the nineteenth century John Lowe was still puzzling with this contradiction. The *Gardener's Chronicle* for the years 1870–80 recorded many instances of cattle and horses dying after eating it, yet there was equally sound evidence of these animals grazing on it with no ill effects. Lowe quotes two informants who probably got near to the truth. A resident at Tintern, where yew is abundant, told him that cattle 'never ate sufficient to injure them unless it was cut'. And an old shepherd on Box Hill, again a place where yews grow naturally, said that his cows 'frequently ate the leaves of the tree, but never took any harm from it, as they were turned out daily, and therefore never took a harmful quantity'.[8]

There is a lot of evidence, too, that small quantities of yew were added to supplement oats for horses, or winter fodder for cattle. The danger seems to be when cattle eat quantities of it, as in winter when with snow on the ground yew may be the only available greenery. There is also danger after a winter in the stall that cattle may gorge on the first fresh fodder they find. The evidence is contradictory but suggests that yew may not have been seen as such a threat to cattle. Perhaps more to the point, there are far quicker and more efficient ways of keeping cattle out of a graveyard than planting a slow-growing tree which may or may not be toxic.

In the case of all the 'common knowledge' reasons given for why yews were in churchyards, there must have been periods of time when and localities where they were, in a limited way, true. People must have responded to the perceived advantages and disadvantages of the yew's situation, and it would be foolhardy to say that a bow was never cut from one or that a dead horse on some occasion did not prompt the hurried fencing of a churchyard. There is no evidence that there was ever any wholesale widespread planting based on these partial truths. The real question behind the curiosity remains and should be rephrased as: why were the churches built beside the yews?

CHAPTER 6

Hidden Clues – the Name
of the Yew

The token of the word unheard, unspoken
Till the wind shake a thousand whispers from the yew.
    T.S. ELIOT, *Ash Wednesday*, 1930, IV

If the yew was considered so important even in 'modern' history –
that is, since Anglo-Saxon times – it might be fair to expect this to
be reflected in the language, and for there to be place-names which
refer to the tree. Maps of the British Isles are certainly dotted with
names such as 'Yew Tree Farm' and 'Yew Cottage', but these do not
necessarily describe much more than a geographical feature. If the
yew was considered so important, might there not be larger areas –
hamlets, villages, towns – to which the yew gave its name? Looking
at the evidence of place-names has brought to light places where
yew trees must have once existed and been considered of significance.
It has even shown up areas of possible 'yew cults'; this is particularly
interesting in places where hardly any ancient yews remain today.

Interpreting place-names can be hazardous. They tend to take on
a life of their own, independent of the rest of the language, and can
change over time. Investigators of place-names may also read into
the name more than is justified; as Oliver Rackham points out in *The
History of the Countryside*, places might be named after unusual rather
than typical features.[1] Similarly, names which seem to have an
obvious root may still remain a mystery; names with 'Stave-' in
them, such as Staveley, may well refer to staves, but does this mean
it was a wooded place where staves were cut, or that it was an open
space enclosed by staves? It could also mean that a stave was planted

from which a tree such as a yew was grown; there are certainly plenty of places where legend tells of a saint planting a stave from which sprang forth a mighty tree. Similarly 'Stoke-' means stock, an ancient name for tree, but again leaves us asking for more precise information. Despite the various readings, however, tracing a place-name to its origins can throw surprising light on our past connections with the yew.

There are many place-names which suggest settlements in or near woods in general. Villages called '-ley' or '-leigh' and '-hurst', for instance (Bromley, Stoneleigh, Leigh-on-Sea, Hawkhurst, etc.), probably referred to an inhabited clearing surrounded by woodland; while names ending in '-feld' or '-field', such as Beaconsfield, seem to have meant not a field as we would understand it but an open clearing as contrasted with nearby woodland. These names probably go back to well before Anglo-Saxon times.

Place-names specifically referring to yew woods or yew trees are also 'disguised', as words have changed over the course of time. The word 'yew' is relatively modern, but it and its counterparts in many other European languages seem to have a common Teutonic root. Dr Johnson said that 'yew' comes from the Anglo-Saxon *ih* or *iw*, or from the Welsh *yw*. Alternatively, it could come from the Latin *iva*, which confusingly also means ivy. Whatever the precise derivation, the name for yew seems to have had very significant meanings ascribed to it. In his nineteenth-century *Notes and Queries*, J.G. Cumming lists these meanings for the word: 'Yew is ancient British, and signifies "existent" and enduring, having the same root as Jehovah, and yew in Welsh means "it is", being one of the forms of the third person present indicative of the auxiliary verb "bod", to be.' In Gaelic, *eber* means 'God's gift to the world'.

The common roots are readily identifiable in many old tongues:

Old English: *iw, eow, ih, ioh, eoh*
Old Saxon: *ih, iw, eow*
Middle Low German and Middle Dutch: *iwe, iewe, uwe*
Old High German: *iwu, iwi, iwa, ihu, iga*

Old Norse: *yr*
Celtic: *yewar* (or *jubar*, pronounced 'yewar'), *ure*
Gaelic: *an-t-iuchar, iubhar, iuthar*
Middle English: *ew, u*
Early Modern English: *yewe, yegh, eugh, yowe*
Welsh: *yw* (singular *ywen*), *yreu-yw*
Middle Latin: *ivus, iva, ina*

There are equivalents in Danish, Spanish, Old Irish and Cornish. *Ivo* occurs in various Celtic languages (Welsh, Cornish, Breton), derived from *ivos*, which is common to a number of other European languages.

In modern languages we find:

German and Swedish: *eibe, eibenbaum, ibenbaum, ifenbaum*
French: *if*
Italian: *taxo*
Spanish: *iva*
Portuguese: *iva*
Irish: *whar*
Dutch: *jeuen, jeuenboom*

It is fascinating to see how close these names are to each other, especially when spoken rather than written. Even though the word has gone through many permutations, the root is still evident. The oldest spelling known of in any Teutonic language is in a seventh-century manuscript, where it is written as 'iuu'. John Lowe carefully chronicled the word's appearance in the English language, and found various literary allusions which show how the spelling changed: *eu* (Chaucer, four times), *ew* (thrice), *eugh* (Spenser), *ewgh, ugh* and *u, ewe* (Ascham), *iuu, yugh, yeugh, yewe, yowe* (Palsgrave), *you* (Brand).[2]

Place-names based on these ancient words for yew, and on others which have been found such as *evo, evor, ivo, ivor, ebur, ibur, ebor, ebro*, and *iver*, are quite common throughout England, although it is usually impossible to pinpoint the date of origin. Considerable caution has to be applied; for instance, there are half a dozen or so rivers in Devon called Yeo, but most of these come from a word simply meaning river, and having no connection with yew.[3] The river Yeo that is joined by the Creedy, south-east of Crediton, however, *is* called after the yew.

Treading warily, then, and acknowledging that some etymologists will disagree with some of these, the following places are thought to have taken their names from the old names for the yew:

Eridge, Sussex (yew ridge)

Ewden, Derbyshire

Ewe Down, Collingbourne Kingston, Wiltshire (referred to in 1241 as Iudon)

Ewell, Surrey (yew well)

Ewen, Gloucestershire (*ewen* is an early name usually indicating a female yew)

Ewetree Green, Lamberhurst, Kent (land adjoining or containing yew trees)

Ewhurst, Surrey, Sussex and Hampshire (yew wood on a hill or yew tree)

Ewshot, Hampshire (projecting land with yew trees, or yew grove)

Hewelsfield, Gloucestershire (yew field?)

Iddesleigh, Devon

Ide, Devon (from *ida*)

Ideford, Devon

Iden, Sussex (yew tree pasture)

Iffley, Oxfordshire (*if* is a Norman reference to yew; however, Iffley could also mean a clearing where plovers are found!)

Ifield, Sussex and Kent (open land where yew trees grow)

Ifold, Sussex (yew vale)

Iford, Sussex (yew ford)

Ivegill, Cumbria (valley of the yew)

Iwade, Kent (yew ford)

Iwerne Minster and Iwerne Courtney, Dorset (a river named yew)[4]

Iwode, Hampshire (yew wood)

Llygad Yw (the eye of the yew)

Ulcombe, Kent (*ul* refers to yew)

Uley, Gloucestershire (yew wood)

Ullingswick, Hereford and Worcester

Ullswater, Cumbria (refers to an ancient yew)

Yeo (river on whose banks yew grows)

Yeoford, Devon (ford in the Yeo river)

Yeovil, Somerset ([place of] dwellers on the river Ivel on whose banks yews grow)

Youlethorpe, Humberside (yew wood)

Youlgreave, Derbyshire (yew grave, near Darley Dale, site of ancient yew)

Youlton, Yorkshire (yew wood)

Ystrad Yw, Wales (the valley or strath of the yew)

This is just a small sample of names which indicate derivation from 'yew'. At the very least it shows that the trees were once far more widespread than they now are.

In Scotland yew is far less common a component in place-names than other species of trees are. Nevertheless, names for yew are reflected in more place-names than the present distribution of yew there would lead one to expect: Udale in Cromarty (the older version of this is Uddall, which comes from the Norse *y-dalr*, or yew dale), Cullivoe of Yell in Shetland, Ulladaill, Ullapool and Ulladill are a few examples. This might indicate that there were once many more yews in Scotland than there are now. This would certainly seem to be the case in Ireland, and also in England where many of the places listed above no longer have any yews. For instance, an ecological study of yews in southern England by Ruth Tittensor found twenty-eight yew place-names around the Hampshire–Sussex borders, of which only one still contained any yew trees.[5]

While this kind of information may be interesting, it does not necessarily say anything conclusive about the trees' significance. It has been suggested by Oliver Rackham that if yews were so important to religious life, there would be plenty of places called 'Yew Church' or something similar. The fact that they do not abound means, according to this argument, that the connection between yews and churches was not so vital, and therefore the trees are not as ancient as Allen claims. It is true that there are relatively few places called 'Yew Church', but it is possible to trace a few, even though the names for both church and yew have changed over time:

- Capel-yr-Ywen (Church of the Yew), near Llandeilo, Powys. The church was ruined as long ago as the 1830s, but a recent visitor to the remote place found traces of yew stumps in a hedgerow.
- Kilnevair (Church of the Yew Tree), near the head of Loch Awe in Argyle.
- Llanbedr Ystrad Yw (St Peter's Church 'in the valley of yew trees'), Powys.
- Killure (Church of the Yew Tree), Ireland. This is recorded in annals of 1015 as 'Arnun's Tree'.
- Cell Iuhbair (Church of the Yew), Kilconnell, County Galway.
- Cell-eo (Church of the Yews), Ireland.
- Tair Ywen (Chapel of the Three Yews), near Llanigon, Hay-on-Wye, Powys. Ruins of a chapel; yew trees were recorded here in the seventeenth century.
- Ibar Cyn Tracta ('the flourishing yew tree', or 'large yew trees near the monastery'), Newry, County Down. Maurice McLoughlin, King of Ireland, founded a Cistercian abbey here in 1157, and St Patrick is said to have planted a yew here.
- Ivychurch, Kent. The words *iue* and *ive* were both used to denote yew at one time, which has sometimes led to confusion between the two. 'Ivychurch' could as well refer to yew as to ivy.
- Killeochaille (Church of the Yew Wood), Ireland. Eochaille, meaning yew wood, was also the ancient name of Youghal in County Cork.

So places known as 'Yew Church' do exist. However, tracking down such names seems a bit of a fool's errand. For if it is usual to have a yew in a churchyard, as it is, it is unlikely that the combination of the two would make a good place-name. Labels are intended to distinguish between things. It is improbable that there would be many places called 'Yew Church' when this was the case everywhere, not the exception.

Some yew trees are mentioned in various Anglo-Saxon charters, such as 'eow cumb' (yew combe) at Stoke Bishop, Bristol; 'Iwwara hagan' (yew-dwellers' hedge) at Havant, Hampshire; 'iww cumbe ealde iw' (old yew) at Michelmersh, Hampshire; 'eow rhyc' (yew ridge) at Upton on Severn, Worcestershire; and 'iwigath' (yew farm) at Martyr Worthy (Itchen Abbas), Hampshire. It is from references such as these that we have records of previous words for yews.

The yew in the church of St John the Baptist at Itchen Abbas appears in an Anglo-Saxon charter of AD 939. In the charter the position of the tree is described in relation to a river with a small island, and these landmarks are still seen in the same position from the tree today; so it is highly likely that the yew there now is the one described in 939.

Yew place-names are, of course, found all over the world, but in Europe there seem to be particular links between names found in areas of northern and western England, Ireland, Switzerland, France, Spain and Portugal. Speculation suggests that nomadic peoples are the common link between the names. For instance, in Switzerland, where yew trees are quite rare (and interestingly 'William Tell's tree' was said to be a yew, despite their scarcity), yew place-names include Eburodunum, which when translated from the Celtic means something like Yew Castle or Yew Fortress, and Yverdon. Switzerland does have a fine yew grove, on a traditionally sacred mountain called Uetliberg, outside Zürich. In Ireland there are many traces of yew place-names; Youghal, to the east of Cork, for example, means 'yew wood', coming from the Irish name Eochaille. There are still yew trees in the town. There is also evidence that many Celtic tribes took their name from the yew, for example the Iverni in southern Ireland _c._ AD 100.

Other European countries carry similar elements of the word for yew in their place-names. An early Spanish word for yew is *ibe*, and yews were once widespread on the Iberian peninsula, where they are now scarce. It is possible that this is the origin of the ancient name Iberia; if so, the yew must have been of great importance in a very large area. In Portugal there are Evora, Ebura and Eburobrittum. A province of Normandy called Eure still contains some ancient yews of great size.

All of these names are reminiscent of the ancient name for York, Eborakon. The history of how Eborakon became York has given rise to suggestions that it may once have been the centre for a Druidic yew cult. Eborakon, which signifies a yew grove or tree, is mentioned in the second century AD by the geographer Ptolemy. It became 'Latinized' by the Romans and known as Eboracum. *The Bloomsbury Dictionary of Place Names in the British Isles* says that both these names come from a Celtic British personal name, Eburos, meaning 'yew man', and no doubt referring to his estate among yew trees. It adds that later the Saxons misunderstood this, and took it as Eofar (*oe.* wild boar) and added *wic* (dwelling place), to give Eoforwic, a name which is recorded in 1060 and not far removed phonetically from the modern 'York'. It is accepted that York's name did grow out of the yew in some way; the name for the whole region of Yorkshire probably comes from Eburach, with similar roots. It is hard to know how far back the association between yews and York went, but in 1835 the writer Thomas Dugdale suggested: 'York was called Caer Ebruac 1,200 years upwards before Christ.'

Yorkshire's yews probably became weapons and tools for the Romans, and then the Saxons and the Danes. Although very few yews now remain in the region, there are still faint traces which add to the evidence that they were once plentiful and highly regarded there. Legends and stories concerning yews still survive. Fountains Abbey has what was once one of the most famous groups of yews in England, known as the Seven Sisters, although only two now remain. It is perhaps a miracle that even these are still there, as they appear to have been forgotten about for the last few decades, and on a recent visit were found to be surrounded by undergrowth of nettles and elder. One of the two trees is in an almost prone position, but is recovering very well.

Fountains Abbey was founded in 1132 by Thurston, Archbishop of York, with monks from the Benedictine abbey in York who wanted to adopt the more austere discipline of St Bernard. It is interesting, given the known association of York with yews, that these monks chose to build their new abbey in a place where yews already existed. The largest of the seven trees came down in 1658, and showed a ring count of 1,200 years. This would date the tree to at least AD 458, and mean that it was probably pre-Roman. The trees stand in a field overlooking the abbey and to the south-west of it. The setting up of the monastery is described by Dr John Burton in his *Monasticon Eboracense* (1758):

they withdrew into the uncouth desert, without any house to shelter them in that winter season, or provisions to subsist on, but entirely depending on Divine Providence. There stood a large elm-tree in the midst of the vale, on the lower branches of which they put some thatch and straw; and under that they lay, ate, and prayed, the bishop for a time supplying them with bread, and the rivulet with drink. Part of the day some spent in making wattles to erect a little oratory, whilst others cleared some ground to make a little garden. But it is supposed that they soon changed the shelter of their elm for that of seven yew-trees, they stand so near each other as to form a cover almost equal to a thatched roof.

This account was based on the words of a monk, Hugh of Kirkstall, who recorded the story between 1225 and 1247, at the request of John, Abbot of Fountains.

The yews at Fountains Abbey, and their gradual demise, have been described by many people over the years. Even in the 1820s they seem to have been endangered; Jacob George Strutt describes them as 'venerable . . . silent witnesses of the changes of time', and adds:

They do not appear to be treated with the reverence due to them: a low wall hides their weather-beaten boles on the side whence they would otherwise be seen to the most advantage, and a paltry little stable is erected almost beneath their branches; on which, worst injury of all, the marks of a despoiling axe are but too visible, and the ground underneath is strewed with fragments of larger limbs, probably torn away for petty purposes to which meaner wood might have been applied with equal utility.[6]

It is to be hoped that the remaining trees, whose origins are lost in time but which may have provided the inspiration for one of the most beautiful of religious sites, will be treated with rather more respect.

Sadly most of Yorkshire's most historic and ancient trees have vanished. Those recorded at Bolton Abbey and Kirkheaton in the eighteenth century are no longer there, nor is the one at Tankersley called Talbot's Yew, in whose hollow trunk it was said a man could turn around on horseback. In 1586 the antiquarian and topograph William Camden recounted a story about a yew in Yorkshire, which again relates to the naming of a town. A young virgin, he says, was beheaded for refusing to surrender her virginity. Her head was hung upon a yew tree until it had decayed, and subsequently the tree was reputed to be sacred. Camden records that the tree became a place of pilgrimage, from which people would pluck branches. The site of the tree, in a small village then called Houton, grew into the town of Halifax, which means 'holy hair'.

The Christian church also harbours remnants of the Yorkshire yews. Does the Archbishop of York know that when he signs himself 'Ebor' he is probably using a name which originated in a distant yew cult?

The holy island of Iona in the Hebrides certainly had close associations with the yew. It is known for having been a centre for early Christianity; St Columba, these days more often referred to by the Irish form Columcille, sailed there from Ireland with twelve companions in AD 563. He set up a monastery which played an important part in the conversion of Britain to Christianity. To suggest that Columcille might have chosen this relatively remote Hebridean isle because it was already a sacred place is more than mere speculation. Tradition says, as the Irish Life of Columcille records, that he found Druids before him in Hi (Iona) and expelled them; Druids are known to venerate the yew.

Even the accepted historical knowledge of the derivation of Iona's name brings in various curious facts. The island itself was originally known just as I or Hi, probably deriving from a Celtic word for yew tree. This element was then incorporated into various forms of the name, and appeared in a document from around AD 700 as 'Ioua insula', 'island of the yew-tree place'. The first word, Ioua, seems to have been misread, or become changed, to 'Iona', and has remained thus. In so doing, the island seems to have become associated with Jonah; 'Iona' is one of the forms of the name Jonah. Even though this association came about 'through accident', it is a curious 'accident', as there is a link between Jonah and yew trees, explored later. It appears that some simple slip managed to bring together the original, and apparently lost, meaning of Iona, as being to do with yew trees, with another yew-tree legend. By 1100 the island was being called something like its present name; a document refers to 'Hiona-Columcille', meaning Columba's cell or church.

It is possible to trace the strange story of Iona further. Irish legend talks of Fer hI who was described as the foster-son of Manannan mac Lir, the Celtic sea god. Various tales connect Fir hI with the islands in which Iona is situated. Professor Watson, writing in 1927, says:

The point of interest is that Fer hI means 'Man of Yew', or better, 'Son of Yew' ... he appears to have been a tree, or rather a yew, divinity. The inference to be drawn from the whole data is, in my opinion, that the 'Iouan island' ... means 'the Yew-isle', and that it may well have been the seat of a yew cultus.[7]

It is hard not to agree with this conclusion. For such a tiny island, Iona has had a remarkable history; as well as being the seat of early Christianity it contains the oldest Christian cemetery in Scotland and the burial place of forty-eight Scottish kings, including Duncan, who was murdered by Macbeth in 1040.

There are, then, many places around the British Isles which have taken their name from the yew, in different ways and for different reasons. There are also some place-names which at first glance do not seem to have any connection with yew – they do not contain any derivatives of the old words for yew – but on looking closer they too reveal this association. We have already seen that Plymtree in Devon is called not after a palm tree, as the name might suggest, but after a yew.

Residents of Heavitree in Devon have often been asked how the curious name originated. Recent work by local historians has produced a convincing answer, and in the course of it has for once brought a happy ending to a story. One of the local historians, Hazel Harvey, tells the tale: 'The name Heavitree comes from the Old English for "head tree". In Anglo-Saxon, head tree was *heafod treow*. And where was this head tree that gave the area its name? The exciting thing is that we think we know.' It is, she believes, the yew tree at Heavitree parish church. She explains that Wonford, now a village near to Heavitree, was once a huge royal estate at which Saxon kings held court, probably near a landmark tree. She says: 'Even before the Saxons came in the seventh century, it may have been a royal centre for the Celtic kings of Dumnonia, and they were there even before the Romans came to Exeter. Wonford stretched over a huge area, so people would say, "I'm going to the head tree", as we say "capital" for London, or "headquarters" for main office.'

Heavitree was the obvious place for gatherings, standing at a main crossroads and visible for miles in all directions. This certainly tallies with the fact that Heavitree was probably the earliest church in the area outside Exeter. However, the idea that the Heavitree yew might have been this original landmark tree seemed at first sight impossible, as it is only about 400 or 500 years old. When Allen, not knowing any of this background at the time, visited the tree he found that it was a side-shoot which had grown from a very much older tree, now gone. It is possible to see the old roots of the previous tree over a wide area around the surviving trunk. It looks as though the original tree was cut down but has regenerated itself from the stump. Hazel says that this is borne out by the fact, which Allen also did not know when he first visited, that the church tower close to which the tree stands was completely rebuilt in 1541. This could have been the time when the original tree was felled. It seems likely that this 'youngster' has grown from the original 'head tree', the Heavitree.

When Allen visited the tree in 1991 it was in a rather sorry state. The hollow trunk had been bricked up, and the Victorians had surrounded it with rubble and old stones, presumably with the intention of supporting it. Local tree lovers have now removed the rubble and replaced it with new earth. In early 1993 Hazel was able to report that 'it is already responding by putting out fresh shoots, and we hope to care for the Head Tree Yew'.

Several other place-names refer to the yew tree from Saxon times. Bicknoller in Somerset has a yew aged about 1,500 years and now supported with metal crutches. 'Bicknoller' is said to derive from the name of a Saxon chieftain, Bica, and possibly from 'the tree of Bica'. So perhaps, as at Taplow, the ancient yew marks a chieftain's grave. Allestree in Derbyshire also probably refers to a Saxon chief on whose territory the venerated tree stood. The ancient yew in Allestree churchyard is about 1,400 years old. Similarly, Oswestry in Shropshire may refer to 'Oswald's tree'; there is believed to have once been a fort outside Oswestry with yew trees growing there. Cholstrey comes from 'tree of the freeman or of a man called Ceorl'. Some place-names, then, refer not just to particular yew trees situated there, but to a person – either real or legendary – who was associated with the tree, as at Ulcombe in Kent, which probably refers to Ullr, the Norse god of the yew grove.

An intriguing connection comes at Wilmington in Sussex, the site of the gigantic figure carved into the chalk hillside. The Long Man of Wilmington, until very recently the largest known depiction of a human figure in the world, has provoked endless speculation about his identity; he has been hailed at various times as Thor, Apollo, Baldur, Muhammad, St Paul and plenty of other disparate characters. One of the most likely explanations has been that he is connected with Waendel, a mythical warrior. Jacqueline Simpson's 1979 article in *Folklore* points out that at the time of the Domesday Book the Long Man lay in a 'hundred', or area, called Wandelme-strei. This was thought to contain the name Waendel and the Old English words *helm* and *treo*, which could be taken to mean 'the tree of the helmeted Waendel'. If this is correct, the tree referred to could be the ancient two-stemmed yew which stands in the churchyard of the parish church, within view of the Long Man.

The yew is believed by the church authorities to be older than the church; Allen believes it is at least 1,500 years old, and that it may be connected in some way with Waendel. Local lore says that a chieftain is buried beneath it. Perhaps the Long Man's two staves indicate the burial, pointing to the yew (with its two stems) in the church. Alfred Watkins suggested that the two poles the Long Man holds could be sighting staves. The position of the yew in relation to the hilltop figure could well bear further investigation. Yet, as Allen says: 'Whatever the real significance of the Long Man of Wilmington, the yew tree of Wilmington is just as much an ancient monument as the figure. Despite metal chains and supports, it has exceptional beauty. Is it, I wonder, a special tree and does it hold the secret of the Long Man of Wilmington?'

The yew at Congresbury in Somerset is another tree that takes its name from a known figure, St Congar. Today the tree is quite mysterious, growing inside a beech tree in the churchyard. According to legend the tree was planted by St Congar (or Congarus), and this seems to be backed up by historical records. The Life of the Holy Congarus in the library at Lambeth Palace says that he was the son of the Emperor of Constantinople, and early in the sixth century AD fled from his father's court in order to avoid a marriage to which he was disinclined. He made his way to Britain and wandered until he came to this part of Somerset. Here he built and dedicated an oratory to the Holy Trinity. It is said that he wished for a yew tree to shade the oratory. He planted a staff in the earth; next day it put forth leaves, and subsequently grew into a wide-spreading tree. The King of the West Saxons, hearing of the miracle, granted land to Congar for the founding of a monastery. Congar is believed to have died during a pilgrimage to Jerusalem, whence his body was returned to be buried at Congresbury. For centuries the tree has been known as Congar's Walking Stick.

When Allen visited Congresbury in 1984 he expected to find at the most a few remains of an old decayed trunk, having read that in 1938 Arthur Mee had discovered that only a stump remained. The tree may have been struck by lightning some hundred or so years ago. However, Collinson's *County History of Somerset* had stated in 1790 that 'In the churchyard is a fine yew tree', so Allen thought it was worth checking. He was armed with an engraving of 1829 which showed the yew and exactly where it was positioned in the churchyard. When he arrived he could see a tree in that position, but, he says:

I could see beech leaves and a fairly ancient-looking trunk. As we hurriedly walked around the church to find our yew, we looked at the old engraving and saw that the yew must have been on the site where the old beech now was. As I approached the tree I could clearly see a familiar sign: the decayed outer bark of a yew. The old trunk of the yew is enclosed by this strange-looking beech tree, which appears to have been around it for at least 150 years. It is a most extraordinary sight. What is left of the old yew is still quite significant; part of the trunk is about 12 feet high.

Allen says that the tree seems to have been decayed and dead for a century or more, but adds: 'Where ordinary trees can be pronounced dead, the yew can never be, and in ten, fifty or a hundred years we may see life again restored to this yew. Only the yew and the mysterious spirit can give away these secrets. We left the site in wonder and marvel at what we had seen and felt.'

As for ancient references to specific yew trees, it is to be expected that few remain. There are many claims for yews, and other trees, having been mentioned in the Domesday Book, but according to the Forestry Commission no specific individual trees are mentioned in it at all, although plenty of woodlands are. Despite this, it has been claimed that yews at Chilcompton, Woolland, Cusop, Ripple, Buckland-in-Dover, Stoke Gabriel, Newlands Corner, Odstock and Rotherfield are all listed. Such a common misapprehension does at least suggest that people value their trees and wish to give them some sort of 'pedigree'.

One further thought on the naming of the yew should be added. In the eighteenth century there was a revival of Druidism which, as will be seen later, was closely connected with the yew. One of those involved in this revival was the scholar Godfrey Higgins, a chief Druid. He wrote *Celtic Druids* (1829) and *Anacalypsis* (1836), which is subtitled 'An attempt to draw aside the veils of the saitic Isis; or an enquiry into the Origins of Language, Nations and Religions'. He was interested in the connections between Celtic societies and the Middle East, and in *Celtic Druids* he set out to compare the letters of the Irish alphabet with the Hebrew, and where relevant also the Greek. In this book he runs through various letters, some of which do have similarities and others not, until he comes to the letter 'jod' to which he gives special attention:

The Jod or Iod or Iota, and Iodha and Yew, are all clearly the same, or as near as can be expected. This will be immediately found on pronouncing the *I* in the word Yew by itself, instantly followed by the other letters. In the Letters of Archbishop Usher, No. 81, it is stated by a Mr Davis, who was employed by the Bishop to procure manuscripts for him in the East, that he learned from the Samaritans, that their nation pronounced the word Jehovah YEHUEH, in Hebrew . . . Ieue. This must be *y*, as *i* in pine; *e* as *a* in ale; *hu*, as *hu* in Hume, or as *u* in use.

Any person conversant with the French and Italian languages knows, that the *i* in them is generally pronounced as the English *e* in queen, as ravine, but that in our language it is mostly pronounced as in the word pine. This is probably a remnant of our Asiatic original language, which we have kept in consequence of our secluded situation. It is the same sound as the *Y* or the *I* in the word . . . Ieue. Perhaps it may be thought far fetched, but, may not the name of the Yew, the very name of the God Jehovah, have been given it from its supposed almost eternity of life? It is generally believed to be the longest lived tree in the world. If this were the case, when a person spoke of the Yew-tree, it would be nearly the same as to say the Lord's tree.

CHAPTER 7

Ankerwyke

One tree can become a forest. Please let it begin at Ankerwyke.

ALLEN MEREDITH

On the banks of the river Thames, opposite Runnymede, there is an extraordinary and ancient yew, whose importance may not yet be fully revealed. Through evidence gathered over the last few years Allen has proved to the satisfaction of many historians that the tree was probably the site of the oath-swearing to the Magna Carta. More importantly than this, however, the Ankerwyke yew was an *axis mundi*, the sacred central focus of ancient tribes of the area. The rewriting of political history is one of the strangest things to have emerged through Allen's work, but Ankerwyke's rediscovery as a tree of historic importance may be but the introduction to a more vital message it wishes to give to humanity.

Over 700 years ago the barons of England found themselves in conflict with King John, who was obliged to concede to their complaints. On 15 June 1215, after nine days of talks, the Magna Carta was agreed at Runnymede. It remains the nearest thing to a bill of rights that Britain has ever had. The Magna Carta has also formed the basis of the constitutions of many other countries, including the USA.

It might be expected that the site of the signing of such a historically important document would now be well marked, and honoured. Visitors to Runnymede, however, are likely to be disappointed. No British memorial marks the spot; the whole site is confusing and was recently described by a daily newspaper as 'a

The Ankerwyke yew in the early nineteenth century

national disgrace' (*Daily Mail*, 9 July 1991). This neglect is due at least in part to no one having previously known the exact spot of the swearing. The Magna Carta itself gives no clue other than 'in the meadow that is called Runnymede between Windsor and Staines'.

Historians nevertheless agree that Runnymede was a special meeting place long before Magna Carta: 'Runnymede, said to be called the meadow of the Runes, or magical charms, the field of mystery, and the field of council' (Gordon Gyll, *History of Wraysbury*, 1861). In Saxon times it was known as Rune-mede, implying a place of council where, originally, the runes would have been consulted. Runes, as will be seen, have deep associations with yew trees.

The Ankerwyke yew today

At first sight it is hard to imagine what made this a place of such significance from even well before the Norman Conquest. Today the area lies in the outer London conglomeration where countryside is barely discernible between criss-crossing major roads and urban sprawl. However, it is just possible to make out the ruins of a Benedictine convent on the small island of Ankerwyke, across the other side of the Thames from what is now known as Runnymede. The convent was founded in about 1160, right next to a yew tree which must have already been there for about 1,700 years and which is still standing.

Allen has also contended, as the result of a dream, that before William the Conqueror many English kings were inaugurated under this tree. While this remains to be proved historically, if this should ever be possible, many of Allen's dreams have ultimately turned out to be uncannily accurate, and other sources have linked the

Runnymede area with the inauguration of early kings. In any case, the yew is now hollow and, like other ancient yews, is therefore difficult to measure.

The first positive measurement of the tree that we know of was in 1806, when Dr Samuel Lysons gave a girth of over 30 feet. In 1989 it was measured at over 29 feet, and it is not much different now to Lowe's description a century ago: 'The base was a good deal broken away, and hollow up to five feet. The trunk above this point, which at one time was hollow, is now filled with a mass of large trunk-like roots, to a degree more remarkable than any I have seen'.[1] It is likely that there has been a great deal of internal growth, and probably little change in the girth measurement over the last two or three centuries. From Allen's work on dating yews, it is clear that this tree must be at least 2,500 years old.

The convent must, then, have been built when the yew was already of a venerable age. It is possible, as seems to have been the case with so many other Christian buildings, that Ankerwyke was chosen for the site of a religious house precisely because it was already a sacred site, thanks to the yew. The word 'Ankerwyke' suggests an early hermitage ('ankerage', a place of retreat). Perhaps in the days before the arrival of the Saxons a hermit or holy man would have used the tree (quite likely hollow even then) as his shelter and his cell. Such practice is known of in other places, and a Saxon–Norman manuscript called the Ancren Riwle, dated around the thirteenth century, gives evidence of a hermitage tree.

Ankerwyke would thus have been the ideal place for the signing of the Magna Carta. Both the barons and King John would have wanted to meet in territory which afforded them protection, as each side distrusted the other. Ankerwyke would have provided some protection from a surprise attack, being surrounded by water. It may well have been regarded as neutral ground, for neither side would have wanted the reputation of having desecrated a convent by acts of violence. More importantly, the tradition of the *axis mundi* may well have lingered, and John could have derived authority from the tree as chieftains and kings had done in the past. To the nobles, too, the site may have appealed as the natural and traditional spot where weighty matters of state were adjudicated. Yet, if Ankerwyke is the most likely place in the area for the swearing of the great charter, how can the fact that it is clearly stated to have been signed at Runnymede be explained?

Allen first visited Ankerwyke in December 1981. He describes his sighting of the yew:

We walked along the frozen track and past a large deserted house. Later we crossed over a steam. The trees which seemed to close in around us were thick with frost, and a slight mist floating near the river added a certain magic to the afternoon. Ian Luckett, a small boy who occasionally accompanies me on my travels, pointed out the tree through the mist. It appeared unreal, as nearly all ancient yews I have seen are on high ground or in some remote churchyard. It seemed almost to be part of a dream, another world. To simply touch it was enough to sense this unique part of history. I would travel miles to see again and marvel at its wonders and mysteries.

Visiting the yew raised many questions in Allen's mind; what was such an ancient tree doing in this flat lowland, not on a hillside or in a churchyard as is usual? He had a strong sense of its importance. In 1989, after revisiting the site, he also began to receive a series of disturbing messages, and dreamt about a coronation ceremony at Ankerwyke. He felt the tree was warning him that its existence was threatened. Allen investigated and found that the area was planned for development. This prompted him to carry out extensive research into the tree, the area and its history. His investigations revealed that, at the time of the signing of the Magna Carta, Ankerwyke was probably part of a larger area known as Runnymede, comprising all the water meadows in the area. He also learned that the Thames has changed course several times since the thirteenth century; Runnymede and Ankerwyke are now on opposite sides of the Thames, but were then probably one united area.

Dr Andrew Brookes, a geomorphologist from the National Rivers Authority, supports this theory: 'Ten thousand years ago, the Thames flowed around a series of islands. It had a braided pattern, and only in the last 400 years or so has its main channel been centralized, widened and deepened for the needs of navigation.' Indeed, the old course of the Thames can be clearly seen at the base of Cooper's Hill, and local historians point out that Langham Ponds were once part of the old river course. The shifting of the course of the Thames may have been caused, at least in part, by the causeway built in about 1250, during the reign of Henry III, on the Egham side.

Allen unearthed some other pieces of evidence which added to the emerging picture. The thirteenth-century chroniclers Matthew Paris and Roger de Wendover gave vital clues in mentioning the ancient yew under which Saxon kings met. The Benedictine monk Matthew Paris wrote: 'propre villam de stanes, juxta flumen Thamasiac, in quadam insula' – indicating that the final agreement of the Magna Carta took place on a small island in the river Thames near Staines. It also became apparent that Sir Gilbert de Montfichet, one of the signatories of the Magna Carta, was a benefactor of the convent alongside the yew.

A meeting close to Cooper's Hill would not have been practical, Allen concluded; it would have been ideal for an ambush with longbows. Since the meadows around Runnymede were open, the only safe place in the area would have been the island of Ankerwyke, not only physically protected by the river but the very sanctuary that neither King John nor the barons would violate. King John is likely to have known of the yew's ancient significance; his chief aide, Gerald de Barri, had written a book called *Topographica Hybernica* which details the importance of sacred yews.

Allen's conclusion that the Ankerwyke yew was the site of the signing of the Magna Carta has been greeted with an astonishing degree of acceptance in a very short time. Some historians have put forward further evidence to support the hypothesis, and older references to it have been unearthed. For instance, J.J. Sheahen, writing in 1862, says: 'Here the confederate Barons met King John, and having forced him to yield to the demands of his subjects they, under the pretext of securing the person of the King from the fury of the multitude, conveyed him to a small island belonging to the nuns of Ankerwyke, where he signed the Magna Carta.'[2]

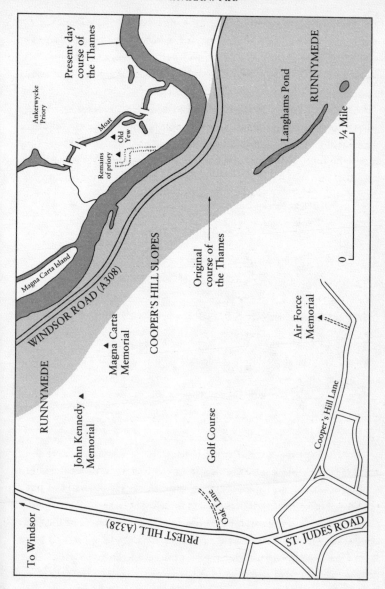

Map showing the Ankerwyke yew and Runnymede

Other historians, of course, have disagreed with Allen. Yet the idea has received much attention; it has been quoted virtually as fact in several articles, books and television programmes. Maybe it has touched on some long-forgotten memory with which we can readily identify.

Even as recently as the nineteenth century there seems to have been some more conscious memory still prevailing, as the following poem about the Ankerwyke yew suggests:

> What scenes have pass'd since first this ancient Yew
> In all the strength of youthful beauty grew!
> Here patriot Britons might have musing stood,
> And plann'd the Charta for their Country's good;
> And here, perhaps from Runnymede retired,
> The haughty John with secret vengeance fired,
> Might curse the day which saw his weakness yield
> Extorted rights in yonder tented field.[3]

And in 1840 the historian S.C. Hall wrote:

It is probable, therefore, that Edward the Confessor occasionally held his witan or council there during residence at Old Windsor, and that the barons chose the site as well on account of its previous association with those very rights they met to assert, as it was a convenient distance from Windsor, sufficiently near for the king, but far enough removed to prevent any treacherous surprises by his forces.

Apart from the ancient yew, there is also a mysterious avenue of around thirty old yews. Nothing is currently known about these, but Allen has teasingly suggested that they might have been planted in 1215 to commemorate the agreement of Magna Carta.

Perhaps more important than the emerging evidence of the links between the Ankerwyke yew and the Magna Carta, more and more people have come to feel the tree's significance in its own right. A Tree Preservation Order was granted in April 1990, and in early 1992 the dense undergrowth surrounding it was cleared. However, the fact that this has only happened so recently is an indictment of our conservation of yews.

Other stories of the tree's history are also slowly emerging. There is a legend that a dove conveyed a bough of the Ankerwyke yew in its bill to Germany, where a convent was built to protect the relic. It was later allegedly transplanted to Spain. Another story links royalty with the tree: Henry VIII is said to have occasionally met Anne Boleyn there, when she was staying in Staines in order to be near Windsor: 'Ill-omened as was the place of meeting under such circumstances, it afforded but too appropriate an emblem of the result of that arbitrary and ungovernable passion, which, overlooking every obstacle in its progress, was destined finally to hurry its victim to an untimely grave.'[4]

On 15 June 1992, 777 years after the signing of the original Magna Carta, a group of people again assembled under the Ankerwyke yew to make an oath. This pledge was as relevant to its time as the first had been; it was a 'green' Magna Carta, drawn up by David Bellamy and setting out to protect the world's wild spaces and wildlife. It reads:

We the free people of the islands of Great Britain on the 777th anniversary of the signing of Magna Carta do: Look back and give thanks for the benefits that the signings, sealing and swearing of oaths on that document handed down to us. Look forward to a new age of freedom through sustainability by granting the following rights to all the sorts of plants and animals with which we share our islands and our planet.

Ten pledges then follow for protecting all forms of life, and allowing them to 'live and complete their cycles of life as ordained by nature'.

Allen may have proved his hypothesis about Ankerwyke and the Magna Carta, but that is only a beginning. The tree has long been under threat from many quarters. A planned golf course which could have endangered it has been halted, but at the time of writing it is still not fully protected. Yet the tree may be one of our most ancient guardians of wisdom, a *deva daru*. This is a phrase which has come to Allen to describe a tree with special spiritual significance; for him such a tree seems to embody or guard a wisdom which is essential to the existence of this planet. He believes it now has to reveal itself because of human greed and ignorance and because of the way the earth is being treated. Allen feels it is vital for the Ankerwyke tree to be granted full protection:

It appears that this tree is becoming the voice for other ancient yews, other trees and much more, so that we may listen and at last recognize what once was and what is to come. It is only a tree but it comes from ages of great wisdom, from times when 'Druid' and 'deva daru' were not just words. This tree stood on this site more than a thousand years before the Saxons came. There would be no Runnymede, no Magna Carta, if the tree had not been there. I hope people will speak out and defend the tree. A *daru* is the most sacred of all trees, and Ankerwyke is the only one in the world I have been given to know.

CHAPTER 8

The World Tree

Again, and maybe the last time on this Earth, I recall the great vision you
sent me. It may be that some little root of the Sacred Tree still lives.
Nourish it then, that it may leaf and bloom and fill with singing birds. Hear
me, not for myself, but for my people; I am old. Hear me that they may
once more go back into the Sacred Hoop and find the good red road, the
shielding tree.

BLACK ELK

Allen became convinced that for further understanding of the yew
he had to turn to mythology and prehistory. He intuitively felt that
references to trees such as the famous oak grove of Zeus at Dodona,
the five sacred trees of Ireland, Pliny's tale of the Druids cutting
mistletoe from an oak, and the many accounts in Middle Eastern
mythology of a Tree of Life held the key to some truth about the
yew. He suspected that many of these traditions had evolved from a
recognition, far further back in history, that the yew was uniquely
sacred. That knowledge may have been lost and found, half-remem-
bered and forgotten again over many thousands of years. In different
periods, at certain places, it coalesced and expressed itself around a
tree, sometimes not a yew, and was lost again. He feels in some
instances that history has simply got it wrong; and the veneration
offered, according to historians, by Druids to the oak, for example,
was in reality given to the yew. A modern chief Druid concedes that
particular point as far as Ireland is concerned, although he holds to
the oak as the tree of traditional Druidism in mainland Britain. Allen
feels, too, that Dodona could have been a yew grove.

At this point, however, a circumspect first step is to examine the beliefs of the tribes who arrived in mainland Britain after the Romans left. For reasons probably only partially grasped by themselves, they saw fit to plant thousands of yews, some hundreds of which are still with us today.

Those Germanic tribes worshipped Odin and Thor, the old gods of the north. At the heart of that mythology, and at the very centre of that world, stood the great cosmic tree, Yggdrasil. There can be few symbols in myth as challenging or as rewarding as this tree, and it seems almost certain that Yggdrasil is a yew. Sometimes in the literature that surrounds the Norse myths the tree is described as an ash, or even 'an evergreen ash'. The *Larousse Encyclopedia of Mythology*, for example, unquestioningly refers to Yggdrasil as an ash, but there have always been commentators who left the question open. Turville-Petrie in *Myth and Religion of the North* (1964), for instance, concluded: 'there can be little doubt that the evergreen yew was held sacred, whether or not Yggdrasil was a yew'.[1] The source of the confusion may be that an alternative name for the yew in Old Norse is *barraskr*, which means 'needle ash'.

The origin of the World Tree is never mentioned in the legends, and even the derivation of the name Yggdrasil is obscure. Most commentators favour 'Horse of Odin', as Yggr is one of Odin's many names, and Odin hung from Yggdrasil for nine days. The Old Norse for yew is *yr*, so another commentator considers 'yew column' a possibility. More significantly, the evidence from all the texts stresses the evergreen needles and Yggdrasil's apparently eternal life. The ash has neither evergreen leaves nor a reputation for longevity.

Yggdrasil is the guardian tree of the gods who maintained the fabric of the universe, and the axis that binds together the three worlds: earth, heaven and underworld. From here the gods preside, and from his seat Odin can look into all three worlds at once. Yggdrasil rises to the sky, and its branches overspread the whole of creation. Three roots support it; one stretches to Hel, the world of the dead, another to the world of the frost giants and the third to the world of humans. At its foot are several springs tended by the

Drawing of a carved head of Odin

goddesses of fate, the Norns, and also the wells of Mimir and Hvergelmir. The Norns – Urd, Verdandi and Skuld (Fate, Being and Necessity) – decide human fates. Beside their spring the gods assemble daily, riding across the rainbow bridge that joins earth and heaven. The Norns take water and clay from the spring daily and sprinkle it over the tree to prevent its limbs from withering. The *Voluspa*, the twelfth-century poem that describes the creation and destruction of the world, says the water is so holy that anything that comes in contact with it will become as white as the film that lies within the eggshell.

It is Allen's view that the gods have their origins in yews, or in groves of yew trees, and are personifications of the trees. That origin is particularly clear with gods such as Mimir, who guards a spring. Yews in the ancient world are invariably found marking a water source and therefore guarding the entrance to the otherworld.

Heimdall, too, performs this guardian role, in the mythology, as it is he who guards the rainbow bridge that leads to Valhalla. The waters of the well of Mimir are the source of wisdom. Mimir was a wise giant who guarded the well and from whom Odin obtained a drink at the cost of an eye. Heimdall has left his mighty horn at the foot of Yggdrasil. He will sound it at the approach of Ragnarok, the twilight of the gods, when all will be destroyed. Hvergelmir's spring is the source of eleven rivers, and serpents lurk nearby. Around the base of the trunk is coiled a huge serpent who continually gnaws the roots, and deer browse on the trunk and lower branches. The trunk is decayed and rotting. A goat feeds here, too, devouring the needles, and her milk makes the mead which is drunk by the slain warriors feasting in Valhalla. Honey-dew falls from the tree and nourishes gods and humans, as the red arils of the yew, syrupy when ripe, drop in autumn. At the top of the tree sits an eagle with a hawk perched on its forehead. A squirrel, Ratatosk, scurries up and down the trunk conveying insults between the eagle and the snake, who are sworn enemies.

Yggdrasil suffers the torment of continual decay from the ravages

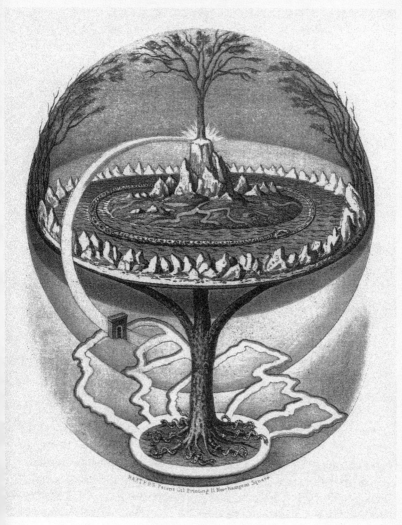

Yggdrasil, the World Tree

Drawing of a carved stone at Lindisfarne Priory, believed to show not only a
Viking attack but also Ragnarok, the apocalyptic end of the world

of the deer and snakes yet is constantly renewing itself. Rain, and
water in all forms, was often seen as the male energy fertilizing
the land. The Norns daily administer the flowing water and clay,
which are expressive of the semen and the receptive earth. For
here, at the centre, the processes of creation and decay must be in
balance.

It is known from a prophecy given to Odin that even the gods are
not exempt from this cycle and must in time perish. The portent of
their doom will be the failure of spring to return, so that the ice,
bitter cold and darkness of winter extend for years. This is the
Fimbulwinter that ushers in Ragnarok, the destruction of the world.
The giants march to do battle with the gods. The fire giant, Surt,
advances from the south, flames springing up around him. Fenris the
great wolf, with blood gushing from his mouth, breaks free and
swallows the sun. His open jaws touch both the sea and sky. The

treacherous Loki sails forth in Naglfar, his ship built from the fingernails of the dead, to wreak vengeance. In the ensuing battle, gods and giants destroy each other, and what is left of humanity is consumed by earthquake, flood and fire. Only Yggdrasil, though shaken to its roots, will survive, so that in time its trunk can open to release the parents of a new race to inhabit the earth. It is the Tree of Life and, to use Joseph Campbell's arresting phrase, 'the umbilical point through which the energies of eternity break into time'.

It is on this tree that Odin suspended himself, an ordeal that culminated in his discovery of the magical alphabet of the runes, which carries in its symbols evidence of yew magic. Odin's experience is very similar to that of the shaman in modern tribal societies. Shamanism seems to have its roots in a world at least as far back as archaeology can take us, and probably much further. It is possible that the psychic world was much more accessible to early people than it is to their 'civilized' successors. The cartoon image of the caveman with a club over his shoulder and lugging a carcass behind him is fading; to hunt and survive in the rigours of Ice Age Europe, he must have been highly attuned to the slightest sounds and movements in the natural world around him. Palaeolithic art, too, where it has survived, shows a relaxed and sensitive mastery in both drawing and sculpture.

The Australian spiritual teacher Barry Long, in a detailed exposition of evolution theory written from a psychic rather than a physical viewpoint, describes how early man 'lived mostly in his psychic double. His body performed on the earth in a totally instinctive way, while the vital feeling part of him lived a completely interiorized though parallel psychic existence.'[2] The upshot of this seems to be that man gained a fully individual sense of himself and his surroundings rather late, the process completing about 10,000 years ago. Prior to that was a very long transitional phase from a stage where he felt 'the world as himself'. Man was the centre of a psychic network where he received and knew the 'feelings' – this may be the most precise word available – being expressed by the environment around him. Hunting therefore was more than the skilled tracking of prey; 'rather, the animal communicated its presence to early man through the psychic network, of which man was the centre'. Instinct, sixth sense and our feelings of love or antipathy towards nature are the vestiges of what was once primitive man's whole consciousness.

Long states that his information comes from the 'higher levels of mind', but it complements and gives depth to the picture being built up by more conventional sources. Statuettes unearthed by archaeologists suggest that palaeolithic people perceived the whole world around them as the mother goddess. From the shores of western Europe to Siberia, over a hundred of these small figures have been found. Considering the great range from which they have been recovered, the figures are remarkably similar. They are female, with the breasts large and distended, the womb and hips round and heavy. The limbs receive less attention, the legs often tapering to a blunt point so that the image could be fixed in the ground. The head is featureless, patterned or abstract. The whole emphasis is focused on the fecundity of the womb and the nourishment of the breasts. Often the figures have been smeared with blood-coloured red ochre; this appears to be a symbol of rebirth, for it is found in graves of the period, too.

One such goddess figure from Laussel in the Dordogne dates from about 20,000 BC. She points to her pregnant womb with one hand and with the other, her right hand, holds aloft an animal's horn, the shape of the crescent moon. The horn is notched with thirteen lines, the number of months in the lunar year and the number of days of the waxing moon. Thus the menstrual cycle of the human womb was mirrored in the phases of the moon during its passage through the great domed womb of the sky.

The picture that emerges is of a people who are an integral part of nature's endless cycle of birth and death. It is not that they stood apart from that cycle and observed it; rather that it flowed through them, and they lived it.

At about 50,000 BC *Homo sapiens sapiens* replaced or interbred with the neanderthals, and this coincided with the slow melting of the last Ice Age. People sought refuge in caves and lived off the great herds which grazed the frozen tundra. Yet the most remarkable remains from this period have been found not in the caves where palaeolithic humanity lived, slept and cooked, but deeper within the earth, in vast limestone caverns which it seems were places reserved for ritual and ceremony.

Several caverns have been found in southern France, and their walls are covered with paintings. They can only be approached through long distances of labyrinthine tunnels, so it must have seemed to the artists who painted them as though they were crawling through the birth canal towards the womb of the mother goddess. On the walls of these caves are magnificent paintings of the myriad forms of life born from that source: the mammoth, rhinoceros and bison, the reindeer and musk ox, the owls, hares and fish. They may have been painted here as sympathetic magic to support the hunting bands, or drawn after a successful hunt so that the spirit of the animal returned to the earth to be reborn, or they may have been simply celebrations of the fecundity of the goddess.

Among these scenes are two which are increasingly being cited as evidence of shamanistic practice. The great cave at Lascaux, discovered as recently as 1940, was in use for at least 20,000 years. The earliest paintings date to 30,000 BC, but over that enormous length of time generations of artists reworked and overpainted, so that most of the existing art dates from about 10,000 BC. Deep in the heart of the cave, down a shaft accessible only with ropes, there is an intriguing and much discussed painting of a man and a dying bison. The bison is in its death throes, pierced by a spear, and the entrails are spilling on to the ground. Close by there is a bird, real or sculpted, perched on a stick. Above this is a man drawn with bird-like features; the head is beak-shaped, and only the four fingers of the hands are visible, rigidly splayed like claws. He may be flying, or possibly he is rigid on the ground in a trance or seizure. Many people believe this figure to be a shaman. The bird on the stick lies out of reach, and if this is a shaman's staff it may have been dropped or discarded. The figure of the man has an erect penis, and the composition of the painting is such as to suggest a link between the dying animal and the bird-man. Trance and out-of-the-body flight are fundamental to shamanism. It may be that the energy released by the dying animal is being harnessed to provoke these states in the bird-man.

There is a second shaman painting that adds weight to the case. In the cave of Trois Frères, high up on the wall above the animal scenes, is a figure about 30 inches high. It is half man and half beast. The antlers and ears are deer-like; the pose is that of an animal perched on its haunches in the manner of a squirrel or rabbit. The legs, feet and hindquarters are definitely human, save for the tail. The painting may depict a man in animal skins and antlers, or one drawing on the spirits of those animals as helpers. Certainly it is the earliest recorded example of a long tradition of human figures wearing stag antlers that travels through Cernunnos, the antlered god of the Celts, Herne the Hunter and many others through to the traditional horn dance still performed today in Abbott's Bromley in Staffordshire. The likelihood is that this figure and the bird-man are shamans.

These paintings, together with Long's assertion that human beings lived easily in a psychic realm, suggest that shamanism was a natural element of palaeolithic life. As the ice retreated and the forests reappeared, the great caverns were abandoned; people presumably followed the herds northwards or make the first tentative steps towards agriculture. The probability is that shamanism remained at the heart of the experience of the tribe; and it seems certain that the Celtic tribes had shamans.

What we know of shamanism comes mainly from the study of tribal societies still existing today, in particular the tribes of central Asia, although the phenomenon has been recorded extensively among North and South American tribes, including the Inuit, and in Indonesia and Japan. Much of our knowledge of shamanism comes from the work of Mircea Eliade.[3] He describes shamanism as 'a technique of ecstasy' whereby the shaman goes into trance and, abandoning his physical body, is able to journey to different realms. He or she may set off on these journeys as a spiritual quest, to seek the aid of the gods on behalf of the tribe, or to guide the soul of a recently departed tribe member who may be disoriented in the spirit world.

Different tribes have particular techniques, but in general a novice would undergo a period of instruction in attaining the trance state and be introduced to the oral lore and experience gathered by older shamans on their journeys. Before initiation a young man or woman may show signs of disordered behaviour, go off alone, suffer epileptic fits or act as if possessed. Such an ordeal is a sign that the young person's soul has been carried away by spirits for instruction. During initiations shamans relate that they die, their bodies are dismembered, their flesh is scraped from their bones. They may receive new bodies. Finally they awake again in their hut as from a deep sleep and can begin to practise their calling. The contemporary North American shaman Arwyn Dreamwalker says that such accounts are far from metaphorical; a shaman's pulse and breathing may stop altogether as he or she enters the gateways of death, from which they must make a conscious decision to return.

In some tribes the initiatory practices mirror closely, as will be seen, the experience of Odin on Yggdrasil. In one case the novice makes a symbolic ascent to heaven up a tree or pole. According to Eliade: 'in a dream or a series of waking dreams, the man chosen by the gods or spirits undertakes his celestial journey to the world tree'.[4] Another tribe has a different variation. A birch tree is set up in the hut, with its roots in the hearth and its crown projecting through the smoke hole. The initiate climbs the tree, emerging from the top to summon the aid of the gods. The procession then goes to another site where the initiate follows his master up another tree into which the master has cut nine notches which symbolize the nine heavens. A further report has the candidate climbing nine birches. For the shamans of the Altaic tribe of central Asia, ascending to heaven with the aid of a tree or pole is also the focus of their ceremony. The birch or pole is representative of the tree that stands at the centre of the world and connects heaven, earth and hell together. By playing his drum the shaman can fall into trance and fly to the centre of the world, aided by his belief that his drum is made from a branch of the cosmic tree that grows there. The cosmic tree is the route of access to the other dimensions.

The account of Odin hanging from Yggdrasil comes from one single precious manuscript which turned up in an Icelandic farmhouse 300 years after it was written in the thirteenth century. This is the poetic *Edda*, which contains 'Havamal', the sayings of Odin:

> I know that I hung on the windswept tree
> For nine days and nine nights
> I was pierced with a spear, and given to Odin
> Myself given to myself
> On that tree which no man knows
> From which root it arises.
> They helped me neither with bread
> Nor with drinking horn.
> I took the runes
> Screaming, I took them
> Then I fell back from that place.

It is clear that Odin has undergone a mystical experience brought about by a period of suffering and sacrifice. It is not the only occasion where Odin shows himself willing to suffer in the search for self-knowledge; he tore out an eye and flung it into the well of Mimir as the price demanded for the gift of prophecy. There are other examples in mythology, such as Tiresias and Oedipus in the Greek myths, where wisdom is gained only with the loss of physical eyesight. The parallels between the story of Odin and the recorded shamanistic experiences are striking: Yggdrasil and the shaman's cosmic tree are both at the centre, linking heaven and hell with earth. Proximity to the tree, either as in Odin's case by hanging from it, or for the shaman by climbing it, or an etheric connection by using wood from the tree in the drum to connect with it, seems vital to facilitate the altered state of consciousness. For the shaman the tree provides the route through which he or she can enter another world, just as it gives Odin access to a deeper level of being. Remarkable, too, is the recurrence of the number nine; the shaman notches his tree at nine levels to signify the nine heavens, and Odin's ordeal lasts nine days, suggesting that he has journeyed through all these inner realms.

There may also be other parallels, for in shamanism the trance state can be induced in two main ways: through the use of hallucinogens and by undergoing a combination of pain, exhaustion and sense deprivation. The first method has been much investigated, and the use of the peyote cactus, which contains mescalin, a powerful hallucinogen, is well known among the Indian tribes of Mexico. Among the northern European tribes the sacred mushroom, fly agaric, is the plant usually associated with shamanistic use. A modern authority on the runes, Edred Thorsson, reports that the yew also contains an alkaloid toxin that affects the central nervous system and when properly prepared is a powerful hallucinogen. In eastern Germany, a medical professor at the University of Greiz, Dr Kukowka, has discovered that on warm days the yew emits a gaseous toxin that lingers in the shade of the tree and can cause people in its shade to hallucinate.[5]

In earlier times there must have been extensive yew groves of vast age created by descending branches rooting and forming new trees. The only place known today that has the slightest resemblance to such groves is a yew wood on a private estate in Wiltshire. Here it is possible to travel across the wood from branch to branch without touching the ground. If Kukowka has recorded such effects under a single tree in the open air, it is not difficult to imagine that the exhalations from many trees in a restricted space, enclosed by a dense canopy of branches that would reduce ventilation, could produce a very potent effect indeed. It may well be, too, that compounds were prepared from the leaves or bark of the tree, to be taken at ceremonies. Nigel Pennick, another rune authority, in fact states this was so, but gives no source for his information.[6]

If yew was prepared in this way, then the shamans must have developed considerable skill, for any ingestion of yew is potentially lethal. If the tribe was aware that the yew could bestow either an ecstatic flight or death, seemingly at whim, then this could only have added immeasurably to the awe and respect in which the tree was held. Even today the toxicity of yew doesn't seem to be fully understood. The number of conflicting observations suggests that the toxicity fluctuates considerably, varying with different trees, time of year, the quantity and part of the tree eaten and so on. Animals fed on fodder may well be more at risk than wild animals that habitually graze on the move and that may well develop some immunity. It is now accepted that an immense amount of herbal knowledge and plant lore has been lost in the last few hundred years alone, burnt with witches at the stake or neglected and forgotten with the rise of science. That shamans possessed a very thorough knowledge of yew which enabled them to use it effectively for their purposes is perfectly feasible.

One curiously synchronistic, and possibly relevant, experience needs to be recorded here. At the precise time that this paragraph was being written, very early one morning, the writer's co-author was still sleeping. She had a dream where she saw 'yew kernels', the highly poisonous seeds contained in the aril, being inserted into an incision made just inside a person's ear. This minor surgery was carried out with some difficulty, but it seemed that in time the flesh healed over the wound, retaining the seed within the flesh, where presumably it deteriorated, allowing the poison to enter the blood-stream. In the serpent temple cults of India immunity to cobra venom was deliberately built up in the devotee over a period of time. It seemed just possible that the dream might have been a pointer to a similar practice.

The other method of shamanistic trance induction, that of pain and sense deprivation, is one that Odin was clearly employing, and his particular form of it, hanging from the tree, was certainly used by the North American tribes in their ceremonies. It was popularized, if that is the right word, some years ago by the actor Richard Harris in the film *A Man Named Horse* and is said to be currently undergoing something of a revival in the USA, where 'body piercers' seek out-of-body experiences by suspending themselves by various parts of their anatomy. Odin was suspended presumably by a rope or by some method of 'body piercing' or a combination of the two. Certainly when in position he was pierced by a spear.

Even today, in the modern city of Singapore, body piercing is the focus of celebrations among the Indian community at annual festivals. Large metal frameworks decorated with flowers and peacock feathers are carried in procession to the temple. They are held in place by skewers through the devotees' flesh. Some have lines of citrus fruits attached to their torsos by fish hooks. Others insert skewers through one cheek and out the other or vertically through the protruding tongue. While for some this is a public expression of faith and devotion, and they remain in a normal state of consciousness throughout, for others it is a well-understood route to ecstatic trance. A cluster of friends support the devotee with incense and percussion, and as the skewers enter the flesh he or she falls easily into a state of ecstatic body movements.

Odin's discovery of his own mortality is a spur to a search for self-knowledge. Once he learns that he will not survive Ragnarok he strives to obtain wisdom. His descent to the underworld, too, to learn the details of Ragnarok from the sibil, is another example of a shamanistic journey. Hanging on the tree, he has undergone 'myself given to myself'. He has surrendered, dropping all the defences that guard one reality of self with its tight framework of personality, to attain a state of being more profound and unified. That achievement is symbolized by his discovery, or realization within himself, of the runes.

Odin's experience on Yggdrasil throws more light on the mysterious symbol of the tree. Its roots extend into other worlds of spirits, giants and hell. The overall impression conveyed by the myths is that a visit to the worlds below Yggdrasil is hazardous. Hel is the goddess of the underworld; she is hideous, a half-black, half-white rotting corpse. The gods Thor, Loki and Thjalfi also went to the land of the giants and were comprehensively outwitted. In a series of trials of strength Thor is unable to lift the giant's grey cat; Loki is beaten in an eating contest; and Thjalfi loses a running race. The gods have fallen victim to the giants' magic, which has highlighted the forces against which the gods are powerless. The grey cat turns out to be the world serpent with whom Thor has had at least one previous combat which has resulted in a stand-off. Loki found his true opponent had been Fire that consumes all, and Thjalfi found himself a poor second to the speed of Thought. Incredibly Thor lost a wrestling match with an old woman – incredible that is, until it is revealed that he has been fighting Old Age itself.

The message is clear. There are forces outside of mortality and nature over which even gods have no control. There are also forces within: the ravaging dominance of thought in the conscious mind, which no person can still or master, and deeper in the depths of the unconscious lurking monsters with whom human beings can only ineffectively spar. It is these forces that will uncontrollably burst out at Ragnarok. Yggdrasil emerges as a symbol of human consciousness. Above ground the gods act with seeming clarity of purpose, but, as in the unconscious, beneath ground they are driven by hidden and disturbing forces.

It is presumably the world serpent that lies coiled at the base of Yggdrasil. Wherever the World Tree has appeared in mythology the serpent has never been very far away, be it – to mention but a few of countless locations – on the cylinder seals of Sumeria, in the Garden of Eden or coiled round the apple tree of the Hesperides in ancient Greece. By itself the serpent is certainly symbolic of water in its undulating movement; indeed, when Odin hurled the world serpent into the depths of the ocean, it could, with its tail in its mouth, encircle the world of humans. Its writhings created the storms, so that humanity was enveloped by serpent and water, at times indistinguishable one from the other. The serpent, with its tail in its mouth and its ability to cast off a skin and emerge anew, has been invoked as a powerful symbol of regeneration and rebirth and thus been linked with the mother goddess. On her images in palaeolithic art there often appears an undulating or meandering line suggestive of a snake or the movement of water.

The serpentine roots of the yew at Waverley Abbey

The serpent can also take the shape of a coiled spiral, sometimes dormant yet remaining a potent reservoir of the life force. In the east the Buddha sits in alert repose on the coils of the cobra, shaded from the sun by the snake's outspread hood. In India the *kundalini* is the serpent power coiled at the base of the spine that will be awakened by meditation. The human body in joy or ecstatic dance often experiences an upwards spiralling energy that seems to arise from nowhere. The DNA molecule, the very basis of all life, has a spiral form; and almost unique in trees, the yew has a spiral spring built into the secondary wall of each cell. The symbol of the serpent seems very much a symbol of the movement of subtle energy and when coiled around the World Tree emphasizes the hidden flowing energies contained within the massive, firmly rooted trunk. Hence the tree is both a fixed point at the centre of the world and a fluid column of energies passing through it.

Sometimes the deep furrowing of the yew's bark is not aligned with the axis of the tree but coils round the tree, snake fashion; the yew avenue at Midhurst in Sussex has some fine examples. A correspondent wrote to Allen about the yew among the remains of Waverley Abbey, south-east of Farnham, in Surrey: 'It is very old and has a root system like none other I've seen ... it resembles dozens of writhing snakes and has an eerie effect. It's huge at the base.'

At the top of Yggdrasil sits an eagle, and this bird, with its effortless grace in flight, acuteness of vision and great talons, is surely an appropriate image of mastery and power; indeed, it has been adopted as a symbol of authority by nations throughout history. It may indeed be Odin, since he had a special seat on the tree from where he could look into all the worlds at once. The eagle was one of the forms that he took when in shamanistic flight, and Snorri Sturluson – whose thirteenth-century prose *Edda* records the myths – relates that Odin could travel anywhere in spirit form, in animal, bird or fish form, while his body remained asleep.[7]

Whether or not the eagle is Odin, there is a curious detail. On the forehead of the eagle is perched a hawk. At first sight this is bizarre; eagles don't really have foreheads, so why having chosen the rightful bird to sit in majesty on top of the world make it slightly ridiculous with a smaller bird clinging on just above its great hooked beak? One possible explanation seems to be that the hawk, whose eyesight is as keen as that of the eagle, is not serving as some superfluous extra look-out, but is looking in. It is therefore a symbol of the faculty known in esoteric systems as the third eye. If this is the case, then it must be assumed that the shamans and priests of the old religion of the north had considerable spiritual knowledge. The centre of the forehead, just above the eyes, is the accepted position of this energy point in the etheric body, but it may also have some connection with the mysterious pineal gland that occupies a similar position in the physical brain.

In the Indian system of *chakras*, which describes an etheric rather than a physical anatomy of the human form, the third eye is the sixth *chakra*, whereas the *kundalini* in its unawakened state remains curled around the base *chakra* which corresponds to the genitals in the physical body. The opening of the third eye marks an advanced stage of spiritual development. The Indian spiritual master Osho said: 'With the third eye functioning you enter a different dimension. If you look at a person you look at his soul, at his spirit, not his body. The body is not there, just the one who resides in the body.'[8]

The Norse stories say that the eagle and the snake are enemies and communicate only through the squirrel, who scurries up and down the trunk carrying the insults traded between the two. The effort of the seeker to unify and integrate his or her being will inevitably highlight that conflict between the eagle and the snake – between the rational and the unconscious; between the desire to dominate, organize and comprehend, and the deeper currents of emotion, intuition and energy that remain hidden. The Norse masters, with wry humorous detachment, visualized that struggle as the tireless commuting of the go-between squirrel. It is the triumph of Odin that he completed that struggle within himself and conveyed the experience within a profound set of symbols called the runes.

A tribal society at a pre-literate stage of development preserves its wisdom in oral tradition, and probably most effectively in stories and legend. In this way the task of memorizing and communicating is easier, and the same story can be understood with different levels of comprehension. Yggdrasil would have expressed a picture of the world view of the tribe and would possibly have also served an esoteric function as the framework and model used by the shamans to convey their inner work.

Allen is insistent that Yggdrasil was a real tree, an actual yew around which the legends and stories grew. There must have been at this time thousands of sacred groves and trees in northern Europe. Most of the continent was still covered with vast areas of virgin forest that would remain unexploited until the development of the heavy plough in early medieval times. Tree worship was widespread. In AD 772 Charlemagne, during a campaign against the Saxons, destroyed Irmensul, which translated means 'the giant column'. This may have been a tree or a pillar made from a tree trunk, for the latter too were venerated as a symbol of the World Tree.

By far the most likely site for Yggdrasil, however, was Gamla Uppsala, in Sweden, which was a political and religious centre for the Svea people in the fourth to sixth centuries AD. By the Middle Ages it was inevitably under attack from Christian forces, such as those of the newly converted King Olaf in 1008. By the twelfth century the Christian Trinity had replaced Thor and Odin in the shrines. What we know of it before that happened is only hearsay recorded by the Christian monk Adam of Bremen, and he, understandably, had a subjective view of things.

Adam describes a temple with three gold statues: Thor in the centre, flanked by Odin and Frey. Every nine years there was a major festival, and the grisly sacrifices are described in detail. Adam's source relates that dogs, horses and men were hung from the trees and that he had seen seventy-two bodies, some animal and some human, suspended side by side.

While human sacrifice was a possibility, there is also the likelihood that at his festival devotees of Odin would act out or undergo the crucial event of his life, especially if they believed the tree there was the very one on which the god had hung. It is always possible, too, that a rite that was once sacred and contained the truth could have degenerated into barbarism. Yet the possibility remains that Adam may simply have put the worst possible interpretation on what he heard. Perhaps his informant had witnessed shamanistic rituals involving body piercing and interpreted them for himself as human sacrifice. It is not a point that is ever likely to be cleared up. A note added in the margin of Adam of Bremen's report of the rites describes the tree: 'Beside this temple stands an enormous tree, spreading its branches far and wide; it is evergreen in winter and summer. No one knows what kind of tree it is.'

In Adam's account the grove was simply described as 'evergreen', but there is no doubt that it must have been a very ancient yew grove, sacred for many centuries. Tradition in Scandinavia certainly bears this out, as a local guidebook to the remains at Gamla Uppsala still records: 'Where belief in the old Nordic gods flourished there was always a sacred grove nearby. Where the aspens now grow stood an immense yew tree ... so large that it was called the "Tree of the World" and symbolized the universe.'

The runes are a collection of signs or symbols etched on to wood or stone. Today they are used for divination and personal guidance, rather as tarot cards are. This modern use of runes is probably very close to their Bronze Age origins. A large collection of runic ideograms has been found carved on to rocks in Sweden. Legends tell of the Volsungr, an ancient tribe that came from the north with the encroaching ice and were guardians of the forest, who brought with them the wisdom of the runes. Allen believes that the very earliest runes were carved into pieces of yew wood, magical sigils encoding the insights realized by cults and tribes in a deep communion with the tree. Much later, probably in about the second century BC, the runes began to develop a practical function. The symbols became connected with phonetic sounds and developed into an alphabet of twenty-four runes which is now known as the older Futhark. This process probably happened through contact that Alpine Germanic tribes had with the Etruscans, who were developing an alphabet at about this time. The use of the Futhark spread through Germany to Denmark and Scandinavia, and extra runes were added on the way. Ninth-century Northumbria used a 33-rune Futhark.

The runes had many practical everyday uses; they were marks for traders and makers, and were used in calendars and memorials. This use continued into the eighteenth century in Scandinavia but it never developed into a cursive script. The likelihood is that the runes began as a system of magical symbols and that this function continued alongside any practical purposes the Futhark was put to.

The word 'rune' in all the old languages – Norse, English, Saxon, High German and Gothic – has the same meaning: mystery or secret. Many surviving runic inscriptions are on amulets and talismans, or treasured personal items such as rings or swords. It is this magical use of runes, inscribing an object with a sigil or formula with the intent to imbue it with psychic force, which has a close connection with the yew.

The Roman historian Tacitus described the use of the runes for divination by the Germanic tribes at the end of the first century AD. Pieces of branch were cut from a tree and marked with signs. These were scattered randomly on a white cloth, and a priest, or the head of a household if guidance was being sought on a family matter, would pick them up and interpret them. Thus the system, at least in this aspect, has clear parallels with both tarot and the I Ching (the Chinese Book of Changes). As to how the selection process worked and what hidden forces guided the priest's hand to a particular stick, the sensible course is probably to follow C.G. Jung's advice, given after pondering the same problem with the I Ching: 'the less one thinks about the theory the more soundly one sleeps'.[9] It is reasonable to assume, though, as is the case with both the tarot and the I Ching, that the signs on the sticks were symbols that represented themes, strands of understanding that reached deep into the collective myths and experience of the tribe, and surfaced to form many of their beliefs and views of the world.

In the older Futhark several of the twenty-four runes have the names of trees; *eoh*, the yew rune, is the thirteenth, with the symbol ⋀. The deeper significance that lies behind the symbol is the subject of this book, and most writers commenting on the symbolism of the runes draw attention to the tree's longevity, its mysterious quality and its links with death through its toxicity and the longbow. Pennick points out that the yew rune has the shape of the pot hook that would have supported the cauldron over the cooking fire. The cauldron has many connections with the yew, as will be seen. There is an Old English rune poem which describes *eoh* merely as 'the yew with rough bark, well rooted in the earth, a guardian against fire, a joy to the home'.

Other runes too are connected with the yew, notably *elhaz*, the elk which browses around the trunk of Yggdrasil. The force of this rune is the concept of protection, and its ideogram Y could represent the antlers of the elk but is also tree-like. The Old Norse word *ihwar* occurs only in runic inscriptions and means either yew tree or yew bow. The bow has obvious protective qualities, but the tree itself has often been planted as a guardian or protective tree around houses throughout Europe. In the younger Futhark, developed later, one of the added runes is *yr*, with the ideogram ⋏ , which symbolizes the bent yew bow, and also the trunk and three roots of Yggdrasil.

Undoubtedly runes were mostly inscribed on wood and have therefore largely not survived. There are a few notable exceptions, however, and these provide strong evidence of the connection of the yew with magic. Some pieces of yew wood with runic inscriptions have been uncovered in the Frisian *terpen* – artificial mounds on the flood plain where the waterlogged conditions have preserved wooden artefacts. One is a short wooden sword found at Arum and dates from the first half of the seventh century. It has the runic inscription 'edoeboda', which may be a personal name or mean something like 'return messenger'. It was probably an amulet to protect a traveller. Another piece of yew, dating from the same period, has scholars in close agreement as to the translation of the runes on it: 'Always carry this yew! Therein lies virtue' (Bugge, 1908); 'Always carry this yew! Therein lies strength' (Arntz, 1939); and 'Always carry this yew in the host of battle' (Buma, 1951).[10] There can be little doubt that this is a warrior's amulet bearing witness to a deep faith in yew magic.

At Westeremden in Groningen, on the Frisian coast, two other yew pieces have been found, later in date, probably early ninth century, as the inscriptions are in the Anglo-Saxon younger Futhark. One is a piece of weaving equipment which is marked with what are assumed to be personal names. There is no reason to believe this item served any magical purpose. The second piece, known as Westeremden B, is a yew wand with an inscription that has sorely taxed the scholars. It contains an intriguing reference to Amluth, who was Shakespeare's Hamlet, and seems to be an invocation to calm the waves of the sea. The survival of these finds is exceptional, due to the favourable conditions of the *terpen* they were found in, but it is unlikely that in their time they were in any way exceptional; they were probably objects in regular use, along with many similar pieces that have perished.

The Frisians were in regular contact with the Anglo-Saxon settlers in Britain and were in time converted to Christianity by missionaries sent from there. Some of them held out and in AD 755 martyred St Boniface. He had been a most ferocious destroyer of sacred trees and groves and at Geismar in Hesse had felled an oak sacred to Thor. It had crashed to the ground and formed the shape of the cross – the standard capitulation of the felled sacred tree, at least according to the Christian chroniclers. There is no reason to assume that yew magic was not a widespread practice throughout the area of north-western Europe and Britain inhabited by the Germanic tribes at this time, but it was bound to yield as Christianity took hold.

There was a long period that produced some remarkable cultural hybrids such as the Ruthwell Cross and the Gosforth Cross where Yggdrasil and Loki exist alongside Christian imagery. The Old English 'Nine Herbs' charm mingles Christ and Odin and contains a powerful display of rune magic. In an incident in the poem, Odin takes nine twigs which have the initial letters of plants inscribed on them in runes. The magic successfully cuts a snake into nine pieces. There is also the beautiful traditional carol, 'The Leaves of Light', which describes a meeting between Thomas, probably Doubting Thomas, and seven virgins, one of whom is the mother of Jesus:

> Oh where are going you seven pretty maids
> All under the leaves of light?
> Oh we are going, Thomas, they said,
> Seeking for a friend of thine.
>
> And they went down into yonder town
> And sat in the Gallery
> And there they saw sweet Jesus Christ
> Hanging from a big Yew Tree.

As the new magic of the rosary, genuflection and the Latin mass replaced the runes, so yew magic drifted into folklore. Examples of that are scattered throughout this book, but what now seem just quaint customs – such as keeping a yew stick behind a door to ward off evil, or circling the Stoke Gabriel yew as a fertility rite – are the remains of an alive and powerful magic. That magic had its roots in a natural religion to which the yew was central. The Christians had little choice but to build their church strategically in its shadow.

CHAPTER 9

The Yew and the Goddess

If they do these things in the Green Tree, what shall be done in the Dry?

LUKE 23: 31

The worship of Odin in the northern European forests led the Saxons to plant yew trees when they arrived in Britain. However, once Allen's dates for the age of the trees are accepted, it is clear that the Saxons arrived in a country where the yew had already been venerated for hundreds of years. The already mature trees at Tandridge in Surrey and at the two Crowhursts, in Surrey and Sussex, as well as others where Saxons settled, are evidence of an aspiration common to Celt and Saxon. As both races had migrated westwards, it would seem possible that knowledge of the yew's significance had travelled with them and can be traced further back to a common Indo-European heritage.

Any migrating tribe originating from a central Asian homeland would have been aware of the yew. The easternmost limit of *Taxus baccata* is the Carpathian Mountains of eastern Europe. Further east the yew is a different, though in appearance very similar, species: *Taxus wallichiana.* It is found in the mountain ranges that stretch through Afghanistan, Pakistan, India and the small Himalayan kingdoms to Burma and the Philippines.

The movements of prehistoric peoples can never be known for certain, and the origins and movements of the Celts are extremely difficult to determine. At their maximum extent, at about the third century BC, they ranged from modern Turkey in the east across to Spain and Ireland in the west. At one time it was accepted that the

Celts arrived in Britain in waves of invasions at about 500 BC. Now archaeologists talk of 'proto-Celts' and use the term to describe peoples such as the 'urnfield culture' of central Europe from about 1300 BC and the Beaker people who arrived in Britain at about 2000 BC from the Iberian peninsula.

The nineteenth century favoured the common Indo-European heritage theory: that tribes moved both west to Europe and eastwards to the Indus valley from a central Asian homeland. That view is again finding modern support. Colin Renfrew, in *Archaeology and Language*, proposes that by about 6000 BC in Anatolia languages were in use which were the ancestors of all the modern Indo-European languages.[1] Certainly at this time on the Konya plain in southern Anatolia, centred on Çatal Huyuk, a remarkable culture was flourishing. Evidence of lead and copper smelting, spinning, weaving and dying of cloth have been found. This culture also had buildings decorated with wall paintings that served as shrines to the mother goddess. Renfrew thinks it possible that the earliest Indo-European speakers could have reached Britain as early as 4000 BC.

The Indo-Europeans who moved eastwards into the Indus valley had established centres at Mohenjodaro and Harappa as early as 2500 BC. They must have revered trees, for a seal has been unearthed from there which shows a tree with its trunk swelling into a womb from which animals emerge. The Tree of Life is a womb, the creative source at the centre, as was seen with Yggdrasil, and much of this chapter is concerned to locate the places in the ancient world where the tree was worshipped as the mother goddess.

The Tree of Life must be the tree through which the life force flows and from which life is born, otherwise the symbol is sterile and abstract. Allen now refuses to be photographed in a churchyard because it perpetuates the distorted picture of the yew as the tree of death. Modern society has viewed death increasingly as an absolute finality. While the goddess has her death aspect, of course, as the crone, or Kali, or the white owl flying from the hollow yew, this was only one face and part of an endless cycle of creativity. It may be a symptom of the dislocation in our psyche that this image of the yew tree as death, as a thing to shrink from and deny, has remained frozen in our minds for so long.

India has a long tradition of tree worship, from the Mohenjodaro civilization to the present day. Countless villages all over the country still have a venerated sacred tree. The yew grows throughout the Himalayas up to 10,000 feet, and John Lowe recorded that

the tree was held in great veneration in some parts of the north-west Himalayas; it sometimes is called deodar, that is God's tree, the wood is burnt for incense, branches are carried in religious processions in Kamaon, and in Nepal the houses are decorated with the green twigs at religious festivals.[2]

Powdered yew bark was also used to make the paste which Hindus place on the forehead. The description of the yew as 'deodar' may cause some confusion because there is also a Himalayan cedar, 'cedrus deodara', commonly known as 'deodar'.

The Tree of Life is a recurrent image emerging from the excavations of the Mesopotamian civilizations. From as early as 5000 BC these cultures flourished along the banks of the Euphrates and Tigris. There were three great goddesses in the region in the Bronze Age: Inanna in Sumeria, known as Ishtar in Babylon; Cybele to the north in Anatolia; and Isis in Egypt. The legends surrounding all three closely link them with the Tree of Life. At this time the goddess was still the dominant deity, but a male figure had appeared, fulfilling the role of both son and lover. He was a vegetation god who died every year at the harvest and was born again in the spring to fertilize the goddess once more so that the earth would be fruitful. These goddesses with their son-consorts will be described in some detail, because of the clear similarities they have with early British mythology, where the goddess was Cariadwen and the yew was very likely a form in which she was worshipped.

The rite of the sacred marriage was celebrated throughout the ancient world. In Sumeria it was the goddess Inanna and her consort Tammuz or Dumuzi whose union was vital for the fertility of the earth. The union of goddess and consort was symbolized and celebrated annually by human representatives in a spring festival. The role of the goddess was taken by the high priestess of her temple, and that of her consort by the king or high priest. It is possible that in the earliest times the king may have been annually sacrificed at the harvest, just as Tammuz died, and replaced the following spring. The physical union of the priest and priestess would have taken place, often publicly, on top of the ziggurat, the stepped pyramid temple.

Several Sumerian hymns have been found that celebrate the sacred marriage, but probably the most familiar description of it is The Song of Solomon. This work may date from Solomon's time, about 1000 BC, but it was written down much later. The urgency and joy of human love are woven into the landscape, and the beauty of the beloved is also the fecundity of the flocks: 'Behold you are beautiful my love, behold you are beautiful. Your eyes are doves behind your veil. Your hair is like a flock moving down the slopes of Gilead. Your teeth are like a flock of shorn ewes that have come up from the washing, all of which bear twins, and no one among them is bereaved' (4: 1, 2).

There are many connections between the Tree of Life as a symbol of the goddess and the sacred marriage. One of the ancient cities of Sumeria was Ur, whose royal tombs were excavated in the 1920s. Among the discoveries was a beautiful statue of a ram. He is reared upright on his hind legs, and his front legs rest on the branches of a golden Tree of Life. The ram is blue and golden; it is the sun god at the spring equinox in the zodiac sign of the ram. The statue represents the union of the sacred marriage, of mother earth and the male heat of the sun, which is vital to ensure the harvest.

In the later kingdoms of Babylon and Assyria the Tree of Life seems to have been the dominant deity. The Assyrian capital was Nineveh; its construction is recorded in the Bible in Genesis and it was destroyed by the Medes in 612 BC. It was excavated in the mid-nineteenth century by the archaeologist Austin Henry Layard. He found the great palace of Aššur-nasir-apli, and in the state rooms he discovered the alabaster panels that are now in the British Museum. The Tree of Life appears in well over a hundred scenes. It is tended by a winged deity who sometimes has a human head and sometimes the head of an eagle. In his right hand this figure holds a pine cone which he points at the tree; in his left hand he carries a small bucket. This may be another depiction of the sacred marriage, as the pine cone is a commonly used male symbol. The winged figure may be sprinkling the tree with water from the bucket both as a practical aid to fertilization and as a symbol of the male god fertilizing the goddess in the form of the tree.

Layard's excavations at Nineveh provide the starting point for an investigation into how yew was viewed at this time. Layard brought back a piece of wood from Nineveh, and this came into the possession of Professor George Henslow, a leading botanist of his day who in 1906 published *The Plants of the Bible*. Henslow examined the wood and found that it was yew. As part of his research Henslow wanted to know the identity of the tree called in the Bible *almug* or *algum*. The word is mentioned only twice:

Moreover the fleet of Hiram, which brought the gold from Ophir, brought a very great amount of almug wood and precious stones. And the king made of the almug wood supports for the House of the Lord, and for the king's house, lyres also and harps for the singers; no such almug wood has come, or been seen, to this day. (1 Kings 10: 11, 12)

Send me also cedar, cypress, and algum wood from Lebanon, for I know that your servants know how to cut timber in Lebanon. (2 Chronicles 2: 8)

So far it is only apparent that *almug* is one of possibly several types of conifer growing on Mount Lebanon, but Henslow was able to take the matter a step further:

A microscopical examination of a piece of wood brought home by Dr Layard, in my possession, proves it to be the wood of the yew tree, a wood which is notorious for its strength, flexibility as for bows, and durability. The yew is not recognizable in any Hebrew word, but was called *smilax* in Greek; and the question arises, can we discover any connection between *smilax* and *almug*?

The word *smilax* occurs in the LXX in the following passage. Jeremiah is speaking of the downfall of the King of Egypt, and says: 'The sword hath devoured thy Smilax. Why has the Apis fled from thee [i.e. Egypt]? The young bull, thy chosen, one, has not remained. Because the Lord has discharged him.' The smilax seems clearly to represent a king supposed to be *firmly rooted* on his throne; while the *great age* to which the yew tree will grow would be a fitting reference to the kingdom of Egypt.

Of course no yew trees ever grew in Egypt; but the tree is taken symbolically, and would be well known to his readers in the more northern Palestine and Syria.[3]

The 'LXX' referred to is the Old Testament known as the Septuagint. In the second century BC a translation was made in Alexandria from Hebrew manuscripts into Greek. The task was performed by seventy scribes, hence the name, who each came up with identical versions. If Henslow is right, then this metaphorical use of yew to denote kingship, with its inference of an *axis mundi* conferring temporal authority, is interesting. It suggests Jeremiah's audience would have readily recognized the reference to the yew and appreciated the range of meanings the symbol contained.

There is no doubt that reading between the lines of the Old Testament reveals a great deal of evidence that there was a flourishing tradition of worship of the mother goddess existing alongside that of Yahweh. Later editors must have tried to convey the impression of an unrivalled, all-powerful male God, but this was not wholly successful. Owen Morgan, a turn-of-the-century writer whose views have influenced Allen, has some perceptive comments on the description of King David and the return of the Ark of the Covenant to Jerusalem found in 2 Samuel 6. David is reproached by his wife Michal for dancing naked in front of the Ark, especially when the servant girls are looking on. In reply David warns her that he will make himself 'yet more contemptible' and that 'I will be abased in your eyes; but by the maids of whom you have spoken, by them I shall be held in honour'. The next verse is very much to the point: 'And Michal the daughter of Saul had no child to the day of her death.' It seems that what is happening here is yet another version of the sacred marriage. David as priest-king has danced naked in front of the Ark, which with its boat shape is, as will be seen, very much a symbol of the goddess. As David and the servant girls clearly understand, the rite is essential for the continuing fertility of the tribe and the earth. By choosing to reject the rite, Michal suffers the consequences and remains barren.[4]

There is little doubt that in the following passage Jeremiah is condemning tree worship: 'Have you seen what she did, that faithless one, Israel, how she went up on every high hill and under every green tree, and there she played the harlot? . . . she polluted the land, committing adultery with stone and tree' (Jeremiah 3: 6–9). The phrase 'on every high hill and under every green tree' occurs regularly throughout the Old Testament. It is clearly a euphemism that acknowledges the continued existence of a goddess rival to Yahweh but wishes to keep the details as obscure as possible.

There are two similar passages in Ezekiel that are of particular interest to Allen. They contrast the 'green tree' with the 'dry tree', and because of the associations attached to the green tree there must be a similar significance alluded to in the reference to the dry tree, or in linking them together. In chapter 17, verse 4, the Lord promises to 'dry up the green tree and make the dry tree flourish'. In chapter 20, verse 47, there are further wrathful pronouncements: 'Behold I will kindle a fire in you, and it shall devour every green tree in you and every dry tree; the blazing flame shall not be quenched, and all faces from south to north shall be scorched by it.'

This prophecy is taken up again in Luke's gospel, where Christ, carrying his cross on the way to Golgotha, turns to wailing women and warns them not to weep for him but for themselves, for many worse calamities are ahead. He concludes: 'If they do these things in the Green Tree, what shall be done in the Dry?'

In many legends from the Middle Ages which Allen has traced these references were picked up and linked with the Tree of Knowledge and the Cross. The Tree of Knowledge was seen as the 'dry tree', barren due to Adam's sin, and the Tree of Life as the 'green tree'. Fruitfulness could only be restored to the dry tree through the sacrifice of Christ upon it. After expulsion from the Garden of Eden, Adam lived a further 932 years and on his deathbed told his son Seth to return to the barred gates of the garden and ask the archangel on guard there for mercy. Seth is allowed three glances into the Garden of Eden, where he sees a dried-up tree with a serpent around the trunk. The top of the tree reaches heaven, and in its uppermost branches is a new-born child. The roots descend to hell. The angel explains that what Seth has seen foretells a future Redeemer for humankind. He gives Seth three seeds from the fruit of the tree from which his parents ate and tells Seth to place these in Adam's mouth when his body is laid in the grave. From these seeds grew three trees, which after many further episodes fused into one tree from which the Cross was made.[5] A fourth-century poem, *De Ligno Vitae*, summarizes the essence of these legends:

> There is a place that we believe to be the centre of the universe
> Where rises the hill that the Jews call Golgotha.
> There was planted, I remember, a branch cut from a dry tree
> And the wood produced the healing fruits of Life.[6]

It is Allen's view that within these legends, and behind the reference to the 'green tree', lies the fruit-bearing female yew. Behind the 'dry tree' is the non-fruit-bearing, and therefore 'dry', male yew.

The connection between the goddess myths of Sumeria and Egypt and the yews planted in the sacred sites of Celtic Britain can be traced through the image of the goddess as Tree of Life and womb. With time the symbol expanded to include related images; a hollowed tree trunk, for example, served humankind both as the first boat and also as the first coffin. When Tammuz died at midsummer he went to the underworld in a moon boat. The male god at this time is in a transitional phase. As with the rest of life and vegetation, he was born from the mother goddess and is therefore a 'son', yet he is evolving to independence, reflecting a changing balance in the human psyche, and is *en route* to becoming a 'sun' god. This gradual tipping of the scales towards a dominant male deity was to continue

The sacrificed god journeys between death and rebirth
on his moon boat, *c.* 22,000 BC

and be completed with the Hebrew and Christian Yahweh forcing the
goddess into a subservient and often buried role. At this time, though,
Tammuz is still an ambivalent figure: both son and lover. The boat that
brings him from the otherworld to be born is shaped like the crescent
moon, a fundamental image of the goddess; it is both boat and womb.
At his death at midsummer the womb boat will again receive him.

In time the cult of Tammuz spread to Phoenicia, where he
became Adonis, and Ishtar became Aphrodite. In that version of the
legend Aphrodite transformed herself into a tree in order to give
birth to him. She put Adonis in a coffer and entrusted him to the
keeping of Persephone, the goddess of the underworld. He was so
beautiful that the two goddesses struggled over custody of him, and
Zeus eventually arbitrated that he should spend six months on earth
and six months in the underworld. Here the goddess is the tree, and
the boat has become a coffer. As part of the funeral rites for Adonis,
baskets and earthenware pots were planted with rapidly germinating
seeds which grew quickly in the June sun. Having no depth of soil,
they soon withered and were consigned to the river and sea, where
they symbolized Adonis's return to the underworld in Ishtar's boat.

The centre of the cult of Cybele was in Anatolia. Her relationship with her consort was much less harmonious than that of Ishtar and Tammuz. She fell in love with a shepherd called Attis but she imposed a vow of chastity on him. He broke this with a river goddess, and the vengeful Cybele turned him temporarily mad. While in this deranged state he castrated himself under a pine tree. When his sanity returned he hanged himself from the tree. Another version of the story has it that after the castration Cybele turned him into a pine tree. Later the Romans took the advice of the Delphic oracle and brought the cult to Rome. In the rites celebrated there, a pine tree left overnight in a crypt had by morning been replaced by a young man who took the part of the reborn god. Another legend says that Attis was born from a virgin who conceived him after swallowing an almond seed. Here too the goddess is closely associ-ated with the tree as a womb of regeneration. Anatolia is a place where the yew grows. The Hittite kingdom was centred on Anatolia from 3000 to 1000 BC, and the Hittites, too, worshipped an evergreen tree.

We know rather more of the ancient Egyptian legend of Isis and Osiris, because Plutarch recorded it in the first century AD. Osiris has similar beginnings to Tammuz as a vegetation god dying annually with the harvest. He is also connected with the Djed pillar, which was considered his spinal column. This pillar was originally a tree trunk and was ceremonially raised at the New Year festivals. It symbolized the return of vitality in spring and was decorated with pieces of cloth tied to it. In the legend Osiris fell victim to the plotting of his brother Set, who invited him to a great feast. Set had prepared a magnificent coffer which he announced would be given to whoever fitted inside it perfectly. The unsuspecting Osiris lay down inside it, and Set, along with seventy-two other conspirators, nailed down the lid. The sarcophagus was thrown into the Nile, carried down to the sea and washed up at Byblos on the Phoenician coast. It came to rest at the foot of a tamarisk tree, which grew so quickly that the coffer was soon enclosed in its trunk.

At this time the King of Byblos was building a new palace and had the tree felled to serve as a pillar for the roof. In its new setting the tree gave off such a marvellous perfume that its fame spread far and wide, finally reaching the ears of Isis, Osiris' wife, who understood the true source of the perfume. She went to Byblos and, having found the coffer within the tree, set sail again for Egypt. On the journey she took the form of a kite, reviving Osiris with the beating of her wings, and she conceived their son Horus. Arriving in Egypt, Isis hid the coffer in the reeds of the Nile delta, where Set, out hunting boar by moonlight, by chance discovered it. Determined to destroy his brother forever, Set tore the body into fourteen pieces. Once again Isis had to search for her husband, and journeying through the delta swamps in her papyrus boat she found all the pieces except one; the phallus had been eaten by the Nile crab. She was helped in this task by her sister Nephthys, with her son the jackal-headed god Anubis. Horus had by now been born, and he also helped, along with Thoth the moon god. With great ceremony the body was assembled, and Anubis, who had the knowledge of embalming, created the first mummy. Isis again fanned the body, and Osiris revived to become lord of the underworld.

The legend had developed over a very long period before Plutarch recorded it, but in his account Osiris is still the son-lover of the goddess. He represents the fertility along the Nile that flourishes briefly and then withers in the merciless June sun. Set remains the ever-present adversary, evil, the arid and encroaching desert, held at bay for only a part of the year. At his annual death Osiris is consigned to a boat for his journey to the otherworld. The coffer, the coffin, the sarcophagus, the hollowed tree are all forms of the womb of the goddess that will receive the life spirit. The otherworld has become Byblos, but the essentials of the myth remain beneath the elaboration of the story. In time Osiris–Horus gestating in the tree trunk and boat will be reborn in spring. Even the subplot of the crab and the phallus tells the same story.

CHAPTER 10

The Yew in Celtic Tradition

The wise people from all over the world knew that we came from the tree, this divinity.

ALLEN MEREDITH

The yew was sacred to the Celts, whose priests were the Druids. Most writing on the Druids stresses that we know next to nothing about them save for a few scattered classical references. The most famous one is Pliny's account of the golden sickle being used to cut mistletoe from an oak tree. The mistletoe falls into a white cloak held beneath the tree, and two white bulls are sacrificed. It is not a story that Allen has much time for, because he holds Pliny responsible for the enduring link between Druidism and the oak. Pliny hazarded the guess that the name 'Druid' was derived from the Greek word for oak, *drus*, and so down the ages Druids came to be linked with that particular tree, resulting in a very distorted picture.

Scholars nowadays query that derivation. Anne Ross rejects it,[1] and Jean Markale suggests the word 'Druid' should be understood as meaning 'the far-seeing ones'.[2] Ward Rutherford reports a connection with the Manx Celtic word *druaight*, which means 'enchantment'.[3]

There is no clear explanation. Allen believes the name 'Druid' comes from *deva daru*, an ancient term for yew trees given him in his dreams, and he thinks that the Hindi word *deodar*, meaning 'God's tree', comes from the same root. He also takes issue with the concept of mistletoe growing on oak. It is extremely rare for it do so, and therefore unlikely to be the basis of a regular festival. Mistletoe itself, though, was undoubtedly a potent symbol of the earth being

Druid high priest. Illustration from Morgan's *Mabin of the Mabinogion*

impregnated. It is airborne, and its berries contain a semen-like fluid. It appears at the winter solstice. The golden sickle with its neat mix of sun and moon symbols may be almost too plausible; gold is an unlikely and ineffective cutting edge. Pliny's information may be very precise, but equally he may have been having his leg pulled.

Allen's most fruitful research into Druidism has centred on the work of a neglected turn-of-the-century writer, Owen Morgan, who adopted or received the further title 'The Morien'. This added name was an act of nailing his colours to the mast. Morien is the Welsh name for Pelagius (*c.* AD 360–*c.* 430), a British theologian who was a contemporary and rival of St Augustine of Hippo. Pelagius had a more relaxed view of things than Augustine. He refuted the latter's doctrine of original sin and held that, as the human soul was created by the Holy Spirit, man was born on earth a member of the kingdom of heaven. Such views show great respect for the dignity and freedom of the individual but they are not the foundations on which to build a monolithic church. In 418 the Emperor banned Pelagius from Rome, and he died in exile, possibly in a Welsh monastery. It has been suggested that he was a Druid.

Owen Morgan's two books, *The Light of Britannia* and *The Mabin of the Mabinogion*, reveal a man steeped in classical learning who is clearly a Welsh-speaker able to draw on a native lore and tradition that must have been disappearing even as he wrote. On occasions he refers to Iolo Morganwg, the great joker in the pack of modern Druidism. Morganwg was an eighteenth-century stonemason-turned-bard who collected genuine ancient manuscripts and bardic relics, but also forged a great deal. He also probably copied works that have since been lost. According to those who have tussled with his vast output, he variously forged, improved, was himself taken in by earlier forgers or, as the modern Druid Phillip Carr Gomm has it, channelled divinely inspired insights into Druidry and complete nonsense[4].

Morgan is probably as sure-footed as most in picking his way through that maze of false trails, and his range of interest is much broader than that of Morganwg. His main concern is to trace the connections between Druidism and the major religions of the Middle East in the Bronze and Iron Ages. His effort is to establish those connections, rather than to hazard theories as to where Druidism developed and how it spread. Occasional references, however, to 'the debased Druidry of the Egyptians', and to a remote period when the Druids and 'their brethren, the learned Chaldeans' lived in an area from the Caspian Sea to the Danube, leave the reader in little doubt. He holds views broadly in line with the theory of an Indo-European beginning outlined in the previous chapter.

Morgan's theory centres around the similarities in the role of the sun god in fertilizing the mother earth that run through the mythologies of the Middle East and the Old Testament, and that are also the core of Druid belief as practised in Britain before the arrival of Christianity. In Morgan's description of the Druids' mythology there was a creator, the origin of all things, given the name Celu, meaning hiding or concealed. He has a feminine partner known as Cariadwen. They are incomprehensible spirits and the source of matter. Matter, in a form of embryonic essence – passive, feminine and known as 'the essence of the five trees' – was brought over the seas by Cariadwen every spring in a crescent-shaped boat. She heated the bottom of the boat so that it served in fact as a cauldron, too; the essence became steam, solidifying once more as the strata of the earth. For countless years she made the journey, departing to the Isles of the Blessed, where she collected more essence and returned again in spring.

The mythology clearly separates three aspects of the sun, the first of which is warmth and heat. This masculine warmth, to which the Druids gave the name Gwyion Bach, impregnated the essence brought by Cariadwen. The equivalent of Gwyion in Greek mythology is Bacchus, and behind his love of wine is the significance that he has brought about the flowing saps and juices of vegetation. The second aspect of the sun is Hu Gadarn, the soul of the sun, the mind of Celu; in Hebrew and Greek terms he is Elohim, 'the Word', and 'the Logos'. When three drops of the male sperm fall into the cauldron of Cariadwen the earth is fertile, and Gwen, or Venus in Greek mythology, is born as the sun's rays activate the sea foam. Morgan points out that earlier forms of the name Gwen in Welsh, such as Gven or Ven, are even closer to the name Venus.

In addition to these two aspects of Celu, the Druids made a third distinction for the body of the sun. The heat in the atmosphere and the soul of the sun are both invisible, but the body of the sun can be seen. Hence the Druids considered that it must be matter, which could only originate from the cauldron of Cariadwen. The body of the sun was given different names according to the time of year. At the vernal equinox of 21 March the young glowing sun was Taliesin, the partner of Gwen, and responsible for the germination of the crops. Apollo would be the Greek equivalent. At high summer he was Tegid, meaning 'all beautiful', and his consort was Blodwyn, the holy flora. By September, though, he had begun to decay and he became Tegid the Bald because he now lacked the rays that were his 'hair'. With the onset of winter he became Said Gwm, Saturn in the Roman mythology. The name is composed of two words: *said* meaning phallus and *gwm* being a burial urn, so the sun was now considered impotent. The sun had many other names, too; Arthur, meaning 'a gardener', was one of the most used. Inevitably some names were interchangeable or used more generally, and 'Arthur' seems to be applied to the sun both at full strength and in winter.

The physical body of the sun approached its death at the winter solstice. As well as giving birth to the earth, Cariadwen had another son, Black Wings, a disembodied spirit. This results in the unending struggle between the forces of day and night, light and darkness. Black Wings is Pluto and on the shortest day of the year he manages to kill the sun as it crosses the tropic of Capricorn. The soul of the sun, Hu Gadarn, flees to the sanctuary of the boat or ark of Cariadwen. In the east this flight was usually symbolized by the dove; in Egypt it was a falcon; but in Wales the bird was a wren, whose nest completely conceals the bird within, just as Hu Gadarn was completely hidden by Taliesin or Arthur, the body of the sun. After forty hours Hu Gadarn was reborn with a new body; this new-born sun was called Mabyn, the 'crowned babe', and grew daily in strength with the lengthening days. Under the old Julian and Egyptian calendars the shortest day was 25 December, and the new sun was born on 27 December. Explaining the period of forty hours poses a difficulty; Morgan speculates that at some time the Druids must have inhabited a latitude where the sun did not appear above the

The battle of light and darkness at the winter equinox. The soul of the Sun
flees to the coracle of the goddess. From *The Mabin of the Mabinogion*

horizon on the 26th. Whatever the reason, he found that the custom of observing forty hours between the death of the sun and its rebirth occurred both in the Middle East, after the summer solstice when Tammuz and Osiris died, and in Celtic Britain after the winter solstice.

Those are the essentials of the Druid mythology, and the parallels between the roles of Ishtar, Isis and Cariadwen are clear enough. Similarly in Egypt the young sun was called Horus and, as the year progressed, came to be called Osiris. The equivalent to Black Wings was, of course, Set. The parallels extend further to the story of Moses, placed after birth in an ark of bulrushes and floated on the Nile. Moses, though, is not the first person to have this experience. The same story is told about the Akkadian Sargon, king in northern Sumeria at about 2350 BC. Morgan says that the babe in the ark of bulrushes is the newly born sun god Horus, or Mabyn. A hero, real or mythic, was likely to have his origins associated with those of the sun god. The ark as womb sometimes developed into a great fish, and Morgan says that Jonah in the whale is 'an Egyptian solar legend made the basis of a romantic Jewish fable'.

A further tale obviously connected is the story of Noah and his ark; the forty hours between the death and rebirth of the sun are rather obscured by the forty days and forty nights that the rains fell, and the forty days that the flood continued upon the earth, but the ark is still the womb journeying on the waters from which all the animals will be born to 'be fruitful and multiply upon the earth'. Noah is the sun god. As the flood waters ebbed, Noah released first a raven, which in Celtic Britain was the symbol of Black Wings, and then a dove, the symbol of Hu Gardarn, the soul of the sun.

Long before Christianity the cross was a religious symbol. In the British Museum are bas-relief carvings of an Assyrian king dating from about 800 BC. He is life-size, and around his neck hangs a great medallion with a large 'Maltese' cross on it. The cross is in fact the symbol of the sun god. The origin of the eastern cross with its equal arms was in the position of the sun at the spring equinox, where, in the centre of the sky, it exactly bisected the north–south and east–

west axes. As for the western cross, on 25 December, the passage of the sun through the tropic of Capricorn crosses the north–south meridian exactly at midday; hence as the sun is lower in the sky the cross has a shorter and higher axis.

There is much evidence that at the equinox and solstice the ancient Britons enacted great rituals at their sacred sites which mirrored the sacred drama they believed to be taking place in the sky and earth around them. There have, for example, been numerous interpretations of the Avebury complex. The author Michael Dames sees the great artificial mound of Silbury Hill in Wiltshire, with its surrounding water-filled ditch, serving as an illustration of the goddess giving birth.[5] Silbury Hill was the pregnant womb, and the reflection of the moon in the water would move as the moon climbed in the sky to present a series of images, from the child's head appearing from the womb, through to an image of a suckling child. This is close to Morgan's view that a moon-shaped barge would have floated on the water at Silbury at festivals. New Grange, the great passage grave and temple in Ireland, is aligned so that at the winter solstice, and only then, a ray of light penetrates the approach passage and illuminates the inner chamber. It appears as if the male ray of light is fertilizing the womb of the earth. Morgan describes several sites in the Rhondda valley where he believes ceremonies took place. He also believes that it is evident that the Druids sometimes represented the body of Cariadwen in the landscape, lying parallel with the sun's path, her belly a mound on the horizon, waiting to receive the virile sun rising due east in spring.

The likelihood is, then, that the line of the sun's passage was the focus of Druid ceremony. Before Christianity this was symbolized by the cross formed if an imagined perpendicular line bisected the path of the sun. This perpendicular may be the origin of the *axis mundi* or World Tree and is certainly inextricably linked with it. There are reports that it was a Druid practice to consecrate a tree by cutting it into the shape of a cross. At the winter solstice, at the intersection of those two lines in the heavens, Black Wings managed to destroy the body of the sun, but the soul, Hu Gadarn, fled to the safety of the ark of Cariadwen, stationed in the sea to the south. There the new body of the sun gestated, prior to rebirth forty hours later.

All ancient churches were built with the nave on an east–west axis. The word 'nave' derives from the Latin *navis*, meaning a boat, and the naves of the early churches were placed on the east–west axis to receive the fertilizing rays of the sun, as Cariadwen's boat had been so aligned for centuries. 'The priest and the church,' says Morgan, 'are now the incarnate son and daughter of Apollo and Venus.' The ancient churches always had a small south-facing door in the direction of the moored boat, and through the door lay the baptismal font, which is again the womb and cauldron of the goddess. As in the old religion Hu Gadarn entered the womb of Cariadwen on the water, and forty hours later was reborn as the new sun, so in the new religion the baptismal font gave symbolic rebirth in the Holy Spirit to the new-born child.

The doctrine of Christianity may have been new, therefore, but significantly the symbols in which it found expression were much older. So also with the yew tree. Allen's work shows that a Celtic site invariably has its yew tree on the axis of the nave. However, the yew tree was there long before the construction of the church; for it was the yew, the hollow tree, regenerating and seemingly immortal, which served as the symbol of Cariadwen's boat, the womb of all life.

There are many unanswered questions about the spread of Christianity and the conflict between the Celtic and Roman churches. The Saxons were converted by the church of St Augustine, and this version of Christianity was markedly different from the church of Pelagius and the Culdees – Celtic Christian monks with roots in Druidism – which retained its independence well into the Middle Ages. Morgan sees the Saxons and the Augustinian church having common interests in conquest and conversion of the Celtic west. As we have seen, the early church was fully prepared to co-operate with and adopt aspects of the original religion. One method of doing this was to take the mythic figures of British religion and attach to them the characters from the Christian religion. Arthur, one of the most popular names for the body of the sun, had lengthy and ongoing treatment of this sort that deserves separate consideration, but there was an early attempt to introduce St George and attribute Arthur's feats to him – the winged dragon being another identity of Black Wings in the annual sky drama. A sophisticated mythology was coarsened into 'real' people of flesh and blood who were the heroes of the early church.

Among the many other names given to the sun were a group of names clustered around the symbol for wings, which is our capital 'A'. Thus Black Wings in Welsh is Avagddu, the Roman Pluto. In opposition to Avagddu, the sun was known as A-dda, Good Wings, A-ddov, Amiable Wings, and A-wen, Holy Wings. The line of the sun, where the Druid stood in worship, facing east, was known as the 'I' station or the 'I' place, Ivan, and as I-wen, Holy I and Iva. The monks were quick to associate A-dda with Adam the first man, and Iva with Eve, from the Garden of Eden. As this was the place where the Christians strategically placed their church, so the church and the area around it also became known as I-wen. Morgan says the monks, planting in each churchyard 'the evergreen *Taxus baccata*, called it Iwen and told the Saxons its name was Yew'. Once again, through this etymological connection, the yew is linked with the equinoctial line and the sacred cauldron of Cariadwen.

This also throws interesting light on the siting of yew trees in Saxon churches. The clearest indication of a Saxon site, as has been shown, is a male and female yew to the south and south-west of the church. Often only one tree remains, but there is sufficient evidence to show that the practice was widespread. The monks linked the name of the sun, A-dda, to Adam, and that of Iva, site of Cariadwen's womb-boat, to Eve, mother of humankind. This may well have resulted in the planting of two trees, representing Adam and Eve, to the south of the church – the traditional mooring of the sacred boat to provide sanctuary for the fleeing Hu Gadarn at the winter solstice. The beauty of the system is that it contains within it tremendous respect for the integrity of nature.

Understandably, considering the popular associations of the yew tree, the foregoing has stressed the connection of the yew with the

Tree of Life and with the womb-boat of Ced or Cariadwen. However, as the images of Tammuz, Osiris and Cariadwen display, life was conceived of as a circular and not a linear experience; the womb that ferried you into life enveloped you again as you left it. The hollowed trunk is both boat and coffin, and in Welsh the same word, *ark* or *arch*, serves both functions. Many Bronze Age and Iron Age barrows contain coffins laboriously hollowed out of tree trunks, and some are more than simply hollowed out; they are shaped to resemble canoes and boats. It will be remembered that Allen found the very oldest neolithic trees oriented to the north of the present church, and Morgan has some remarks that may throw light on that. The oldest burials discovered have the skeleton aligned north to south, with the feet southwards. This was favoured by the Druids, who believed life returned from Annwyn, the underworld, to the south. The later burials with feet eastwards imply an association with the sun in spring as an agent of resurrection.

At the creation of the world Cariadwen brought from the Isles of the Blessed the protoplasm which, heated in her cauldron, became steam and solidified as the earth. The action of heat, that is Gwyion Bach, in time produced vegetative matter, but the evolutionary leap to creatures of flesh and blood was provided when Celu the creator let fall 'three drops' into the cauldron. One legend has Gwyion Bach, set to watch the cauldron containing the three drops, placing his scalded fingers in his mouth. The experience is rather like Adam and Eve eating the fruit of the Tree of Knowledge. Something of the Word or the Logos has been imbibed. Cariadwen is furious, but as the experience has given Gwyion knowledge he can stay one step ahead of her, changing form first to a fish and then, when Cariadwen becomes an otter, to a bird, whereupon she changes to a hawk. Finally he changes into a grain of corn on a winnowing floor, and she to a hen who swallows him. The grain of corn, though, makes her pregnant, and Gwyion is reborn from her and after further adventures pronounced to be Taliesin. So the three drops bring a rapid advancement as Gwyion progresses from tender of cauldron to sun god, and man and woman tumble from the cauldron which previously had produced only vegetation.

The three drops are always symbolized by the three golden apples. The Celts, like the Greeks, had a belief in Elysium, the Isles of the Blessed, a paradise inhabited by those who found favour with the gods.

The Celtic hero Bran, for example, hears mysterious strains of music while asleep and on waking finds a silver apple branch with blossoms beside him. A goddess appears and sings of the magic of the land, its freedom from pain and death and its marvellous trees; she disappears, taking the branch with her. Bran sets sail and meets Manannan the sea god riding the waves in his chariot, who gives him directions. The god tells Bran that the sea is a plain of flowers and that all around, although invisible to him, people are relaxing and drinking. Bran sails on to the Land of Women, where the goddess welcomes Bran and his companions with feasting. They stay a year, or what they believe is a year, but the goddess warns them that in human time it has been many centuries and that if they return to Ireland they will age immediately and crumble to dust. Despite this they set sail and arrive off Ireland, but the first sailor who attempts to go ashore proves the prophecy of the goddess to be true. Bran can only wander continually in his boat, writing his story on wooden sticks in ogham, the ancient British script, and casting them into the sea.

Greek myth, too, tells of the golden apple tree of the Hesperides. It grew at the edge of the world where the setting sun touched the horizon. The apples were given as a wedding gift to Hera, a goddess with very early origins, both sister and wife of Zeus. They were protected at some stage by Medusa, and in some stories by the serpent coiled around the trunk. The waters of life emerge from springs at the base of the tree and are collected by the Hesperides, who are nymphs born from the goddess Night. There is a similar legend in northern mythology, where golden apples, needed by the gods to ensure their eternal youth, are guarded by the goddess Idun.

Morgan believes that the whole of Britain, as the westernmost

The Golden Apple Tree of the Hesperides. Vase painting *c.* 700–400 BC

land known, was at one time regarded as the Garden of the Hesperides. Britain as a mound, surrounded by water, was an emblem of the Isles of the Blessed, and there were also local sites that served the same purpose. The obvious one is, of course, Glastonbury in Somerset, around which so many Arthurian legends, and speculations about the site of Avalon, have collected. Glastonbury Tor was in early Britain an island surrounded by the river Brue and by waterlogged marshland. Morgan's theory about the golden apples is very much in line with the guiding ideas of his work; the tree from which they hang is the sun-cross imagined as a tree. On this cross-tree hung apples that were symbols of the divine essence that had produced humankind. Morgan makes his connection with the Tree of Knowledge in Eden – Adam and Eve knowing they were naked being a development comparable with Gwyion Bach's new knowledge gained when he placed his scalded fingers in his mouth. The mounds surrounded by water, the barrows with their ditches, the stone circles, were all symbols of the garden of the sun. It is likely that on at least some of these sites the yew was planted both as a Tree of Life and as a Tree of Knowledge. The red berries are 'the apples of immortality' beyond death, symbols of the three drops, the Logos, the Word, the male essence of creation that fell into the cauldron to bring humankind to birth, and annually, as Hu Gadarn, slipped from the dying physical body of the sun back to the moored sacred barge of Cariadwen.

There is a curious postscript to this. Morgan makes an effort to prove that the name Eden is a corrupt form of the ancient Celtic 'Y Dinor', meaning 'The Mound'. In a very early British poem Arthur's Seat near Edinburgh is called 'Ei Din' or 'His Din', and in Welsh the personal name Hu is pronounced 'Ei'. Morgan suggests that the word is derived from Hu's Din, Hu's Mound, the Hu of course being Hu Gadarn. He traces some Eden place-names to modern Athens. It seems at first to be one of Morgan's more ambitious speculative forays until one remembers that at Crowhurst in Surrey, on high ground, there stands a 4,000-year-old yew tree. Not far away runs the river Eden.

Allen points out that there are islands whose names suggest a connection with yew trees and which may therefore have had this special significance. The connection of Iona with yew has already been looked at, but there is also Eubonia, an early name for the Isle of Man. The Isle of Arran in the Firth of Clyde was previously known as Eamhain Ablach or Avallach. In Irish legend this island was presided over by Manannan, the sea god that Bran met. Eamhain has the meaning 'place of yews' and Ablach 'apple'. Avalon is the Elysium of Arthurian romance, the place where his sword Excalibur was forged and where Arthur was taken when fatally wounded. Avalon may literally mean 'apple orchard', although Morgan says that in Welsh or Gaelic the name means 'everlasting apple'. There are certainly words in several languages that are close to it, the Celtic *avallo*, Middle Welsh *afall*, Middle Breton *avallenn* and Old Irish *aball* all mean apple. The twelfth-century historian Geoffrey of Monmouth referred to Avalon both as Avallo and as Insula Pomonum, that is, 'Island of Apples'.

Medieval legend related by William of Malmesbury in the twelfth century may go some way to explaining the derivation of the name Glastonbury and connecting it with the apple. A man called Glasteing had a prize sow which escaped and, after giving him a long chase, was finally caught under an apple tree. Glasteing liked the spot, brought his family to settle there, and called the place 'Insula Avalloniae'. It is also possible that Avalon is simply the home of Avallach, a god of the dead or simply an early Glastonbury landowner. On the whole, though, the evidence clearly points at a connection with 'apple'.

The significance of Glastonbury as an energy centre linked with many spiritual traditions is well known. Legend has it that Joseph of Arimathea came here shortly after the Crucifixion, bringing with him the Holy Grail, but it may well have been a spiritual centre for the worship of the mother goddess long before that. The Tor has a coiling pattern built into its slopes; and, as the spiral and serpent were goddess images, it is speculated that the Tor was the site of an artificial maze. Within it there may be limestone caverns. The Tor and the rounded Chalice Hill beside it are seen by some as male and female shapes, and from the side of Chalice Hill flows a natural spring of red-coloured chalybeate water that may well have been seen as the menstrual flow of the goddess. The Christian Holy Grail associations have been added to by the history of Glastonbury Abbey, which is believed to contain in its structure evidence of a knowledge of alchemy and sacred geometry. Later researchers have suggested Glastonbury is the centre of a giant zodiac in the surrounding landscape and a crossroads for ley lines. The reports of psychic experiences connected with the place are innumerable.

The Chalice Well is situated on a hillside adjacent to the Tor, and is one of the main spiritual sites of Glastonbury. It is filled by the spring through which water with a high chalybeate content flows unceasingly at 25,000 gallons a day. The flow has never been known to fail. Around the well today there are female yew trees of no great age, but excavations carried out around the well in the early 1960s revealed exciting evidence that yews grew on the site at a much earlier time. At a depth of 11 ft 9 in archaeologists found the stump of a yew tree with the remains of a root system still intact. It was apparently *in situ* where it had previously grown. It was examined by the biophysics department at Leeds University, which concluded that the tree would have been growing in mid-Roman times, at about AD 300. The existing trees suggest there was a ritual avenue of yews leading from the well up to the Tor, but Allen considers it more likely that a female yew would have grown directly above the spring itself. He has found several places where a yew grows above a spring, and it has always been female. The churchyard at Hope Bagot in Shropshire has a fine example.

Allen has several times sought to examine the Glastonbury stump to get some idea of the tree's age. It was conserved for the Chalice Well Trust by Taunton Museum. It may have been displayed at one time and then consigned to a loft. Its present whereabouts are unclear, and if it has disappeared then that is not unusual for significant finds at Glastonbury; the lead cross the monks found in 1190 with the inscription in Latin 'Here lies the renowned King Arthur in the Isle of Avalon' went missing some time after it was sketched in 1607. An omphalos or egg stone, another prehistoric goddess emblem, was unearthed during the abbey excavations early in the century, and that too seems to have disappeared.

Today on the flanks of the Tor there are apple orchards, but the significance of the yew stump, along with the name Avalon and the depiction of the apples on the Isles of the Blessed in Celtic literature, all add weight to Allen's theory that many seemingly straightforward ancient references to apple trees in fact refer to female yew trees. Avalon is the island of the yews, not the island of the eating apple. Yew grew on the sacred mound as it grew on the tumulus and barrow, as the symbol that the deceased had returned to an eternal womb outside of nature. In Celtic literature the apple belongs in the otherworld, as the silver apple bough that Bran finds shows; silver and glass seem to be images used to convey a dream-like and otherworld state. One of the other early names for Glastonbury was Ynys Witrin, the Isle of Glass. Sometimes apples are poisonous or drive people mad if used wrongly. This is not to say that Celtic society did not revere and celebrate the eating apple, too; customs such as apple bobbing may well date back to the Samhain festivals. But the yew berry as apple has a different quality, of the unknown, the otherworld and eternity.

There may have been a historical Arthur who, with cavalry skills learned from the Romans, organized Celtic resistance and harried the Saxons after the legions withdrew in the fifth century. If there was such a man it is likely that tales of his exploits mixed inextricably with those remembered stories and dramas that celebrated the older Arthur, the sun god. The Arthur of romance may have fought twelve battles, but the sun, too, struggled continually with Black Wings in all twelve houses of the zodiac. His journey across the sky culminated when his physical body died at the winter solstice and his spirit found refuge in the barge of Cariadwen on the water. There are echoes of this in Arthur's final journey. He lies fatally wounded as the boat takes him to Avalon; but Morgan le Fay, placing him on a golden bed and examining his wound, announces that health can be restored if he stays with her. That too recalls the older Arthur, mortally wounded at the winter solstice, just as Morgan Le Fay recalls the mother goddess who would give him rebirth. Arthur's journey is the journey of Adonis and Osiris.

Legend tells that Joseph of Arimathea arrived at Glastonbury in about AD 60, bringing with him the chalice used at the Last Supper and in which blood from Christ's wound was caught at the foot of the Cross. In Arthurian romance Perceval arrives at a mysterious castle of the Fisher King, who is wounded and whose castle is surrounded by wasteland. He sees a magnificent jewel-studded bowl that has supernatural powers. A single holy mass wafer eaten from it is sufficient daily nourishment for the King's father. Courteously Perceval refrains from questioning his hosts but he later discovers that if he had done so he would have broken the spell, the King's wound would have healed, and the land would have become fertile again.

Owen Morgan is very frank in his view of the Joseph of Arimathea legend: 'It is a striking example of the pious fraud of the early ecclesiastics. They lied to popularize Christianity.' It is strongly suggested, in different versions of the Grail story, that the Fisher King's wound has left him impotent, and this along with the waste-land points to a tale that has developed from fertility legends. Morgan favours a widely held view that the origin of the Grail is pre-Christian, rooted in the deep reverence for the cauldron as the symbol for the feminine. It is a view that Allen largely shares. To that cluster of images with which the yew tree has merged itself – the boat, cauldron, coffin and barge – must be added another: the Holy Grail.

CHAPTER II

Groves and Lone Trees

Where Yews, though dead, were often seen to rise again, and not a bird
could be heard singing in this dark grove, nor animals would stay too long,
neither Silvan priest would enter such a wood when sun had gone.

LUCAN, first century, AD

Most of the yews considered so far in this book are found in
churchyards; but this, of course, is not their only habitat. Yews are
found in many parts of the world, yet Britain is unique in the
number of ancient trees that now remain. Yews occur naturally
throughout the British Isles, although they are quite choosy about
the conditions in which they will grow.[1] Large areas of yew are rare;
the tree tends to occur alongside other species or standing alone
rather than in woods dominated by the species. This was not always
so. Fossil evidence has shown that three Ice Ages ago yew was very
widely distributed throughout the British Isles. The trees did not
survive under the ice, but gradually crept back north again across
the land bridge which still linked the British Isles with continental
Europe. In fact, the yew was one of only a handful of species that
spread back to Britain before the land bridge was breached by rising
seas. Since then, yew has had to fight for its survival with other flora
and fauna, and particularly with humanity, whose love–hate relationship with the tree has radically affected its distribution.

Allen believes that a map of where ancient yews exist or once
existed could help to establish the location of Celtic tribes, although
this would have to be interpreted with caution. There are no ancient
yews in East Anglia, for example. This may be for climatic reasons,

but the writer Vaughan Cornish attributes it to the fact that the invading Danes would have destroyed them as a Christian symbol and as the *axis mundi* of the local people.

Of the few ancient yew woods and groves now surviving in the British Isles, nearly all were probably planted by people, most likely for sacred purposes, rather than occurring naturally. Yews have also been planted outside churchyards for more mundane reasons. There is a long association between yew and homesteads, where they have been used to supply weather protection, wood and even camouflage for outside privies, and they have been used as markers for track-ways and boundaries. It is sometimes impossible to tell whether particular trees have occurred naturally or been planted, and the distinction becomes further blurred when a 'natural' tree has been used by people for their own purposes, whether sacred or secular. Allen has looked at many yews growing outside churchyards, and has found that these can also be of historical and spiritual signifi-cance, and that many are in perhaps greater need of protection than those in churchyards.

For the purposes of this chapter, yews growing outside church-yards have been sorted into three groups: yew woods and groves; yews planted near to human habitations; and yews on ancient hill forts. This is only a rough-and-ready categorization, as most sites outside churchyards where ancient yews occur remain very much a mystery. We can only guess their original purpose, if such they had, and hazard a guess at why they have managed to remain in those particular sites. It is, for example, a mystery how the Ankerwyke yew, with its lowland site unique among the ancient yews of Britain, has survived in such an unlikely spot on a Thames islet. Some yews, such as those at Snoddington Manor and Middleton Scriven, may also have originally been on the site of a church which has now gone, and others may have once been sites of sacred signific-ance of which no other trace is now left. It is important that this is kept in mind, and it goes some way to explaining the special atmosphere people talk of even around many yews which are not in churchyards.

The yews at Borrowdale

Most visitors to Keswick in Cumbria visit Borrowdale, but many do not realize that at the end of the dale they pass by the remains of a grove of yews containing what may be some of the oldest living trees. In the nineteenth century the grove was far better known than it seems to be today, perhaps because it had recently been brought to people's attention by Wordsworth:

> But worthier still of note
> Are those fraternal Four of Borrowdale,
> Joined in one solemn and capacious grove;
> Huge trunks! And each particular trunk a growth

Of intertwisted fibres serpentine
Up-coiling, and inveterately convolved.[2]

Wordsworth's description of the yews as 'those fraternal Four' stuck, and this is how they are still known, even though there are now only three. The steep, craggy slope looks unable to support much life at all, yet the yews, though gnarled and windblown, have managed to cling on and survive. The largest one has a 24 foot girth, a remarkable size considering that they grow from out of the rocks and in one of the wettest and windiest climates of the UK. Because of these conditions it is impossible to date the trees, but comparison with other trees growing elsewhere in harsh conditions suggests that they are extremely ancient. Allen believes they could be neolithic.

The missing fourth tree was blown down in the great gale of 1883. A description of its remains suggests that this was an even mightier specimen than the largest one now remaining:

A little way up the hill ... lay the trunk of a yew tree, which appeared as you approached, so vast was its diameter, like the entrance to a cave, and not a small one. Calculating upon what I have observed of the slow growth of this tree in rocky situations, and of its durability, I have often thought that the one I am describing must have been as old as the Christian era ... In no part of England, or of Europe, have I ever seen a yew tree at all approaching this in magnitude, as it must have stood.[3]

A local guide of the time is reputed to have told visitors that there could be no doubt of this tree having existed 'before the Flood'.

John Lowe, writing in 1897, also marks his appreciation of the trees. He quotes a Professor Knight whose description of the grove summarizes the awe that early worshippers may have felt: 'a natural temple ... an ideal grove, in which the ghostly masters of mankind meet, sleep, and offer worship to the destiny that abides above them, while the mountain flood, as if from another world, makes music to which they dimly listen'.[4] We also know from the professor that in the great gale the trees which were left standing lost many of their main branches.

Thankfully Professor Knight's gloomy prediction that the trees would soon vanish has not proved correct, although they have suffered considerable weather damage in the last few years. Surprisingly, however, the trees' fame seems to have dimmed since the time of the evidently more appreciative Victorians. One recent visitor to the area was unable to find anyone who had even heard of them, until an aged local claimed that 'the Four Brethren' had been destroyed by wind and flood early this century. Yet a Borrowdale pub is still called the Yew Tree Inn, and there are still those who go to the yew-dotted crag to be with the trees. One such visitor in 1993 reported a dramatic reprieve from a painful chronic illness after spending several hours there. The trees have a powerful effect on those who visit them, and Allen feels that the mystery of why and how they have survived in this setting is still to be solved. It is good to be able to say that the Borrowdale yews, unlike some other naturally growing ones, are endangered only by the forces of nature.

The majority of Britain's surviving yew woods and groves are in the south of England, predominantly in Surrey, Sussex and Hampshire. Yews thrive on the chalk downlands and are now quite common on the South Downs and the Hampshire–Sussex borders. They favour high ground, and in this area the yew woods have grown from trees which once marked parish boundaries. However, these thriving colonies of yew found in small pockets in the British Isles contain almost only *young* trees. Ancient yew groves or woodlands are rare.

Merrow Down near Newlands Corner in Surrey has the remains of one of the largest and oldest such groves. A local Victorian by the name of Martin Tupper once suggested that the trees had been planted to mark the Pilgrims' Way to Canterbury. The idea must at first have seemed obvious, for, as John Lowe put it: 'the trees' dark foliage offers a fine contrast to the bright tints of the neighbouring woods, and to the snowy masses of blossom which in early summer clothes the boughs of the gnarled old hawthorn trees that are studded over the hillside'.[5] Lowe and other yew researchers of the time contended that the trees had grown naturally in what was once an area covered in yew trees, and that these trees later survived destruction in order to mark the Pilgrims' Way. Allen suggests that the trees are about 2,000 years old. He contends that many – but not all – of the original trees may have been planted by people. If this is so, then their purpose may have been, not as suggested by Tupper to guide pilgrims to a holy place, but to create a holy place themselves.

A description of the trees at Merrow Down given in the 1882 *Journal of Forestry and Estate Management* still stands good today:

A number of great yews, sheltered by many acres of jungle, or native forest of thorn and furze, stand in what would be called in America a 'wood opening'. A bit of primeval forest covers this secluded part of the North Downs; the lesser native shrubs and trees are sprinkled freely round – the butcher's broom, ivy, holly, elder, birch, maple, hazel, crab, sloe, bullace, thorns, and hedge fruits, and the mistletoe, with oaks and ash trees. These yews are in a sheltered site, known as Yew-tree Vale. They are by far the noblest plantation of great yews that I have seen for size and number.

Most of the trees at Merrow Down are now hollow and decayed. One particularly striking tree is reputed to have been mentioned in the Domesday Book, although as previously stated no individual tree is listed there. This is probably another example of people honouring the tree in their own way; this particular yew, which appears perfectly solid, has a service tree growing out of it. The yew's girth is some 21 feet; that of the service tree is over 4 feet. Close by stands another hollow yew, but most of the other yews are set well apart from each other.

Like the Fraternal Four, the Newlands Corner yews encouraged poetry, although in William Watson they seem to have found a new McGonagall:

> Old emperor Yew, fantastic sire,
> Girt with the guard of dotard kings,

What ages hast thou seen retire
Into the dusk of alien things?
What mighty news hath stormed thy shade,
Of armies perished, realms unmade?

Ah, thou hast heard the iron tread
And clang of many an armoured age,
And well recall, the famous dead,
Captains or counsellors brave or sage,
Kings that on kings their myriads hurled,
Ladies whose smile embroiled the world.

Wiltshire also has an impressive yew wood, on a private estate at Great Yews, Odstock. The mysterious silent wood has probably survived because of its remote setting, and the thickly wooded area contains a good number of yews which are most likely of the same age as those at Newlands Corner. Apart from one large opening, nearly all the yews are, unusually, within touching distance of each other; this may be the oldest dense yew wood in Britain. One visitor described the wood as having 'one of the most sacred atmospheres I have experienced'. The writing of Lucan quoted at the beginning of the chapter would make an apt description of the place.

It is worth noting that Great Yews is within an area rich in ancient sites; it is close to Stonehenge and Old Sarum, and there are also yews at nearby Cranbourne Chase. Close to that, in turn, is Knowlton, with its single line of yews on a Bronze Age ritual site.

Kingley Vale near Chichester in Sussex is one of Britain's best-known yew woods. In terms of age it is, says Allen, 'not very impressive', but it is an important site because it is one of the few remaining yew forests in Britain. Many woods such as this have been cleared in just the last two or three decades; this wood is now a National Nature Reserve. The original trees at Kingley Vale are also reputed to have been deliberately planted, possibly to commemorate a battle fought there in AD 859 by the inhabitants of Chichester against invading Vikings. Some Victorians had a slightly different version of the yews' origins, although agreeing that they were planted in

Saxon times. According to this account, they were set to commemorate the death of Sygbert, King of the West Saxons, who was stabbed here by a swineherd. The 1882 *Journal of Forestry* was not convinced, however:

It is quite as probable that Nature whose hand formed the hollow by the agency of water, laid down grass for a carpet, clothed the steep sides with thorn trees and sent the blackbird to the spot to sing, and the tawny owl to hoot at night, planted the yews here in clumps and single specimens, so that landscape gardeners might be furnished with a perfect model of their art. To this spot she certainly invites them, and here high and low have often come for picnic, the Prince and Princess of Wales when staying at Goodwood and the million from all the world – Portsmouth, Brighton, London, America. One might say of each old yew in Kingley Vale:

'What scenes have passed since first this ancient yew,
In all the strength of youthful beauty grew.'

Even mere adolescent yews seem to inspire ponderings on ages past.

The twenty-odd oldest trees at Kingley Vale are at the heart of the wood; the oldest one has a girth of about 17 feet. Further trees appear to have grown naturally from seeds spread by birds. Other species of tree such as ash, oak, holly and spindle grow alongside and often take advantage of the space left by yews which fall in bad weather. The oldest yews are probably only, at most, 800 years, the majority of them considerably less. A tree which came down in the 1950s had a ring count of 500. It is interesting, even so, that people have still connected such relatively 'young' yews with ancient ways; some of the trees have been dubbed 'Druids' trees', and local folklore says that the grove has been used for witchcraft.

Allen has received a good deal of correspondence about yew trees from people recording trees which they know and love. One of these correspondents says that there are 'a number of yews, including some which appear quite old', in Rectory Wood, Church Stretton, Shropshire. They are mostly situated around the pool there. A writer from County Donegal, Eire, writes: 'Near to where I was born, at a place called Drumoghill (from the Irish Drumeochaill, meaning the ridge of the yew woods) there is an old yew tree. This tree is unusual in that it is an English yew and every other yew tree in this locality is of the Irish type.' These trees have not been investigated by Allen, but the growing correspondence he receives suggests that as our awareness of yews increases more may present themselves.

Perhaps the most famous yew grove in Britain is Druid's Grove in Surrey. It consists of what appear to be the remains of an ancient avenue of yews, plus many scattered ones, growing in dense, mixed woodland containing many box trees. The oldest trees here have long been considered ancient. The novelist George Meredith lived nearby from 1867, and he encouraged his visitors to visit the trees, telling them that 'anyone walking under them should remember that they were saplings when Jesus Christ came to earth'. It is not surprising that Allen was particularly interested to visit Druid's Grove and wondered whether the name held any significance.

Allen first went to the grove in 1981 and has returned several times since to document the trees. He writes:

We came across twisted, shattered fragments, the skeleton remains of ancient yews. In the main avenue we saw enormous yews, some upwards of 24 feet in girth. I found a particularly ancient yew, much of it a mere shell, with rotten decayed wood inside, but as so often with aged yews fresh growth has occurred over many centuries. This relic is still a large tree, over 20 feet in girth. Of the most significant trees, five are over 22 feet in girth and four over 20 feet. For the trees to have reached this kind of size in such a crowded area must have taken many years. This is one of the few remaining ancient woodlands which has trees that would date back to Roman times.

Measuring and cataloguing the trees here is difficult. Many of them are surrounded by impenetrable undergrowth, and some are on steep, slippery inclines, as Allen has found to his cost. Although the uprooted and decaying stumps of trees which may have been in that state for centuries can be seen, there is also plenty of evidence of vigorous growth. The yew's ability to regenerate itself by putting down an aerial root inside the hollow trunk is seen here.

The severe storms of 1987 and 1990 caused considerable damage in Druid's Grove. Many yews were uprooted, including one of the

Druid's Grove

largest ones in the avenue, and others lost branches. Surrey County Council and the park rangers have fortunately decided to leave the fallen trees where they lie, wherever possible. It is likely that some will still regrow, while those which do not will join the other fallen yews which, lying prostrate and gathering moss, give life to other creatures and plants.

Druid's Grove can be hard to find and is in parts almost impenetrable, but it has exerted a strong pull on visitors for a long time. Brailey's *History of Surrey* (1850) says: 'Many of these yews are of great age and venerable aspect; and of a girth seldom equalled.' Brailey conjectures that 'under their sombre shade the Druids themselves might have wandered, in their most abstract hours of gloomy meditation'. John Lowe documented the trees in 1897 and found several measuring over 22 feet. He, too, was intrigued by the grove's name, but confined his speculation about the trees to recording that

'There is no history concerning them which can be relied on. They are not mentioned in Domesday Book, which resulted from a census which took little account of any growths in field or forest, except those which fed swine.[6]

Lowe is correct that there is no known historic evidence to tell us how Druid's Grove got its name. Allen believes that some of the trees are over 2,000 years old and that the name is no coincidence. The trees certainly seem to form an avenue, which suggests purposeful planting rather than natural distribution. The intended use of the grove is much more open to speculation. Many people have commented on the unusual atmosphere of the place. Some strange things have happened there which, although not dramatic in their own right, when added together suggest that this a special place. Allen has twice found that he has 'stepped out of time' while in Druid's Grove – that when he has left the grove his watch has shown the same time as when he entered it, despite the watch apparently working perfectly. This also happened to him when he visited Knowlton. On another visit to the grove he came across just one other person, whose name was also Allen Meredith.

Ancient yew woods such as this are now scarce in the British Isles, as are single ancient yews growing outside churchyards. Yews face a common hazard: man. Many yews have been destroyed by farmers and other people worried about them poisoning animals, to the extent, according to Bowen, of radically affecting and diminishing the distribution of yews. In fact, a good many animals do eat yew regularly and to no ill effect. Deer and squirrels eat the bark, as well as the twigs and leaves which rabbits and hares favour. A wide range of birds including robins, pheasants, redwings, thrushes and fieldfare eat the arils, and even the seeds which are poisonous to humans are consumed by bullfinches, hawfinches and mice.[7] Yew can be toxic to cattle and horses, though, especially when pruned branches have been left to wither, because of the enzyme action of the taxines generated in the decaying process.

While there are enough recorded cases of cattle and horses dying from eating yew to make it a real fear, it seems to have become more of a paranoia. Bowen reports that many of the yew saplings he has planted have been uprooted by a fearful neighbour, even though the grounds of Bath University are unlikely ever to provide grazing for a herd of cows. The problem is something of a vicious circle: the less yews are grown, the greater the ignorance is about them. For example, the recent death of two ponies after having been tethered to a yew tree for several hours by someone ignorant of the yew's toxicity, perhaps because yews are uncommon, could have done little to encourage the planting of more yews. Yet when Allen visited one parkland containing yews he noticed several horses chewing greenery from the tree. It may seem surprising that yews have been allowed to remain in parklands where animals may graze, but presumably small amounts of yew will not harm the horses.

Given this widespread fear of yew, it is all the more surprising that the trees have been so closely connected with houses and habitation. Yet they are found in close proximity to many old farms, manors and houses, as well as along trackways and in parkland. Here a distinction again needs to be drawn between *Taxus baccata* and its cultivars. It is largely the Irish yew which has been used for the topiary that was once so fashionable in 'hedges or pyramids, cones, spires, bowls, buttresses and ramps, little square towers, finials of various forms, archways and canopies'.[8] And while yew in all its varieties is still a popular garden ornament, it is *Taxus baccata* which is found in the old gardens of places bearing the tree's name.

An investigation of all the Yew Tree Cottages, Yew Tree Farms and Yew Tree Inns could make a book in its own right. This is not to dismiss the significance of such trees, as they are often of historic interest, even though the vast majority are nowhere near as old as the ancient ones in churchyards. Some of the letters Allen has received give fascinating information on these 'domestic' trees and also demonstrate people's love and veneration of them:

At the border of our garden stand two large and, we are led to believe, ancient yews. Estimates of their age by villagers vary from 500 to 800 years. There is a stump in the lawn which we think was also a yew. We have been told that it is known as the oldest house in the village. The trees are subject to a preservation order. In any case we would never dream of touching them; they have given their name to this house ... I feel a respect for a venerable tree, particularly a yew.

(The Yews Farm, Melton Mowbray, Leicestershire)

Our yew tree is on the south-west corner of the house, which we are told helps to 'keep away evil spirits'. The name Toots means a look-out from the Saxon. We are on top of a hill. It is perfectly dry under the branches, forming a sanctuary for birds and animals.

(Toots Farm House, Caversham, Berkshire)

The farmhouse is a seventeenth-century listed building and must have been named after the yew tree. You will see the name on all old Ordnance Survey maps. Someone who admired the tree and seemed to know a little about them suggested that it could be approximately 700 years old, but I think that is an exaggeration.

(Yew Tree Farm, Tonbridge, Kent)

There are several mature yews in my garden. I feel a great affinity with the trees and feel physically sick when I hear chainsaws in the locality.

(Swinton, Manchester)

A yew with a girth of 13 ft 8 in grows in the grounds of our house. Extensive alterations were made to the house in the 1690s but a house is known to have been on the site for a long time before that. Roman coins have been found in the garden. A Roman pottery kiln is within 200 yards.

(The Manor Farm, Compton Bassett, Wiltshire)

The yew trees in our garden are 150 yards due north of the church, which was originally twelfth century. The cottage is sixteenth century. There are four yew trees in the churchyard and marks on the church where the bows (cut from the trees) were sharpened.

(Yew Tree Cottage, Bolton-by-Bowland, Lancashire)

When I lived at the Dower House at Riseholme near Lincoln during the war we had some old yew trees. Many a time I climbed up into their dusty branches to hide. Very distinctive scent. Outside the kitchen door was one of the deepest wells in Lincolnshire ... I wonder whether you have found that large yews are tied up with underground water courses?

I live next door to the site of a now demolished old farmhouse. Fortunately a neighbour had the foresight to put a preservation order on the trees – one of which is an ancient yew. This area was part of Clapham Park.

(London)

The yew in my garden is only 7 ft 9 in round, but it towers above the surrounding houses. The farm buildings which occupied the area before the 1930s were named on old maps in the local museum as Yew Tree Cottages so it would seem to have been an established tree for some time.

(Caterham, Surrey)

We live in an old schoolhouse that is nearly 300 years old. There is a beautiful yew in the garden that village folk say has always been there.

(Wigan, Lancashire)

Our cottage is sixteenth/seventeenth century and has a magnificent yew tree in the grounds. We estimate it is 900–1,000 years old. My family and I feel it an honour to own such a beautiful tree.

(Yew Tree Cottage, Hythe, Hampshire)

Taxus baccata is, of course, still being planted by people in their gardens:

We moved here in 1976 and on our journey down we stopped where tractors were turning into a wood. Many small trees were being run over by the big wheels and we asked if we could take some to try to save them. Three of the trees were small yews. We wrapped them in wet paper and planted them into our garden the following day. We now have three healthy yews nearly 20 years old.

Perhaps some people's reason for planting a yew is still influenced, whether consciously or not, by the tree's ancient significance; a woman who recently planted a yew in her garden said she was told by a gypsy that it would give her protection.

What must primarily interest us here, however, is where *ancient*

Taxus baccata appears in domestic situations, and just a few do still remain. Since most dwellings are relatively modern compared with the potential age of yew, it is not surprising that known ancient yews, those over 1,000 years old, near to farms and houses are scarce. Some examples follow.

In an isolated part of Wales, Panillydw in Dyfed, a yew tree grows to the east of a house and is cemented in. The branches grow right down to the ground, and the tree is at least 1,200 years old.

A female tree on a farm at Barlow, Sheffield, is aged 1,500 years.

At Burcott Farm in Hereford and Worcester a 1,500-year-old tree grows in a hedgerow on an old trackway. It may once have been a boundary marker.

There is a sturdy yew at Keffolds Farm in Surrey whose 29 foot girth is remarkable, given that it grows on a high, exposed slope. It was once hollow, but over the years it has grown within the hollow, and it now looks almost completely intact again. The tree is female, and there are a stream and a well nearby.

A particularly intriguing site is at Temple Farm, Corsley in Wiltshire. The tree's girth has been measured since 1780 and at 32 ft 7 in has changed little in that time. Allen measured the tree in 1982 with the help of the farmer, whose family has lived at Temple Farm since 1886, and who said that the tree lost some of its main branches in 1900 and in 1981. Nevertheless the tree is still solid and healthy, and new bark has grown over parts that seem at one time to have been decayed and hollow. Allen says: 'It is strange to see such an enormous tree in someone's back garden.' He dates the tree at 2,000 years and draws attention to the name of the farm. The origins of Temple Farm are not known, but its name may be significant. As at Keffolds Farm, a stream and a spring are nearby. The farm is close to the Longleat Estate, which was mentioned in reference to the yew in 1870, and which has retained its connection by now supplying yew clippings for the production of anti-cancer drugs.

There are also some fine old yews in manors and parklands. At Snoddington Manor in Hampshire the magnificent tree which stands in a field near the manor has a girth of 26 feet. It was probably once even larger, as some decay has now set in on its west side. Inside the hollow tree another yew is forming, with a girth of 7 ft 7 in to date, and it is possible to walk around it within the hollow yew. Given the common association of ancient yews and churches, it is possible that this was the site of a church. Ancient burial sites surround the area.

At Brackley in Northamptonshire, in fields across the road from the present church and where the old village is thought to have been built, a yew grows close to medieval earthworks and remains of fish ponds. A letter writer comments: 'Local legend has it that the tree, which has a girth of 24 feet, is over 2,000 years old. About twenty-five years ago there used to be two other very big yew trees in the village. One lady always felt they had something to do with witchcraft.'

In the deer park at Kentchurch Court in Hereford and Worcester are many large yews, one of them over 35 feet in girth and believed to be about 2,000 years old. This is another intriguing site, as Kentchurch was once the home of Owen Glendower, the late-fourteenth-century Welsh chieftain who led a revolt against Henry IV's rule in Wales.

At Knowle Park in Kent a 20 foot tree aged 1,000 years stands in park grounds at some distance from the house.

More writers tell of yews at other manors and parklands:

There is a yew in Clayton Manor garden, which dates at least from Roman times [not checked by authors]. The branches used to lie on the ground all round and grew up again and we used to clip it like a hedge, but the present owner cut off the branches and cleared it all out except for three that had taken root and grown as three separate trees, their joining branches cut and removed. How can people mutilate such a beautiful tree that had taken so long to grow?

(Sussex)

There is a yew in front of the old hall which was built in the 1100s for Thomas à Becket.

(Rancliffe, Preston)

The earliest written record of a house here is in 1251. In the walled garden, a large yew used to stand. Our predecessors cut it down around 1981. The stump was approximately 6 feet in diameter, 6 inches above ground. We waited to see if it regenerated but it did not do so. We would like to replace it.

(Field Place, Warnham, Sussex, birthplace of Shelley)

In the 1930s several very old yews were removed from close by the old dwelling. Four were left in the garden and these I am told may have been planted by the monks who kept the great bible (Pitliver, from the Old French 'place of the *livre* or book'). There is a secret passage from this place to the abbey.

(Pitliver, Fife)

Yews at Hanchurch in Staffordshire have long been a matter for speculation. They surround a rough square of about an acre and are believed by many different sources to be around 1,500 years old. It is likely that a church stood within the trees before the ninth century, possibly destroyed by the Danes; the fact that no remains of it have been found is immaterial, as churches were often built only of wood. It could also have been a monastic site, and Roman remains have been found in Hanchurch. Clearly it was some kind of sacred site; a strange tradition, noted in the nineteenth century, said that the original church was removed from Hanchurch to Trentham by four swans.[9] This may be a throw-back to Celtic mythology, in which swans are associated with mystical, shape-shifting rites through characters such as Cu Chulainn, Oenghus and Midhir. If Hanchurch was, as seems likely, a site hallowed by the Celts long before it was consecrated to Christianity, this may make us question the origins of other sites whose history has vanished.

On the edge of a wood at Wintershall in Surrey is a large yew aged about 2,000 years. Little is known about this tree, other than that it was a boundary marker and that it was cut down about a hundred years ago and has since sprung up again. It is on the very edge of a wood, and Allen reports having found it to have a very spooky feeling around it. Old folklore says that certain trees were inhabited by tree elves, known as 'green ladies'. They were said to live in elm, oak, willow and yew. An old English folksong suggests they ensnared passers-by with skinny white hands which seemed to clutch at the wind:

> Ellum do grieve, oak he do hate,
> Willow do walk, if yew travels late.[10]

These trees, it was implied, should be treated with respect in order not to offend the green lady. In particular, permission was to be sought from her before lopping a branch from her tree. Perhaps this was not done when the tree at Wintershall was cut years ago, and the vegetation spirit still emits her displeasure at this dishonouring. As someone wrote to Allen: 'There is far more to yew trees than just bark and foliage.'

To return to yews as boundary markers, the tree's quality of permanence makes it very suitable for this purpose, and a few particular yews do still remain which are known to have been boundary trees. Acton Burnell Park in Shropshire, for example, contains yews of which the largest closely follow the parish boundary, which goes across the ridge of a hill.

This use of yews for boundary markers has also been speculated on by a correspondent who wrote following the demise in the 1987 storm of one of two old yews which straddled a road at Haywards Heath in Sussex: 'I can well remember as a small boy in the 1940s the dexterity of the bus driver as he manoeuvred through the archway of overhanging branches between the two trees.' The correspondent suggests that the trees may have been planted as boundary markers:

These two are the last in a straight line of six ... possibly this line stretched even further across land now taken up by a building and the railway line. Most probably the area's only claim to fame was that troops mustered here during the Civil War, and whatever little history there is, it would seem the line of yews are the only living witness.

Another boundary tree still remains at Discoed in Powys (where there are also two huge and ancient churchyard yews). This tree is on a farm close by the ancient way, Offa's Dyke. A track runs close by, and the yew could well have been used as a border marker.

The tree at Aldworth in Berkshire was also a boundary tree according to the Ordnance Survey, on whose old maps the tree used to be indicated.

The Wintershall tree was used as a boundary marker in Saxon times; but this, of course, may not have been its original purpose, if it ever had one, as it would obviously have been a mature tree to be used in this way. Allen asks: 'It may have been a boundary tree, but what was its origin? Was it once part of an Iron Age hill fort? Is it the remains of a yew wood? Or of some other sacred site? We easily fall into the danger of categorizing things, as I have to some extent.' We are always eager to put labels on things, which may or may not be right, but that can be a distraction from the 'essence' of the tree.

In late Victorian times the knowledge of yews as boundary markers – by this time specifically parish boundaries – was still intact. Today the name Gospel Oak may be familiar to us, even if only as a British Rail station on the North London Line; we probably do not stop to question what it referred to. Just a century ago the name Gospel Yew would have been equally familiar. Both refer to trees beneath which the Gospels were preached, as part of the marking of the parish boundary, and were therefore important and deeply meaningful features of the landscape, both legally and spiritually. A Victorian writer, George Piper, devoted an essay to the subject of Gospel yews. He wrote that a yew of 'great antiquity', known since 'time out of mind', marked the junction between the parishes of Bosbury, Castlefroome and Canonfroome (Hereford and Worcester): 'It stands in the boundary fence of the Fishpool Coppice, at the south-west corner of a tillage field, part of the old Birchend Farm, and near to the fifth mile post leading from Ledbury to Bromyard – the field is known as "The Gospel Yew"; it has no other name.' The tree is still there now.

'Gospel trees' such as this marked the limits of the parish's jurisdiction. The trees were acknowledged as such every year, when a procession of parishioners would go 'on perambulation' to the tree, and the clergyman would read the Gospel of the day beneath it. Interestingly, Mr Piper reports that the processionists carried not just the cross, as might be expected, but also staves. Did this stem from an ancient memory? Perhaps so, for Mr Piper also describes it as an 'old Celtic practice'. Unfortunately for the young boys of the parish, this endearing-sounding ritual had a darker side: 'Boys were taken to be flogged at the boundaries, for the purpose of infixing in their memories ... that the boundaries might not be mistaken. They were subjected to this discipline upon the spot in a severe form.'

As well as marking boundaries, yews were used as ancient route markers. A writer in Battle, East Sussex, has a tree in splendid condition with a girth of about 15 feet at the back of the house:

We have been told it was between 700 and 800 years old by someone interested in yews. He thought that yews were sometimes grown in alignment for the sake of travellers in ancient times. Also that ours has some connection, in that respect, to the one at Crowhurst. Whether or not this is so, ours is in line with an ancient hedge that may have been the boundary for the monastic grounds. There is only 30 feet of the hedge left, but the alignment could be traceable to the Church of St Mary in Battle.

The writer adds that the lane in which the house is situated follows the line of an ancient path or road once called the Wasingate, which in turn at one time crossed the ridge where the 1066 battle was fought.

The use of yews to mark the Pilgrims' Way to Canterbury is taken up by a correspondent living in a Yew Tree Cottage at Sittingbourne in Kent, with two yews on the grass verge outside the garden: 'They overhang the lane that runs between the A2 and the A20 and might have been a route between the Pilgrims' Way on the North Downs and Watling Street. I have noticed other pairs of yews in this part of Kent and I understand that they were "markers" for pilgrims on their way to Canterbury.'

Whether planted or already growing, yew made excellent markers for travellers along tracks. Alfred Watkins in *The Old Straight Track* found that yews were often an indication that a track had once existed nearby: 'There is every reason to surmise that trees were planted in prehistoric times as sighting marks.' He adds that 'trees are joined with stones, water [wells], mountain-tops, mounds, and fire as objects of ancient reverence and even worship; all these are found as sighting points on the ley ... the yew is an early British tree, and the mound at Capler Camp is packed with them and no others near.' They may also have been used as meeting points (as at Heavitree), and even as a venue for court hearings. Watkins reports: 'On a high roadside point nearly three miles from Hereford is a spot called the "Yew and Ash", where on the law day the Herefordshire sheriff met with his javelin men the judge of assize, on his way from Shrewsbury, and the present yew and ash trees were planted in 1855 to mark the spot.'[11]

A phenomenon which appears around houses is the yew tunnel or avenue, formed from trees which have interlinked to form a dense walkway. The idea of a 'green gallery' is a direct survival of the medieval garden, where walled sections and tree-lined walkways were perfect backdrops for the ideal of courtly love which fascinated medieval society and was portrayed in works such as *The Romance of the Rose*. Green galleries made of yew can eventually form an impenetrable vault of branches overhead which will even be proof against rain.

At Aberglasney in Dyfed a large yew tunnel stands close to the old mansion. Although there is no known planting date for the avenue, it must be of considerable age, as it has hardly changed since its depiction in a painting of 1800.

Yew avenues, of course, also exist in churchyards. There is a particularly fine one at Bentley in Hampshire, which was recorded by Gilbert White in 1793. The largest yew, which may be 400 years old, is a curious sight with its huge limbs extending so far that it has needed many wooden supports.

Further valuable information about avenues and tunnels has come from correspondents. One writes: 'The Woodland Trust arboretum at Kingston St Mary, outside Taunton, has a wonderful yew tunnel. The atmosphere is magical.' Another tells of the garden of Pinbury Park, Cirencester in Gloucestershire, where there is an ancient avenue of yew trees:

The avenue is known as the Nun's Walk since it is said that the yews were planted at a time when the site was occupied by nuns resident in a small community. It is said that at the time of the Dissolution the nuns were required to vacate the premises but that the housekeeper was permitted to remain and, loving the place as she did, has continued to perambulate the avenue notwithstanding her intervening demise. The last occasion upon which it was said she was seen was during the Second World War. The avenue is approximately 100 yards in length. Pinbury is, so it is said, named after Penda King of Mercia who was no friend of Christians and who used to treat Pinbury as his summer house from which he launched periodic attacks on Cirencester.

The fact that unlike most other trees yews are either male or female has produced some curiously touching alignments. Behind an old tithe barn at Englishcombe near Bath in Avon a row of yews perches on a steep ramparted bank. Two of the trees stand quite close to each other but are distinctly two separate trees, being a male and a female. The trees are about 600 years old, and over time the male has sent out a lancet branch into the top of the trunk of the female tree, where it has become embedded. The trees are not just entwined with each other, they are completely fused from the lancet branch upwards, male and female combined.

At Watcombe, between Hungerford and Oxford, is a group of yews which have long been known as Paradise. Interestingly the name was also used for groups of trees at Gresford, Chichester and Winchester. *Chambers's Journal* of 1892 describes Watcombe:

A fine pair of trees standing together a little to the rear of the group are known as Adam and Eve, and represent, according to the local legend, our first parents driven out of Paradise. They are of the male and female species, while the foliage of Adam is of a darker shade than that of his companion Eve. Standing still farther from the group is a solitary specimen 20 feet in circumference, which, in the emblematic language of the legend, is the Serpent. This tree shows the effects of time more than any other, the trunk being now nearly reduced to a shell ... A lateral opening in the trunk is large enough to afford standing-room for six or eight persons.

Paradise still exists today, but the 'serpent' tree is now almost completely hidden away in undergrowth.

In spring of 1993 Allen received a letter asking if he knew of the existence of yew trees at Old Enton, near Godalming in Surrey: 'We have two great yews on the top of one of our hills hidden from view. One has a girth of 28½ feet and the other 23 feet.' The writer expressed his wish to preserve the trees and 'to do something positive' with them. When Allen visited the trees he found that they are on the site of what could be an ancient hill fort. Having recently been to two other hill forts where ancient yews are growing, this discovery added to Allen's suspicion that yews may once have been an important feature of hill-fort sites. Merdon Castle in Hampshire, a hill fort dating from about 100 BC and now on a private estate, also has several very old yews growing on its steep slopes.

These are relatively recent discoveries, and considerably more work will have to be done to discover if there is any meaningful pattern. At the moment we can only conjecture that yews and hill forts may well have been connected in some way. Allen believes that the tracing of ancient yews will be of great assistance to archaeologists and historians, as the importance of yew to humanity in the past comes to be appreciated. The position of ancient yews may lead to the discovery of many more historic sites and provide insight into their use.

Wychbury Hill in the West Midlands has so far revealed the strongest evidence about yews on hill forts. On the site are an Iron Age fort and the remains of other earthworks. It dates back to approximately 2000 BC, possibly much earlier, and also contains

Celtic agriculture and an eighteenth-century folly-temple. Twenty-eight yews grow on the hill, within the fort's ramparts. A group of them appears to form some kind of ceremonial avenue and leads up to seven yews believed to mark a sacred spot. One of the earthworks on the hill, a mound called the Round Hill, is known from previous archaeological reports to have had a yew growing on it before the 1930s, but this is now gone. The yews around the central fort are in varying condition. The largest, a 17 ft 6 in female tree outside the earthwork ramparts, is in an excellent state, but some of the others appear to have been burnt and otherwise quite badly vandalized in recent years. However, even the most severely damaged one, a 16 foot tree within the earthwork, shows signs of regrowing by sending up new growth from a branch which has embedded itself into the ground.

At the time of writing, Wychbury Hill is at the centre of a fierce controversy. It is threatened by a proposed six-lane bypass road which could tunnel under it and cut into the edges of the sacred and historical site. Whatever the outcome of this, Wychbury Hill appears to be acting as another catalyst for us all to look at what we want for our future in the British Isles, or indeed the world. It is a particularly apt place for this debate to centre on. From the 700 foot summit a wonderful sweep of rural Worcester, Hereford and Shropshire right up to the borders of Wales can be seen in one direction, and in the other the sprawling mass of the industrialized West Midlands. Wychbury Hill lies above a geological triple fault line containing coal, sandstone and Permian strata; standing on the borderland between two great physical divisions, the Severn and Trent valleys, it is on the watershed of England, and these and other attributes suggest it may be a power point of some kind.

This area of the British Isles gave birth to the Industrial Revolution through its rich supply of all the right kinds of mineral deposits – coal, ironstone, limestone, fireclay, sand, dolerite and quartzite. Perhaps these materials were not rightly honoured when they were taken from the earth to create what was expected to be a golden era of prosperity but which has become a threat to our very existence. As the shaman Arwyn Dreamwalker says of another resource from the earth, uranium: 'If we had come to it in peace instead of in war then we would be using it in its sacredness, instead of being so out of balance that we don't know what to do with it any more.'

One opponent of the bypass scheme comments: 'From Wychbury you can see and ponder where we are all going – on one side the Black Country, on the other rural England. Take your choice for our future. The Industrial Revolution was born in the Black Country; hopefully the antidote to our environmental ills lies here.'

The whole area is obviously sacred. Even the road running around one side of the hill is called Wassel Grove (Wassel being a singing celebration, Grove a holy place), and many local people have reported the sounds of battle and apparitions.

Objection to the bypass has invoked one of Britain's most powerful ancient guardians. Wychbury Hill, it has been claimed, may be the site of King Arthur's battle of Mons Badonicus. Arthur's later death and what became of his body are shrouded in mystery, and it has also been suggested that he may be buried beneath one of the yews on Wychbury Hill, alongside other warriors. These ideas have been put forward by a local historian and archaeologist, Granville Calder, who has researched the area for forty years. His theory has been disputed, but nevertheless it has been given enough credence for archaeological investigation to have been set in motion. Certainly a local record called *The Affairs of Hagley* does tell of a three-day battle in the right area between Celts and Saxons. Further evidence comes from the name of the place; the Battle of Badon appears to have been fought in AD 493 in the 'county' of Hwicce, the name of the Saxon tribe occupying Gloucestershire and Worcestershire at the time and from which the name Wychbury derives. All the same, anything to do with claims of Arthur's battles and death is fraught with difficulties, as any factual basis has long since been hopelessly, from a historian's point of view, enmeshed with myth and legend. Other places such as Glastonbury have better claims to be his last resting place. While Wychbury may well prove to have been an ancient battle site and even to contain warriors' graves, it is probably best to look on such claims about Arthur in a more symbolic way.

Arthur is the epitome of the sacrificial king who must die in order to regenerate the earth, but who on some level remains alive in hiding. This idea lingers today in stories that President Kennedy, Haile Selassie and even Elvis 'The King' Presley are still alive somewhere. In many versions of the legend of Arthur it is said that he never did die, but that he will return at the hour of Albion's greatest need. No wonder he is being invoked at Wychbury Hill. Arthur's connection with the yew has been considered earlier; at Wychbury the yews which have been ignored and neglected over the centuries are now being seen as a possible living link with Arthurian legend.

A likeness also exists between tales of Arthur's death and yew trees which can appear dead for years but are able to regenerate. Some of the trees may date back to Arthur's day, a time when Druidism with its veneration of the yew had not completely disappeared; Merlin was clearly in the Druid tradition originally, before later accounts in a more Christianized era started suggesting he had a Satanic aspect. Arthur's half-sister, Morgan le Fay, was also gradually connected with the 'dark arts', yet it is she and her sisters who took Arthur to the Isle of Apples to minister to him before he died or otherwise disappeared. There is a reminder here of the Scottish poet Thomas the Rhymer, who was buried on Tom na Huriach – 'boat-shaped hill of yews' – in Inverness and who was said to have met the fairy queen through a hallucination produced by eating yew berries. Morgan le Fay is a potent healer versed in shamanistic ways; she can fly and change shape; she is a 'medicine woman' to be treated with respect and epitomizes the power of the goddess. The earliest account in literature of Arthur's death says: 'I will are [sic] to Avalun, to the fairest of all maidens, to Argante [Morgan] the queen, a fay most fair. She shall make my wounds all sound, make me all whole with healing potions. Then I will come again to my kingdom and dwell with the Britons with great joy.'[12]

The connection between the yew and Arthur can be seen on

many different levels, and the most likely site of the burial of an 'actual' Arthur – Glastonbury – is now known to have had a yew in one of its sacred places. Symbolically Arthur and the yew both represent ancient truths and mysteries upon which we are now calling again for our much-needed regeneration.

CHAPTER 12

Under the Greenwood Tree

Before there was a law of a pope or his trouble
Each one made love without blame to his loved one.
Free and easy enjoyment will be without blame,
Well has May made houses of the leaves –
There will be two assignations, beneath trees in concealment
For me, myself and my dear one.

THE RED BOOK OF HERGEST

Of the few ancient yew trees now remaining in Derbyshire, the one in the churchyard at Doveridge connects us with a whole tangled web of yew lore. According to legend and a fourteenth-century manuscript, it was beneath this tree that Robin Hood and Maid Marian first met and were later betrothed. It was also reputed that the couple actually married beneath the tree. Such a wedding, in the open air and beneath a female yew, is superficially Christian but may well have had echoes of pagan ceremonies. Prior to the coming of the Saxons and the Normans the red berries of the female yew were used as part of the dowry, as the *Cad Goddeu*, a Welsh bardic tale that relates to the battle of the trees, says: 'The yew is the judge, his berries are thy dowry' (vv. 98–9). The red berries of the yew were used to symbolize the fertility of the marriage.

The wedding beneath the yew may strike us as strange today, so closely has the tree become associated with death. It is possible that the stories of Robin Hood were themselves a response to this; as knowledge of the yew's aspect of everlasting life faded, so other figures representing the vitality of life emerged to express a fundamental idea.

The Doveridge yew now has a girth of 20 ft 8 in. When Lord Waterpark measured it in 1872, he wrote: 'This yew tree is quite hollow all the way up, about one third of the stem completely gone, which will account for its girth appearing small. It is perfectly healthy, and has grown in the circumferences of its branches, in the last 30 years, from 167 to 212 feet.' Allen dates the tree as Saxon, probably 1,600 years old; this would make the Robin Hood connection feasible.

Places associated with Robin Hood are legion. They range from inns where he is supposed to have slept to Little John's alleged burial site and many places called after him. Yet most of these are relatively late 'discoveries', from around the seventeenth and eighteenth centuries, and nearly all of them were just exploiting a legend which was still changing and becoming increasingly popular. It is, then, interesting to find in the Doveridge yew such an early mention of Robin Hood in connection with one particular place. The Doveridge story also suggests that the yew tree had embedded itself in the legends, traditions and folklore that still persisted in Robin's time, many of them originating in cultures such as those of the Celts, Druids, Norse people and Greeks.

Scholars have for years debated whether Robin was a real person. It seems likely that he was, but that more significantly he provided the starting point for the legend: a lusty character through whom all sorts of ancient tales could be revitalized, and new tales added. Robin's origins have been traced by the historian J.C. Holt to a Robert Hode who lived in the archbishopric of York, and who was outlawed by the justices of York in 1225.[1] A Hood family lived in Wakefield and Barnsdale in the thirteenth century, and at this time most of Robin's adventures are still recorded as taking place in the Yorkshire area. However convincing the historians' arguments are for there having been a 'real' Robin, it is striking how rapidly the tales took on a life of their own. The stories spread quickly, probably by means of the minstrels who plied their trade among aristocratic and knightly families, and who added their own touches along the way. The legend drew some of its incidents from thirteenth-century tales about real-life outlaws, but the tellers of the tales gradually incorporated many other themes which have turned the original stories into the ones we know now from pantomine, television and cinema.

The earliest known written ballads of Robin Hood do not include many of the main characters and incidents which we now take for granted, such as Friar Tuck, Little John and the stories centring on the Sheriff of Nottingham. Holt is right that 'a story is not fixed in time and place. It provides a continually shifting point of focus.' There was, though, something about Robin Hood which appealed to people as soon as the tales began, and even today he is a symbol of some powerful concepts. The tales also tapped into a rich vein of mythology which the church was then doing its utmost to oust. Perhaps their popularity is due not just to their ability to adapt to new times, but to the fact that Robin represents one of our most ancient archetypes; he is a mythic figure who recurs throughout history in different forms. The tales of Robin Hood kept alive the traces of an ancient mythology.

It has already been established that some kind of yew cult almost certainly existed in Celtic times in and around York. By the thirteenth century it was probably at the most a distant memory, but it may well have been woven into customs, folklore and stories. So it seems significant that this hero of the forest should have emerged from an area where trees were once worshipped, and in particular that he should have been outlawed for his activities by the representatives of the new authority in York. Even quite late versions of the Robin Hood story bring in a York connection, despite the fact that Nottingham and Sherwood Forest were soon claimed as Robin's territory; eighteenth-century tales say that Friar Tuck came from Fountains Abbey in Yorkshire, the site of some very ancient yews.

The most direct connection Robin has with yew is through his bow:

> Make glad chere, said Little John,
> And freshe our bowes of ewe,
> And loke your hearts be seker and sad [firm and resolute]
> Your strynges trusty and trewe.
> Good soothe it was a gallant sight
> To see them in a rowe,
> With every man a keen broad sword
> And eke a stout ewe bowe.

This ballad is probably relatively late, but it is typical of the tales in which references to the 'stout ewe bow' abound. These may partly be trying to evoke a 'merry old England' of the past, but one of the very earliest written accounts of Robin also alludes to the yew bow. In 'Robin Hoode his Death', Robin is treacherously killed by his prioress cousin, and as he dies he asks to be buried thus:

> And sett my bright sword at my head,
> Mine arrowes at my feete.
> And lay my yew bow by my side.[2]

It is, of course, not surprising that Robin's most valued possessions include a yew bow. A fine bow was vital to his way of life. Nevertheless, it is interesting that yew, and no other material, is singled out.

Robin's wish to be buried with yew alongside him could be an echo of more ancient burial rites. We know that the traces of such rites still persisted well after his time, as the well-known extract from Shakespeare's *Twelfth Night* demonstrates: 'Come away death . . . My shroud of white, stuck all with Ew, O prepare it' (Act 2, scene iv). Yew is often cited in the sixteenth and seventeenth centuries as being carried by mourners at funerals and strewn over the grave after the ceremony. Such customs are still documented in modern times, for instance at Fortingall.

In later tales this theme is taken further when Robin is said to have been buried beneath a yew tree. Even now one of the most popular legends about Robin is of him shooting an arrow from his bow as he lies at death's door:

the dying man asked for his good yew bow and arrows. 'Bury me where this arrow falls,' he entreated; then, fitting an arrow to the string, he shot. The missile fell at the foot of a yew which might have yielded such a bow as he held in his unconscious grasp. A sigh, and Robin Hood was a memory. The mortal part of him they buried, as he had bidden, under the yew.[3]

Allen believes that Robin's last act on his deathbed hints further at early rituals which may be the last memory of a dying yew cult, and which he may even have been aware of. The request to be buried beneath a yew tree also still persists; T.S. Eliot and Lewis Carroll are two examples of this.

The way Robin meets his death in the early stories, from about the fifteenth century, is also interesting. His cousin is not only a close relative but also a Christian prioress, yet she deceives her kinsman into trusting her and poisons him to please her lover. There is an echo here of the way Christianity gradually took over the ancient religions; the early Christians were told not to destroy the ancient ways, but rather to build upon them. Their apparent 'kinsmanship' served to gain the people's trust, but the old ways were gradually 'poisoned' and killed off, and dubbed pagan or even Satanic. Witness, for example, the later burning of 'witches' in the name of Christianity. Although Robin is never portrayed as a religious figure, he *does* enshrine a religious quality. Robin epitomizes the life force of the forests and of nature – often unruly and certainly beyond taming by human's laws, yet vibrant and energized. And although he defies the law of the courts, he always pays allegiance to the king, suggesting his ultimate honouring of the 'rightful' laws of nature and human society.

Another figure to appear at around the same time as Robin Hood is the Green Man. This can be no coincidence; the old ideas of the vegetation cults were seeking new expression in the face of the church's opposition. It is not surprising to find that Robin has frequently been likened to the Green Man, and has often been used to symbolize him. The Green Man is frequently depicted in European cultures as a figure sprouting vegetation and representing the regenerative power of nature. Vestiges of the spirit of paganism, or nature worship, survived through the centuries. The edicts of the early church campaigned against it; and the Green Man, banished to shadowy corners in the church roof, behind the rood screen or on top of pillars, was 'Christianized' in a way. Yet, even in stone, his verdant head springs forth as a promise of life appearing anew every year.

There are many obvious parallels between Robin and the Green Man, and another suggestion for Robin's origin is that 'Robin Hood' was a contraction of 'Robin of the Wood'. Robin and his Merry Men dress in green and depend on the forest for life. The woods provide their safe retreat as well as being the setting for their skirmishes. The forest has both a nurturing and a fearsome aspect, as the Green Man can have, too.

Robin's appeal to those who heard the tale was not just to do with his natural justice – the tales centring around the Sheriff of Nottingham appeared quite late – but is to do with just the kind of qualities symbolized by the Green Man. Robin epitomized the kind of life of which ordinary people might only dream: dangerous, certainly, but answerable to no one (except perhaps the king), carefree and spontaneous. In their comprehensive book on the Green Man, William Anderson and Clive Hicks sum it up: 'As Robin of the Wood he also appealed to atavistic instincts, the inner certainty that the woods were wakeful and alive. He is the watcher through the leaves, the burst of laughter in an empty clearing, the joker in the ambush.'[4] At a time when the church was doing its utmost to kill off the ancient religions, Robin Hood must surely be the form which the Green Man assumed. Robin does count one man of the church among his companions: Friar Tuck. He has the simple qualities associated with a religious person, forthright, honest, good-hearted and earthy. He is, for example, a far cry from the wealthy corruption of the monasteries epitomized in Chaucer's portrait of the worldly and well-fed Abbot.

Despite the fact that the church clearly tried to get rid of the old vegetation gods, there are many stunning examples of the Green Man in churches in Britain. The church seems to have had an ambivalent relationship with him. If the yew in the churchyard was

The verdant face of the Green Man

the living presence of an old spirituality which revered the regenerative power of nature, the Green Man carved in the church could be said to be its representative in permanent man-made form.

In several churches these two symbols that remind humanity of its connection with nature – the yew tree and the Green Man – are found together. At Langley, for instance, the church's chancel pillars have three medieval Green Men sprouting foliage from their mouths; the yew in the churchyard, described in 1853 as 'the shell of a tree', still survives and is at least 1,400 years old. Clearly it was there long before the carvings. Similarly the yew at Darley Dale in Derbyshire is at least 1,600 years old, while the Green Man there could be about twelfth century.

The fine fifteenth-century Green Man on the chancel arch at Llangwm triggered the twentieth-century revival of interest in the Green Man. An influential article in the 1939 *Folklore* gave figures such as these the name by which we now know them. When Lady Raglan visited the church she was shown a carved stone head situated behind the rood, in the choir. From its rather crude but powerfully carved mouth foliage springs forth and wraps itself around the man's face. Lady Raglan carried out detailed research and wrote:

the question is whether there was any figure in reality from which it could have been taken. The answer, I think, is that there is only one of sufficient importance, the figure variously known as the Green Man, Jack in the Green, Robin Hood, the King of the May, and the Garland, who is the central figure in the May-Day celebrations throughout Northern and Central Europe.[5]

The large yew tree at Llangwm stands next to the path to the south entrance. Lady Raglan must have passed by it on her way into the church.

Surprisingly, the Green Man appears at Fountains Abbey, which was constructed beside yews now 1,500 years old by monks who were seeking a more rigorous monastic order. Considering the legacy of vegetation cults in the Yorkshire area, however, it is perhaps inevitable to find the Green Man here.

Stoke Gabriel in Devon is also something of a mystery. The yew tree is magnificent but at 'only' 850 years old has achieved a fame beyond its years. As Allen says: 'Why is it one of the most famous yews in the country? It is certainly not one of the largest or oldest by any means, yet over the centuries many authors have written about it.' Even books one might not expect to be given to flights of fancy, such as *The AA Guide to Britain*, cheerfully state that it is at least 1,000 years old; many put it at over 1,400. The tree has been associated for years with a fertility rite. Beside the yew, on either side of the church door, are thirteenth-century carvings of Gabriel and Herne the Hunter, who, as will be seen, is a reappearance of the Green Man.

Broadwell in Gloucestershire should be mentioned here, although the 'Green Men' are of a rather different type. The position of the church, near to a monastery, moats, a tumulus and an old manor house, suggests it has been a sacred site for hundreds of years. The churchyard once contained a Saxon pagan cemetery. The 1,300-year-old yew tree is close to the Broad Well spring from which the name comes. Two Saxon carvings have been unearthed from the churchyard; one shows what appears to be a Tree of Life, and the other, which is very worn and hard to decipher, depicts figures perhaps dancing around a tree on a mount, from which two crucifix shapes also emerge.

At Crowcombe in Somerset the Green Man appears three times, in carvings on bench-ends. One of these shows him in the normal way, with foliage growing from his mouth. The other two carvings are more unusual; from their ears come mermen and fish, perhaps honouring the gods of the nearby sea as well as those of vegetation. Bel Mooney writes of the Crowcombe Green Men: 'I always thought the Green Men would be rotund, jolly creatures, full of a spirit of pagan celebration ... but these at Crowcombe are not. There is something vaguely sinister; something in the flare of a nose, and the slit of an eye ... Whatever, he is something to be feared and placated under a threatening sky.'[6]

The time that the Green Man appears in churches with a fresh burst of vitality coincides with just the time that the Robin Hood ballads were spreading and becoming so popular. Given the close identification of Robin Hood and the Green Man, there must surely be a reason why they put in such strong appearances simultaneously. It may be to do with the fact that the yew tree was becoming gradually identified, through the growth of the church, as the 'graveyard yew'. This close identification with death may have meant that the yew's other aspect – that of everlasting life and regeneration – had to find another outlet, namely through the Green Man and Robin Hood. Similarly, Jack-in-the-Green figures appeared during the Industrial Revolution, at a time when the Green Man was no longer being carved in churches and when there was a massive shift of the population from country to town. This figure representing vegetative resurgence has also survived to today through May Day ceremonies.

Unearthing the presence of the Green Man in the Robin Hood tales is only the beginning of finding Robin's roots, for the Green Man himself contains many different aspects. Similarly the figure of Robin and the tales about him are composed from many different legends. The search here is not for a real person but for something deeper. Delving into mythology to find Robin's origins provides a different kind of truth: 'Events which can be dated and analysed, and placed at a proper distance from the present, can also at some stage begin to appear far away; can fade. Myths are fresh; they never lose their force' (V.S. Naipaul).

The name 'Robin Hood' may give further hints about his origins in our mythological past, and about some more ways in which he has brought aspects of the yew right into the twentieth century. Allen has argued that the name 'Robin Hood' came from the term 'Red Wood', which may have indicated some early Celtic divine cult relating to the yew tree, and existing perhaps around 2,000 years ago. Yew was at one time referred to as 'the red one'. Its wood is of a rich red colour. The third-century Gaelic bard Ossian compares the hue of health on his hero's cheeks to a 'red yew bow', suggesting that such a simile would be readily understood by his readers. Yews sometimes exude a red liquid; this usually comes from rainwater having gathered in a hollow in the wood, then trickling away infused with the colour of the wood. The famous 'bleeding yew' at Nevern, Dyfed, for instance, exudes a red resin. The berries on a female yew add to this description of yew as 'the red tree', and the berries and red 'blood' of the yew were considered to be powerful forces against witchcraft. The connection here with Robin Hood is that the name 'Robin' signifies red. 'Robin the hooded man' could have also been 'the red wooded one'.

The 'Hood' element of Robin's name also contains some intriguing possibilities. The 'hooded one' or the 'hidden one' is mentioned in various Celtic tales and references to gods, and the hood is a symbol which crops up all over Celtic Europe at about this time in an image known as a Genius Cucullatus (*cucullus* means hood). An eighth-century manuscript links the Irish hero Finn, who has a strong affinity with the natural world and is also a hunter, and the 'man in the tree', 'The peaked red one, Derce Corra mac hui Daighre', whose face was never seen. A well-known example is the carved stone found at Housesteads on Hadrian's Wall, at the civil settlement attached to the Roman garrison and dating from around the third century AD. It shows three figures wearing heavy hooded garments which reveal only their faces and feet. It has been suggested that these figures could represent three ages of life, or different aspects of one god. The name Genius Cucullatus comes from an inscription in a Romano-Celtic shrine in Austria, where two altars are dedicated to 'genio cucullato'. The hooded figures also have a strong fertility aspect; those found in the Cotswolds carry eggs and are often shown alongside a mother goddess.[7] Many from the Continent are phallic.

There is no doubt that the cult of the Genii Cucullati was widespread in Romano-Celtic Europe, and Allen believes that it denotes the hidden mysteries of death and birth. These meanings could be likened in various ways to the yew; 'hooded' or 'hidden one' could indicate the hidden trunk of the yew, obscured by its vast canopy of branches, or hiding the new birth inside its trunk. What is more probable, though, is not that symbols such as a hood were some kind of secret code for the yew, but that the tree was their original inspiration long before.

The hood appears in other European mythologies, too. Odin was referred to as 'the hooded god', perhaps because of the golden helmet he wore, or the wide-brimmed hat in which, as his early form of Wotan, he was said to hunt through the night skies for game. Odin possibly became connected with Robin Hood via Merlin; Robert Graves suggests that Robin is a Christianized version of Merlin and that his name is a variant of Merlin's Saxon name, 'Rof Breoht Woden' or 'Bright Strength of Odin'.[8] There may be something in this, for Merlin was also known as 'Man of the Woods'.

Returning to the derivation of the name 'Hood', this word, or *hod* or *hud* in Saxon, meant 'log', specifically the log at the back of the fire, the yule log. According to Robert Graves, popular superstition held that Robin Hood resided in this yule log, and when it was burned he would escape up the chimney in the shape of a robin to do battle with his rival, Bran or Saturn, who had been 'Lord of Misrule' at Yule-tide. This is strong evidence of Robin not only being connected with the yew tree (the yule log being a yew branch), but also restoring the proper balance by annually killing off the Lord of Misrule. This is a clear reminder of the idea found in many cultures, and already discussed, of the weakening sun dying and being reborn after the annual struggle with darkness at the winter solstice. Here the spirit of Robin comes out of the yew, in the form of a robin. Almost every yew tree is home to a robin. At some point the bird was 'Christianized' with the folklore that its red breast resulted from a drop of Christ's blood. Robin Hood is seen not just as the restorer of natural order after the Lord of Misrule has been allowed full rein; he is here the god in the wood who must die so that his spirit may return again, just as the yule log continues to the next year. *Hod* being Saxon for 'wood' therefore adds yet another dimension to the likely derivations of Robin's name, and to the possibility of him being a resurgence of an ancient tree cult which in some areas of Britain had been maintained into the Saxon period.

Interestingly Red Riding Hood has marked similarities to Robin

Hood. The names of the two are very similar, and the tales also have some strong parallels. Just as Robin in the early tales was poisoned by his cousin, so Red Riding Hood is duped by what she believes to be her grandmother, but is actually a wolf, who devours her. Red again appears as an important element, and in both stories the forest setting is fundamental.

In the same way that Robin took his name from a wide range of mythological and even spiritual sources, it may be that he also absorbed some of the other attributes from these gods and heroes. Robin's prowess as a hunter and bowman is well known, and this aspect as the hunter connects him with many hunter-gods. Hunting appears in the attributes or legends surrounding many pre-Christian gods and goddesses: Blodeuwedd, Diana, Janus, Maia, Athena, Minerva, Artemis, Heimdall and Odin, to name just a few. Hunting was a revered activity, as its success was deemed to depend on some kind of affinity between the hunter and the hunted. This can be seen right back in the earliest cave paintings which show human figures and their quarry. The Celts had many deities connected to the animals which they hunted, suggesting a reverence for the animals on which they depended for food.

Hunting also has a more profound meaning: the 'divine hunt' in which the killing of an enchanted beast endows its killer with immortality. The hunter, especially in Celtic mythology, signified not only death but also rebirth through the act of hunting in a way which gave honour to divine forces. The Christians again adopted an ancient symbol for their own purposes, as Professor Stephens writes:

The stag ... early on the hart, was a symbol for Christ and gave way to the lamb. But the stag symbol was too old and deeply rooted to entirely disappear. In the early Middle Ages in the West it was utilized with a new meaning ... it became the sign of the natural man, the wandering or wild or worldly soul, erring homeless in the thickets of care-filled time. Hence the stag or other wild animals tokened pagans or the unconverted. They were hunted by men and dogs – holy servants of Christ, till they were driven into the fold of the church.[9]

These concepts of hunting again bring us to the yew, so identified with death in modern times but which also contains the potential for rebirth and regeneration. Perhaps this is why the 'white goddess' of whom Graves writes was depicted in her death aspect as an owl emerging from an enormous hollow yew tree. As Allen says:

The white owl, bird of the yew, is symbolic of hunting and death, and the resurrection to come. White can also mean pure, virgin-like, fresh; in Welsh white is *sanctus*, and the yew is often referred to as *taxus sancti*. The yew tree is associated with death, and also with the hunter. The yew bow which comes from the tree *becomes* the hunter, just as it is also the owl, Cernunnos, Robin Hood and many others.

The Celtic god Cernunnos is particularly connected with Robin Hood as the hunter. Cernunnos is a crucial figure in Celtic mythology. His name means 'horned' or 'peaked one', and he is generally depicted with horns or antlers coming from his head; occasionally he is shown with three heads, as in a statue at Condat in France. He is one of the few Celtic gods from before the Roman period whose image has survived. The first known depiction of him contains the main components ascribed to him; a fourth-century BC carving from northern Italy shows him with antlers, torcs denoting divinity on each arm, and accompanied by a small figure with an erect penis, and a snake. He is sometimes also shown carrying a sack from which grain pours forth. Cernunnos is closely related to the animal world, and to fertility and growth. Joseph Campbell says that in the Irish epics he is called the Dagda, from *dago devos*, the good god. Despite the fact that he is sometimes unsettlingly god/man/animal, his beneficence is clear. His rapport with untamed nature may be rather alien to us today, but he embodies some of the qualities which the Green Man came to symbolize, and which western society is seeking again.

While Cernunnos's associations with the animal world are obvious, through the beasts that are often shown alongside him and his stag's antlers, he is also a god of vegetation. Perhaps the most famous image of him is that on the wonderful Gundestrup bowl from Denmark; one panel of the bowl shows him with the familiar stag's horns, but elsewhere on it he appears with leaves growing over his head. Cernunnos may well have been the origin for the Green Man. In some other images of him the antlers could as easily be the branches of a tree as the horns of a stag. Even where they are unmistakably antlers they imply the life of the forest. Many carvings of Cernunnos leave a pair of holes at the top of his head for the insertion of horns or branches, possibly on festival days.

The idea of a 'horned' god continued long after Christianity tried to ban it. In the fourth century AD St Augustine spoke of 'that most filthy habit of dressing up as a horse or stag', and the Christians' Devil was probably forged from an unholy alliance between Cernunnos, Pan and various other earthy deities. Nevertheless, Cernunnos survived in folklore and legend; he appears in various folk dances, and certainly left his mark in many place-names in Britain, such as Cerne Abbas.

Cernunnos can be equated with the Teutonic god Heimdall, god of light, of the dawn and beginnings. He is the 'guardian of the door' and of the rainbow bridge, which he protects against the giants. Heimdall is the guardian of the apple of life-in-death, which he was given by Iduna, the equivalent of the Celtic Blodeuwedd, born of flowers. Heimdall has a more nurturing aspect than Cernunnos, and his senses are acute – he can hear the grass growing, and the wool growing on the sheeps' backs. As already seen, Heimdall is connected with the World Tree, and he is linked with the yew through the apples which he guards. As 'guardian of the door' Heimdall may have been represented by the Saxons in their planting of yews in churchyards. The church porch or portico was an innovation of the Saxons, and most of their churches have a yew next to the porch. One other explanation for this is that guardianship is suggested by this positioning, and it is appropriate that people entering and leaving the church would have passed beneath these protecting yews.

Gathering together all these elements from assorted mythologies is hazardous, as Allen himself warns: 'It is difficult to simplify legends and stories which come to us from a mysterious past; but

Heimdall holding the horn. Drawing of part of the Gosforth Cross

this hunter, sometimes in a male and sometimes in a female role, adds to the mystery.' There is a reminder here of figures such as Janus or Diana, both of whom are sometimes shown with two faces. The yew also has two aspects, those of life and death, and the more we delve into these things, the more strange connections appear.

One example of this might be the death of William II, known as Rufus the Red, King of England in the late eleventh and early twelfth centuries, who was shot by one of his own archers while in the New Forest. There have been suggestions that his assassination was a ritual sacrifice; Robert Graves, for instance, hints at this. The hunting and slaying of the King were carried out by use of a bow which, according to still current legend, came from the yew at Brockenhurst in Hampshire. It was an ancient site, and it is possible that a more ancient yew existed there prior to the one planted in Saxon times. The site, and the tree on it, would probably have been considered very significant locally, which gives added emphasis to the theory about the yew bow. Rufus the Red was killed on 2 August 1100, a most significant date as this was associated with Lammas Day or Lugnasadh, a time when sacrifices were once part of the rites.

An interesting footnote to this tale is added by a current resident of Chandlers Ford, Hampshire. Norma Pruden says of the yew tree in her garden that 'There is a story in the area that when they took King Rufus's body to Winchester Cathedral via Chandlers Ford they camped overnight and planted a yew tree. This is the present one now in the garden, some 15 feet in girth.' It is possible that the murder of Rufus drew on elements of pre-Christian mythologies of hunting and associated ritual.

The concepts that Cernunnos and others such as the Green Man and Robin Hood epitomize seem to be so basic to our understanding of the world that such figures keep reappearing. In Tudor England there was something of a revival of Celtic matters, one aspect of it being the 'reinvention' of Cernunnos in the form of Herne the Hunter, who was supposed to terrorize the grounds of Windsor Great Park. Shakespeare speaks of Herne in *The Merry Wives of Windsor* through Mistress Page:

> There is an old tale goes that Herne the Hunter,
> Sometime a keeper here in Windsor forest,
> Doth all the winter-time, at still midnight,
> Walk round about an oak, with great ragg'd horns;
> And there he blasts the tree, and takes the cattle
> And makes milch-kine yield blood, and shakes a chain
> In a most hideous and dreadful manner.

(Act 4, scene iii)

Like Robin Hood, Herne was sometimes said to have originally been an actual person, as Shakespeare implies. According to this version he was a forester who had offended the king and been hanged, appearing afterwards as a shaggy man wearing stag's horns and blowing a trumpet, ugly beyond description and usually portending ill luck. It is much more likely that he is a reappearance of Cernunnos – the name Herne sounds very similar to the first part of

Cernunnos – and could also have drawn on myths of Odin. Here again the connections, though tangled, are there. From Cernunnos he has inherited the stag's horns, while from Odin comes the idea of being transformed through hanging; Herne takes from both deities his identity as the hunter. He seems to be an involuntary resurgence of an enduring archetype.

Shakespeare's picture of Herne is far from flattering, but he also appears in some stories as helpful and kind, the master of the woods and animals, and a 17 foot giant. This is a curious reminder of an old idea that the original inhabitants of the British Isles were giants.

In Celtic times the most dramatic form that hunting took was head-hunting. A severed head was a revered object, and warriors bedecked their horses with strings of them. Once again we find in the early tales of Robin Hood an echo of ancient practices. When Guy of Gisborne (originally a yeoman, not a nobleman) is sent to capture him, Robin decapitates him and then mounts the head on his yew bow, as recounted in this fifteenth-century verse:

> He tooke Sir Guys head by the hayre,
> And sticked itt on his bowes end:
> 'Thou has beene traytor all thy liffe,
> Which thing must have an ende.'

> Robin pulled forth an Irish kniffe
> And nicked Sir Guy in the fface,
> That he was never on a woman borne
> Could tell who Sir Guye was.[10]

In another fragment of a story from 1475, Robin's encounter with Guy of Gisborne takes on a new twist. A knight promises to capture Robin for a fee, and the two men compete at archery, presumably with yew bows, and wrestling. Robin defeats his opponent and beheads him. He then uses his horrific trophy to disguise himself:

> This knyghtys clothis wolle I were
> And in my hode his hede woll bere.[11]

Robin later shed much of this more gruesome side, and became increasingly linked with May Day. May Day celebrations as we think of them today developed only in the late fifteenth century. Robin was adopted into the May games during the fifteenth century, at the end of which the tales about him began to be written down, and it was probably through the games that he became so renowned. He was soon established as the principal player in them, but was actually just a newcomer to a long-existing rite. The May Day festivities celebrate the physical return of the creative forces, of fertility and birth, and as such their origins are to be sought in Maid Marian.

If Robin Hood was the King of the May, naturally Maid Marian was the Queen. Maid Marian, or May Marion, was originally the Roman goddess Maia, an incarnation of the earth goddess. Vulcan her husband was one of the original Latin gods, preceding even Jupiter. He was the god of fire and the sun, in particular the life-giving aspect of heat. Faunus, her father, was a fertility god, and the orgiastic annual fertility festival held in his temple was one of the most important in the Roman calendar. Maia's own fertility ceremony was in May, celebrating the coming of spring. The Faunus festivals continued until at least the end of the fifth century AD, when Pope Gelasius banned them in favour of the ritual Purification of the Virgin. As the Romans were in Britain for about 450 years before the ban, it is likely that such ceremonies would have been performed in the British Isles.

Over the centuries the Roman deities became intermingled with those of Greece. The goddess Maia had her Greek counterpart in Cybele. From what we have already seen of her and her beloved, Attis, she made her own contribution to May Day even though it is not her name which came down to us through Maid Marian.

The fir tree, symbolizing the resurrection of Attis, seems a likely source of the origins of the maypole, although the custom of erecting one probably contains elements of many such celebrations involving sacred trees. The maypole could equally have come from the yew, which would once have been at the centre of a tribal territory. Even now we know of yews around which people danced until quite recently. The impulse to dance around a tree seems to be innate; Allen reports that when he took a party of schoolboys to the Tandridge yew, they linked hands around the massive tree without any prompting and moved around it. Many old folksongs refer to this, such as 'Hey Down, Ho Down, among the Leaves So Green', which according to Professor Burnett is a Druidic chant. The annual ceremony at Painswick in Gloucestershire is a further example; people join hands around the church on Clipping Sunday, following the clipping of the yew trees – said to number ninety-nine – in the churchyard. In fact, the clipping probably originated in a clapping, not a clipping, dance around the trees.

All this is not to say that the maypoles themselves would once have been made of yew. What is more likely is that the yew was the inspiration, the original source. It is a remnant of an ancient reverence, even worship, of trees generally and the yew in particular. In post-Freudian times the maypole tends to be seen almost solely for its phallic symbolism and its implied fertility. This, of course, is there, and the disc on top of the pole represents the female aspect; but the obvious symbolizing of sexual awakening is far from incompatible with the Green Man, Robin Hood and the yew tree. Yews planted in barrows, for instance, seem to have been symbols of regeneration, the western version perhaps of the oriental *yoni* and the *lingam*. The maypole signifies not just fertility and sexuality, it also represents the *axis mundi*, the never-changing centre or pole around which the world revolves.

Perhaps a memory of the original May Day celebrations under living trees remains in this seventeenth-century verse from 'Robin Hood and Little John':

> Then musick and dancing did finish the day;
> At length, when the sun waxed low,
> Then all the whole train the grove did refrain,
> And unto their caves they did go.

Some of the ninety-nine yews of Painswick

May Day in the Middle Ages was a far merrier event than Christmas was. Greenwood marriages blessed by a Friar Tuck figure would be made on May Day. These weddings would often be afterwards confirmed in the church porch, but the offspring of such 'unofficial' unions might find themselves rejected by their fathers. As well as the beribboned maypoles, the festivities included drinking and game-playing, including archery contests. The bow has its own symbolism which makes its use at May Day games particularly appropriate; it represents both man and woman, the man through the sending of an arrow, the woman through the crescent-moon shape of the bow. This symbolism is far older than the Christian idea, which usually sees it as a symbol of worldly power as in images of St Sebastian being martyred by archers. Many other cultures associate male/female ideas with the bow.

The Green Man probably acted as a balance between the old

pagan ways and the new Christianity for a long time, but by the early sixteenth century both the church and the civil authorities were ardently opposing May Day celebrations. In 1517 the suppression of May Day riots in London culminated in fourteen people being hanged, drawn and quartered, and another 400 people were reprieved only when Henry VIII granted clemency, even as they stood with the nooses around their necks. Henry VIII himself was not averse to a little May Daying. Just two years before these hangings, he and Queen Catherine had been fêted by 200 bowmen dressed in green on Shooters Hill in London; and, under the direction of 'Robin Hood', archery demonstrations and merry-making had proceeded.

Generally, however, by this time the old ways were considered a legitimate target by the Protestant church. Indeed, our knowledge of many of the old customs which still existed in the sixteenth and seventeenth centuries comes to us through its denunciations. In a passage in one of his sermons to Edward VI, Bishop Latimer tells how he visited a certain church to preach on a holy day, only to find when he got there that the door was locked, and nobody to be found: 'And one of the parish comes to me and says, "Sir, this is a busy day with us, we cannot hear you; it is Robin Hood's day. The parish are gone abroad to gather for Robin Hood. I pray you let [prevent] them not." I was fain there to give place to Robin Hood.'

The Puritan writer Philip Stubbes, in *The Anatomie of Abuses* of 1583, wrote in shocked tones:

Against May, Whitsunday, or other time, all the young men and maids, old men and wives, gadding over night to the woods, groves, hills and mountains, where they spend all night in pleasant pastimes; and in the morning they return, bringing with them birch and branches of trees to deck their assemblies withal. And we marvel, for there is a great Lord present among them, as superintendent and Lord over their pastimes and sport, namely Satan, prince of Hell. But the chiefest jewel they bring from thence is their May-pole, which they bring home with great veneration as thus. They have twenty or forty yoke of oxen, every ox having a sweet nosegay of flowers placed on the tip of his horns; and these oxen draw home this May-pole (this stinking Idol, rather) which is covered all over with flowers and herbs, bound round about with strings with two or three hundred men, women and children following it with great devotion. And thus being reared up with handkerchiefs and flags hovering on the top, they strew the ground round about, bind green boughs about it, set up summer halls, bowers and arbours hard by it. And then fall they to dance about it, like as the heathen people did at the dedication of the Idols, whereof this is a perfect pattern, or rather the thing itself. I have heard it credibly reported (and that 'viva voce') by men of great gravity and reputation, that, of forty, three-score, or a hundred maids going to the wood overnight, there have scarcely the third part of them returned home again undefiled.

The reference Stubbes makes to the presence of Satan at the May games suggests that Cernunnos was indeed linked in people's minds with these festivities. Even at this late date there are also echoes of groves and, therefore, of yew trees. Behind Stubbes's suggestion that the maypole was an idol, that it was 'the thing itself', are traces of tree worship. Maypoles were eventually banned in England during Cromwell's time, but they almost certainly never vanished completely, judging by the puritanical condemnations of the practice which continued to appear. Nevertheless, it is noticeable how the wild and passionate dances to which the Puritan writers referred have since been replaced by really very formal ones, in which ribbons are interwoven in strict geometric patterns, often by primary-school children. Little remains of the very adult, ribald and fecund Green Man here.

Although May Day now appears to us as an old festival, it is just an echo of more ancient customs, such as those found around Maia and Attis. It also grew out of the Celtic festival of Beltane, which celebrated the coming of the summer months. Beltane and Samhain marked the two halves of the year, the months of growth and the months of winter respectively, and were the two major festivals of the Celtic year.

At Beltane fires were lit beneath a sacred tree. It is this tree, too, which has survived as the maypole, a symbol of the regeneration of nature. People danced around the sacred tree-fire in a sunwise

A woodcut from an old English chapbook shows the Green Man appearing
through the leaves, as fairy folk dance near a toadstool and a tumulus

direction and carried lighted brands around the fields. They jumped
through the flames, encouraging the crops to grow as high as they
might leap, and drove the cattle and flocks through the fire to purify
them of winter infestations. There was a serious side to the festival,
which, like Samhain, was seen as a transitional time when the
underworld was more accessible and hence more threatening. The
struggle between the dark and the light forces was honoured, and
this may have included animal sacrifices in some places. A game in
which one person was chosen to act as if dead was probably a resi-
due of even older human sacrifices. Yet Beltane was also a time of
great celebration, ecstasy and excitement, a time when the promise of
summer was clearly visible on the trees, and the people could again
meet in the open air after the long winter months. In Ireland it was
also the time for the divorce of trial marriages which had been made
at Lughnasadh the previous year and had not survived the winter.

The sacred tree

It is easy to see that Beltane would be the time for new partner-
ships to be played with, and that this is what the Puritans later found
so abhorrent in May Day festivities. Perhaps the continuing attraction
of the Stoke Gabriel yew is that it still retains some of these old
fertility rites; it is said that fertility for a woman is achieved by
walking forwards around the tree, and for a man by walking back-
wards around it.

Various explanations have been given for the origins of the name
Beltane. One is that it has to do with the trees which are such an
important part of the festival. *Bile* is the word for a tree, and *bel* is a
sacred tree; *tan* can mean red or fire, and *tann* is a sacred tree;
Tandridge, site of an ancient yew, means 'the red tree on the hill'. In
Cornwall the compound *glastann*, green sacred tree, meant an evergreen holm-oak or yew tree. Thus the word Beltane reveals connections between sacred trees and fires, both of which were present in
the ceremonies. Other Celtic festivals such as Imbolc and Lughnasadh
contained the elements of the lighting of fires, the burning of faggots,
and children jumping over the glowing embers. This happened until

recently in remote areas of Normandy and Scotland. It is perhaps no coincidence that such places as Fortingall, in the very centre of Scotland, and La Haye de Routot in Normandy, have on their ancient burial sites two of the oldest and most famous yews in Europe.

Allen has carried out a good deal of research into Celtic festivals, and believes that their origins are more than coincidentally connected with the yew tree. He concludes: 'No matter how I go about it, it always presents a familiar pattern, a pattern that always seems to be entwined with the yew, at first remote and as I proceed it becomes more of a reality. This mystical tree will forever remain a mystery, and any writing about the yew could never do it justice.'

One of the most ancient yews in the British Isles is at Llanfaredd in Powys. It is estimated to be about 3,000 years old, and although decayed on one side is still a fine large tree. There are tumuli on top of the hill, and a spring or well just to the east of the church. The river Wye is across the road from the tree, and recently another huge yew was discovered at Alltmawr, just across the river on a hilltop. The evidence points to Llanfaredd being a site of great antiquity. In 1944 a visitor to the church recorded that the cross and the candlesticks on the altar were made from yew. He also found that the vases had been filled with sprigs of yew, and learned that this was the custom at this time of year; it was the third Sunday after Easter. With such a length of time having elapsed since the marking of the death of Christ at Easter, it is curious that yew, which so often symbolizes death in churches, should have been there at the time of resurrection and renewal. Perhaps the yew in the vase at this time of year was the remnant of many ancient customs, coming down to us via Beltane, Robin Hood and the Green Man, and representing original rites and celebrations beneath the sacred yew.

CHAPTER 13

The Sacred Trees of Ireland

In the eleventh century when the Ulstermen cut down the sacred trees at Tullughohoge, County Tyrone, their behaviour was considered so outrageous that the men of Kinel Owen retaliated by carrying off three thousand cows.

ANNALS OF TIGERNACH

The deforestation of Ireland from late medieval times onwards was extreme. During the eighteenth and nineteenth centuries firewood became so short that fossil timber from the bogs became a major source of fuel. Before that process gathered momentum, though, Ireland was densely covered with mixed woodland, broken only by mountains and bogs.

That the yew was plentiful we know from Gerald of Wales, who made four visits to the country between 1183 and 1204.[1] Gerald was a well-connected Norman cleric who clearly saw a visit to Ireland as a matter of leaving civilization behind and entering a world of barbarians. He made no attempt to hide this prejudice in his *History and Topography of Ireland*, where he relates a bizarre collection of 'the wonders and miracles' of Ireland with varying degrees of amazement and indignation. To this fondness for disdainful gossip, for which the Irish have never forgiven him, is added a lot of keen observation, particularly of geography and natural history. He found the woods full of yew and, like the classical authors, thought this discouraged bees. 'Yews,' he writes, 'with their bitter sap, are more frequently to be found in this country than in any other I have visited; but you will see them principally in old cemeteries and sacred places, where they were planted in ancient times by the hands of holy men, to give them what ornament and beauty they could.'

Gerald also notes how, when the soldiers of Henry II landed, they were delighted at finding a good supply of yew for bow staves and cut the trees disregarding the superstitious fears of the local people. In another passage he tells that several troops of archers were billeted for a time at Finglas, County Dublin. There, 'the illustrious abbot Kenach and other holy men in succession, through whose fervent piety the place became celebrated, had formerly planted with their own hands ash trees and yews and various other kinds of trees, round the cemetery for the ornament of the church'. The soldiers cut them down for firewood, but 'in retribution for their impiety they were smitten by a sudden and singular pestilence so that most of them perished miserably within a few days'.

The strong connection between trees and holy sites in Ireland is recorded elsewhere. According to the eighth-century *Book of Armagh*, St Patrick established a church near Bile Tortan, one of Ireland's five legendary trees, and what evidence there is suggests that churches were sited next to sacred groves for the same reasons that they were built next to yews in Britain. Some saints are recorded as having great respect for trees. Of Columcille it was said: 'Much afraid as he was of death and hell, the sound of the axe in Derry frightened him even more.' Manus O'Donnell's Life of Columcille, written in the sixteenth century, records the yew tree in front of the 'black church' as a special favourite of the saint. He believed a thousand angels were keeping watch among the foliage, yet another version of the yew as a guardian tree. Some verses on the tree are attributed to Columcille:

> This is the Yew of the Saints
> Where they used to come with me together
> Ten hundred angels were there
> Above our heads, side close to side.

Dear to me is that yew tree
Would that I were set in its place there!
On my left it was pleasant adornment
When I entered into the Black Church.

In the annals there are several references to the destruction of yews, and it must be reasonable to assume that these were significant trees or groves, or the event would not have been worth recording. In the year 1077 Gleann Uiseann with its yews was burned. In January 1149 the yew tree of Ciaran, at Clonmacnoise, possibly planted by the saint himself, was struck by lightning, and 113 sheep sheltering beneath it were killed. Some years later in 1162 the monastery at Iubhar Chinntrechta, the modern Newry in County Down, was burnt, along with all its furniture and books, and also the yew tree which Patrick himself had planted. It has been suggested that Iubhar Arnum, Arnum's Yew, mentioned in the annals in 1015, was the yew at Cell Iubhar, now called Killure, in County Galway. 'Cell Iubhar' means 'church of the yew', but there are six places with this name in Ireland, so the association is only tentative. Nevertheless, the emerging strong association between the yew and early Christian settlements is important to establish, because the situation in Ireland is very different to that in Britain. Allen does not know of any really ancient yews in Ireland. They must have been there, because the evidence for the yew cult is very strong, but for a variety of reasons they have not survived.

There was a celebrated yew in the cemetery at Glendalough, County Wicklow, until the middle of the nineteenth century. It was believed to have been planted by St Kevin, but there are few other records. There may be a clue in the record of three yews long gone in Kilcomin, County Offaly. Near this place there is a rock bearing what the devout believe are the impressions of the hands and knees of St Cuimin. In the nineteenth century there were three remarkable elm trees called 'Cuimin's trees' growing close to the rock. It was said at the time that they were planted many years before in place of three yew trees of unknown age, but straight as an arrow, which had previously grown in the same spot and which were supposed to have been planted by the saint himself.[2]

The fact that yews on a sacred site were replaced by elms suggests that the significance of the yew may have disappeared into a general sanctity surrounding trees, because there is certainly, even to this day in Ireland, a living tradition of respect for sacred trees. Elms, after all, pose no threat to horses or grazing livestock. It may be that ancient yews have not survived because they proved too difficult to incorporate into Christianity. Perhaps they were felled by rival tribes or marauding Vikings, or succumbed to the need for fuel, or fell victim to social pressures different to those in Britain. Or it may be, as is still happening in Britain, that there are ancient yews in Ireland waiting to be rediscovered.

The sacred tree and the sanctity in which the yew was held are deeply rooted in the language, literature and folklore of the country. Irish has a special word for a sacred tree: *bhile*, sometimes Anglicized as 'bell' or 'bellow' tree. Place-names derived from this word, and from the names of specific trees, abound throughout Ireland. Towns such as Aghavilla, Aghaville and Aghavilly can all be traced to *achadh an bhile*, in Irish 'the field of the tree'. Knockvilla is another common place-name, in this instance combining the Irish *onoc*, meaning 'hill', with *bhile*. From the word for oakwood, *doire*, comes the modern Derry, and *ros*, meaning 'forest', is a constituent part of place-names all over Ireland. The word for 'yew' has several forms: *iubhar*, *eo*, *whar* and *og*. Newry took its name from two yews said to have been planted by St Patrick and cut down by Cromwell's soldiers.

Altogether Allen has found nearly two dozen place-names that directly relate to the yew:

Aghadoe, Aughnanure: field of yew trees
Ahoghill: ford by the yew trees
Anure: lake by the yew trees
Aughall: yew wood
Ballinure, Ballyure: settlement at the yew trees, yew farm
Clonoe: meadow of the yew tree

Donohill: port at the yew wood
Emly: lake-marsh of the yew tree
Glenoe: glen of the yew tree
Killenure: yew-tree corner
Killeochaille: church of the yew wood
Killure (Cell Iubhar): church of the yew tree
Longhanure: lake of the yew trees
Newry: the yew tree at the head of the strand
Nure: yew tree
Oghil, Oghill, Eochaill, Youghal: yew grove
Rathnure: ring fort of the yew tree
Terenure: land of the yew tree
Ture: yew tree

Allen believes, too, that the name Ireland really means 'Yew Island'. Aristotle and the Greeks called Ireland 'Ierne', and the Romans had a variety of forms in Latin, all close to the Greek, such as 'Iubernia' or in Caesar 'Iuvernia'. By the ninth century this has become, in the Latin of the historian Nennius, 'Eumonia' or 'Euboniam Insulum'.

In Irish mythology place-names have a special significance because of the collection of stories written down from the middle of the twelfth century onwards and known as the 'Dindshenchas'. These tales explain the origins of place-names in terms of the actions of the gods by rooting the myth into a geographical location where the god may have done some heroic deed, or may now be buried, or may live on within the earth.

In the mythological history of Ireland, too, the yew appears to have a central role. In an early Irish tale, the *Aislinge Oenguso*, there is a supernatural heroine called Caer Ibormeith; the name means 'yew berry'. Then there is the tragic story of the the two lovers Ailinn and Baile. From the grave of one sprang a yew tree, and an apple tree from the grave of the other. The apple tree is, of course, the female yew, not the crab or wild apple. After seven years the trees were cut down and turned into ogham writing tablets. On the one made from the male yew that grew over Baile's grave were written the 'visions, espousals, loves and courtships of Ulster', and on the tablet from the female yew, the 'apple' tree that grew on Ailinn's grave, similar information relating to Leinster was written. At a later date, when King Conn of the Hundred Battles was examining these tablets, they sprang together and could never be separated. There is a similar tale of Naoise and Deirdre. After their deaths yew stakes were driven through the corpses of these lovers to keep them apart. The stakes sprouted and became trees whose tops embraced over Armagh Cathedral.

As yew was the medium on which the runes were first carved, so ogham, the linear alphabet used by the Irish, and coelbren, the similar Welsh alphabet, were also first carved into yew. There are many references in Irish tales to ogham being written on wands of yew. Dallan, the Druid of Eochaidh Airemh, cast yew wands with ogham inscriptions to discover the whereabouts of Etain, wife of the human Eochaidh but also of the god Midir: 'Dallan cut four wands of yew, and wrote or cut an ogham in them; and it was revealed to him, through his keys of science and his ogham, that the Queen Etain was concealed in the palace of the fairy chief, Midir, in the hill of Bri Leigh.'

The combination of yew and ogham for magic and divination must be much older than the emergence of the ogham alphabet, which is a series of lines drawn across and at angles to a central stave. It was in use by the second century BC and may be much older. There is dispute over whether some lines found on chalk slabs at Windmill Hill in southern England are an early ogham or not, but if they are this would place use of the script back as far as 2200 BC. The script, with its absence of curves and loops, was clearly designed to be incised easily into wood or stone. The main focus of modern interest in ogham is that the whole alphabet appears to have been based on associating various letters with specific trees, and so it is sometimes called 'the tree alphabet'. The fourteenth-century manuscript *The Book of Ballymote* attributes the invention of ogham to the god Ogma, and pairs the letters to the trees. Here Ida, Ioda or the yew is once again the central vowel *i*, and other sources also attribute the ogham *edhadh*, which is *e*, to the yew as well as to the aspen.

The mastery of the complexities of ogham must have taken a great deal of time in the Druid and bardic academies, and it seems to have existed in various forms as a sign language and in codes that would have allowed secret messages. Since an alphabet is such a fundamental organization of consciousness and concepts, one based on trees which clearly had a magical and divinatory purpose promises insights into the inner experiences of those who devised it. There have been several attempts to elucidate the characteristics and meanings involved in linking each tree to a particular sound and letter. Inevitably these efforts have been very personal; Robert Graves in *The White Goddess* examined an early Welsh poem, *Cad Goddeu*, meaning 'The Battle of the Trees', and emerged with a system that extended ogham to a tree calendar. Others have developed this further, trying to reconstruct a whole system of Celtic magic.

The names of many of the gods reveal that they are closely linked with yews – more than linked, in fact, because the gods have emerged from the trees, and the further they are traced back the less formed is the personification and the nearer they are to the trees themselves. The greatest of the Irish gods was Dagda, always associated with the cauldron and hence with fertility; he may also have been known at an earlier time as Crom Eocha. Three of his descendants were the brothers Brian, Iuchar and Iucharba, who were the sons of his daughter, Danu. One of the important records of Irish mythology is the twelfth-century *Book of Invasions*. This is a mixture of oral tradition and both pre-Christian and Christian learning. It describes five waves of mythic invaders arriving successively to colonize Ireland prior to the first historical invasion by the Celts. The fifth invasion was that of the Tuatha De Danann, the people of the goddess Danu. These people are much identified with the landscape, with the fairy hills called the *sid*, which are the ancient burial mounds, or with natural geological features. In some legends the gods live inside the *sid* in wonderful underground palaces which are often also versions of the Celtic Elysium.

Danu, or Dana, is known by many names; she is also Aine, Ana and Anu. She was both sun goddess who rose every morning from the bed of the sea god off the coast, and earth mother. It is said that she nursed the gods, and in County Kerry there are two hills celebrated as the 'paps of Anu'. Some attempts have been made to trace Danu and her father, Dagda, back to Osiris and Isis. Robert Graves in *The White Goddess* thought that the history given in the *Book of Invasions*, which describes the Danaans as a Greek tribe forced north-westwards by an invasion from Syria, and finally reaching Ireland in the mid-Bronze Age, is plausible enough to have some basis in fact. Whatever the origins, though, Danu is clearly a great mother goddess who gives birth to three sons who are yew trees.

Munster seems particularly related to the yew and is the site of the *sid* or sacred hill of Danu called Cnoc Aine. Here her festival was celebrated annually at summer solstice. Nearby is the equally sacred Lough Gur, which before nineteenth-century drainage was a circular ring of water surrounding an island and forming the typical Celtic sacred mound discussed elsewhere. On the hill were four mounds; one, now destroyed, was that of Aine herself, and the others were dedicated to Eogabal, Fer hI and Uainide. In the legend associated with the site the father of Aine was not Dagda but Eogabal. The name means a crotch or fork in a yew tree. The myths and images have become very mixed, for, although both Dagda and Eogabal are gods, the images associated with them are feminine; Dagda is the guardian of the cauldron and Eogabal suggests the tree as a womb. Michael Dames, who has investigated the legends of the area, found that Uainide represented the green foliage and was the brother of Eogabal.[3] The name Uainide too sounds as if it is derived from *eo* or yew. Both brothers claimed the sacred hill. It was believed that Lough Gur would magically disappear once every seven years, revealing a supernatural tree growing from the lough bed, and there are stories of a giant eel living in the water. Such associations suggest the lough as a site of the Isles of the Blessed, the Celtic Elysium, which as well as being located across the ocean was found within the hill and under the waters of the lough.

The third mound on Cnoc Aine was that of Fer hI, Aine's brother, and his name means simply 'Man of Yew'. Another tale about him is told in a poem, 'The Yew of the Disputing Sons', which is found in the mid-twelfth-century *Book of Leinster*. The poem is one of the Dindshenchas, for it sets out to explain the name of a particular tree and to connect it with the historical Battle of Mag Mucrama. The poem tells how a relative of Fer hI, Eogabal Ane – so presumably his brother – is killed. In the poem's confusing plot the family of Fer hI makes a magical yew to trap the three brothers who committed the crime. The three brothers all want to claim the tree as their own, and they become rivals and end up destroying each other. The poem ends with contradictory images of the yew; it is both a shelter from the elements for many warriors, which is a common medieval description of the tree, but also magical and dangerous, definitely something of the otherworld, to be feared and dreaded: 'It is hidden secretly by the elves with mysterious control; only one in a hundred finds it; it is a lasting injury, a misfortune for ever.'

The barrows on Cnoc Aine, then, contain the mythic genealogy of Ireland. The father, brother, uncle and sons of the mother goddess are all yew trees, so it is reasonable to expect that Danu, too, must have been seen as a yew. The family of kings that ruled Munster from the seventh to the middle of the tenth centuries were also called by a name closely connected with the yew, the Eoganacht. They must have been anxious to gain divine right for their rule by associating themselves with the yew, because in the saga *The Exile of Conall Corc*, written in the eighth century, a swineherd relates a prophetic vision which describes the Rock of Cashel in Tipperary as the foundation stone of a new dynasty:

I saw a wonder today on these ridges in the north, I beheld a yew bush on a stone and I perceived a small oratory in front of it and a flagstone before it. Angels were in attendance going up and down from the flagstone. 'Verily,' said the Druid of Aed, 'that will be the residence of the King of Munster for ever, and he who shall first kindle a fire under that yew, from him shall descend the kingship of Munster.'

Here kingship is sanctioned by Christianity, by angels and by the yew tree, which is clearly the *axis mundi* of the kingdom and the sacred tree at the inauguration site where the king was crowned.

There certainly remained in Ireland a concept of kingship akin to the sacred marriage that existed in the earliest Indo-European civilizations. The human king was 'married' to the goddess; her divinity invested him with temporal authority and ensured the fertility and fortunes of the people. Often the name of a Celtic tribe clearly shows its relationship with the yew. On the Continent there were the Esuvii in Calvados and the Eburones between the rivers Main and Rhine. There were also the Eburvices, the Eburobrigen, in Aude the Eburomagus, and in Switzerland the Eburodunum. In southern Ireland the Celtic tribe was the Iverni. The yew was the focus of the inauguration site, and there was no worse catastrophe for a king and his tribe than to have his territory invaded and the sacred tree felled. Several instances of this are recorded in the Irish annals.

In ancient Ireland there were five very famous sacred trees: Bile Tortan, Eo Mugna, Eo Rossa, Craeb Daithi and Bile Uisnig. Allen believes all these trees to have been yews, which is not the accepted view. Nobody disputes, however, that Eo Rossa was a yew, believed to have grown in Old Leiglin in County Carlow. In the Rennes Dindshenchas its qualities are described in a series of epithets:

Tree of Ross, a king's wheel, a prince's right, a wave's noise, best of creatures, a straight firm tree, a firm strong god, door of heaven, strength of a building, the good of a crew, a word pure man, full great bounty: the Trinity's mighty one, a measure's house, a mother's good, Mary's son, a fruitful sea, beauty's honour, a mind's lord, diadem of angels, shout of the world, Banba's renown, might of victory, judgement of origin, judicial doom, faggot of sages, noblest of trees, glory of Leinster, dearest of bushes, a bear's defence, vigour of life, spell of knowledge, Tree of Ross!

Some of the epithets obviously refer to the tree as the centre of the social fabric. The 'king's wheel' is the *axis mundi*, but the picture conveyed is that the tree imbued and strengthened both the individual and the community. The tree will protect the crew and bring a good catch, and its bounty and energy flow through the environment; it is in the joyous crash of the wave and the security of the roof pillar. Other epithets highlight the tree as a source of wisdom. It is known that the Druidic fire was kindled by yew faggots, and perpetual fires honoured Brighid as both Celtic goddess and Christian saint. 'Door of heaven' and 'spell of knowledge' suggest the tree is able in some way to impart its wisdom through the intermediary of Druid or poet, who probably had some of the abilities of the shaman. Professor MacCulloch thought that phrases such as 'word pure man' and 'judgement of origin' could refer to the custom of writing divinations in ogham on rods of yew.[4]

What is remarkable here is that even after some hundreds of years of Christianity the worship of the yew is dominant despite the Christian imagery; it is the tree, not Christ, that is 'the Trinity's mighty one' and 'Mary's son'. The vitality of the poem is in stark contrast to the rather lifeless stock formulas that describe the felling of the trees. Eo Rossa's end is described in the Life of St Laserian. The saints of Ireland wanted the wood for church building, and gathered around the tree fasting and praying that it would fall. As each saint prayed, the roots shifted, but it was not until St Laserian's turn came that the tree finally fell. St Moling received sufficient timber from Eo Rossa to roof his oratory.

Yet there is a further story from the Life of St Moling that suggests that at a deeper level the transition from tree worship to Christianity was protracted and uneasy. Soon after the felling of Eo Rossa, Moling went to the forest to fell another tree. The first blow of the axe sent a chip flying into Moling's eye, and he was blinded. After an encounter with the Devil, disguised as a student, he was finally cured by a priest. The complacent tale of Laserian and the power of prayer were clearly insufficient to smother thousands of years of reverence for the tree and forest that had gone deep into the psyche. The chip that blinds Moling is a concentrated missile of suppressed feelings that easily tears through the hastily spread blanket of the new dogma. The episode is a shocking reminder of other truths and allegiances that have for the meanwhile been pushed underground. Before Moling can be healed he has to endure suffering, go on a journey and be tested. In fact, his 'healing' is probably only a larger recognition of the inner conflict and a more sober resort to dogma.

Another of the sacred trees is Eo Mugna. Although *eo* means yew, the general view of this tree is that, despite its name, it is an oak. The reason for this conclusion must be that Eo Mugna is described as having a crop of three fruits: apples, acorns and hazel nuts. The acorns are the one obvious fruit, and the oak does often have an 'oak apple', the name given to the round galls that are not a fruit but an aberration of the plant tissue of the tree, usually caused by wasp larvae. Commentators, having successfully explained two of the fruits on Eo Mugna, conclude it is an oak. They thus ignore the hazel nuts and the straightforward evidence of the name 'Yew of Mugna'; and they suggest that, although *eo* usually means yew, it might sometimes just mean tree.

In having a crop of three fruits, however, Eo Mugna is simply exhibiting the characteristics of its parent tree. Certainly four, and in one source all five, of the sacred trees are said to have grown from berries from a single branch which were planted in various parts of Ireland. To Allen's mind this single origin is sufficient evidence to view all the trees as the same species, and that species as yew for reasons that will become clear. In autumn the branch of the female yew carries an acorn and cup which are the undeveloped form of the red aril containing the small kernel. It is normal for a single branch to carry the fruit in both stages of development side by side. Thus a branch of yew could carry both 'acorn', the 'red apple' and a 'nut', although obviously not a hazel nut.

Hazel nuts have been found interred in Celtic graves and they have a long association in Irish myth and literature as a source of wisdom and poetic inspiration, but the odd thing is that they are often described as crimson. There are magical hazel trees that grow in the otherworld at the site of Connla's well. These trees, reminiscent of Eo Mugna, have blossom, foliage and fruit that appear simultaneously. The nuts fall into the well, where they are eaten by salmon and the juice stains their bellies. The normal hazel nut has a yellow catkin, then a brown shell with an off-white kernel, quite unable to stain anything crimson. Suspicions therefore focus on these crimson hazel nuts with their juices able to stain, by implication, the flesh of salmon pink.

There is also one other puzzling piece of information. The Irish word for salmon is *eo*, the same word that is used for the yew. There can hardly be in nature a more splendid symbol for regeneration than the life cycle of the salmon, with its journey downstream to the ocean and its final return that must be achieved at all cost, to spawn at the precise spot where it was born. In Irish myth, though, it is the salmon that embodies and disseminates wisdom; it has eaten the hazel nuts that fell into the well and is thus the much-sought-after 'salmon of knowledge'.

The hero Fionn meets at a river bank an ancient Druid called Finegas who has been seeking this salmon for seven years, because the prophecy is that whoever eats the salmon will immediately obtain knowledge and wisdom. The arrival of Fionn is immediately followed by the capture of the salmon, and it is entrusted to Fionn to cook, although he is warned not to eat it. As when Gwyion Bach tends Cariadwen's cauldron, a mishap occurs in the cooking, and Fionn thrusts his burnt thumb into his mouth to relieve the pain. He immediately finds all knowledge revealed to him. Thus Fionn's knowledge may originally have derived from the *eo* that is both salmon and yew, and from the 'hazel' berries that, unaccountably, contain a crimson stain.

The salmon of knowledge caught by Fionn also has a name; it is called Fintan. Fintan is worthy of further investigation, because he appears again, in human form, as the central character of the story which tells how the branch with three fruits, from which the sacred trees sprang, arrived in Ireland. The tale is related in *The Settling of the Manor of Tara*.[5] This part-prose and part-verse narrative is set in the time of Diarmait mac Cerball, King of Tara in the mid-sixth century. Diarmait was an historical figure living at the time when

Christianity was taking root in Ireland. At a great gathering of kings from throughout Ireland the issue was raised that the upkeep of Tara was excessive and this should be dealt with before the feast began. Advice was needed, particularly to explain why Tara had been established in this particular way from the beginning. Diarmat called a succession of sages, among them Cennfaelad, who had 'the brain of forgetfulness' removed, and Tuan, 'he who passed into many shapes'. All declared themselves unworthy and called for one greater than themselves, until finally Fintan, 'son of Bochra, son of Bith, son of Noah', was sent for.

Fintan relates, in the story, how he came to Ireland with the first invaders, how he survived the Flood and lived with the various people of the successive invasions as a noble sage down to that time. At that point Fintan breaks off to deal with a query from an audience who do not seem to have fully grasped the length of time that he has just described. 'We should like to know from thee,' they ask, 'how reliable thy memory is.' Fintan is not being asked to prove that he isn't suffering from the forgetfulness of old age, but simply to explain the passage of time from his arrival in Ireland before the Flood to the present in a more comprehensible way. For an analogy he uses the yew tree:

'One day I passed through a wood in West Munster in the west. I took away with me a red yew berry and I planted it in the garden of my court, and it grew up there until it was as big as a man. Then I removed it from the garden and planted it on the lawn of my court, and it grew up in the centre of that lawn so that I could fit with a hundred warriors under its foliage, and it protected me from wind and rain, and from cold and heat. I remained and so did my yew flourishing together, until it shed its foliage from decay. Then when I had no hope even so of turning it to my profit, I went and cut it from its stock, and made from it seven vats and seven ians, and seven drolmachs, seven churns, seven pitchers, seven milans, and seven methars with hoops for all of them. So I remained then and my yew vessels with me until their hoops fell with decay and age. Then I remade them all, but could only get an ian out of a vat, and a drolmach out of an ian, and a churn out of a drolmach, and a pitcher out of a churn, and a milan out of a pitcher, and a methar out of a milan. And I swear to Almighty God I know not where those substitutes are since they perished with me from decay.'

'Thou art indeed venerable,' said Diarmait.

Fintan's yew is clearly the sacred tree at his kingdom's inauguration site, for when it had reached a suitable size it was transplanted from the garden to the centre of the lawn of the court. The fact that warriors assembled beneath its boughs shows its significance as the focal point of the kingdom's power. Much less obvious is how the audience, hearing *The Settling of the Manor of Tara* recited by a bard, would have understood the role of Fintan. Allen is convinced that Fintan is, originally at any rate, the yew tree and he believes that the meaning of the name Fintan is 'red tree' – a combination derived from *fionn*, tree, and *tan*, red. The narrator has already made a passing reference to 'Tuan son of Cairoll from Ulster, he who passed into many shapes'. He was one of the many sages summoned by Diarmait who deferred to the greater authority of Fintan. We know from other stories that Tuan, though younger than Fintan, had been alive for hundreds of years. He had been born in human form, living at the time of one of the pre-Celtic races, and changing shape in old age had become a stag and, successively, a boar, a hawk and a salmon; finally, when that fish was caught and eaten by the Queen of Cairoll, he was born again as a human being, Tuan.

It has been seen from the tale of Fionn that he cooks and tastes the salmon of knowledge, Fintan. There is another remarkable poem that emphasizes this shape-shifting ability of Fintan himself. *The Hawk of Achill* records a conversation between Fintan and the hawk of the title. There is no doubt that the Fintan of both works is the same man, for both call him 'son of Bochra'. In *The Hawk of Achill* both the hawk and Fintan were born on the same day, and Fintan reveals that he has passed through different transformations as eagle, falcon and salmon. In one revealing incident Fintan describes how when in salmon form he lost an eye to a swooping hawk, and the hawk of Achill readily admits that he was the hawk concerned. The loss of an eye, as was seen with Odin in Nordic mythology, always suggests a deepening inner wisdom.

The lengthy description of planting the yew berry is only an oblique answer to the question posed him, but it establishes Fintan's authority beyond doubt. This and the various other clues – *eo* meaning both salmon and yew, Fintan meaning 'red tree', Fintan's ability to become a salmon and the salmon's capacity to imbibe the crimson 'hazel nuts', his close connection with the tree of the three fruits and the likelihood that it is the female yew, his personification of wisdom and immense longevity – all contribute to the view that Fintan is the yew tree and embodies all the religious traditions that centred upon it.

The watershed of the poem is Fintan's description of the appearance of Trefuilngid Tre-eochair. Once again a great assembly of Irish nobles was in progress when there appeared a giant of a man with golden-yellow hair falling down to his thighs. He had 'a shining crystal veil about him like unto raiment of precious linen'. In his right hand he carried the branch with the three fruits – nuts, apples and acorns – which is described as a 'golden many-coloured branch of lebanon wood'. From his appearance and his task he would appear to be a sun god, but later Fintan describes him as either an angel of God or God himself. His mission concerns the sun, and he is responsible for its rising and setting. That day the sun had sidestepped the Jews and not shone on them, and so he had travelled to the west to discover the reason for this strange event from the sun as it set. The reason was that a man had been crucified that day. Trefuilngid chose to stay forty days, but there was concern that entertaining him might cause hardship. However, he explained, 'the fragrance of this branch which is in my hand will serve me for food and drink as long as I live'. When he left, Trefuilngid gave Fintan some berries from the branch; he planted these and they grew into the five sacred trees of Ireland. There then follow lengthy details of the boundaries and divisions of Ireland according to the instructions Trefuilngid had given, and it becomes clear that Fintan's role is coming to an end, and in the new Christianized Ireland his fate is linked to that of the sacred trees.

As in the first half of the poem, where Fintan plants a yew berry, and the history and fate of the tree are an example of the span of his life, so in the second half he plants berries from Trefuilngid's branch, and the growth, prime and decline of the sacred trees are mirrored closely by Fintan's life:

> Bile Tortan, Eo Rosa
> One as lovely and bushy as the other
> Mugna and Craebhh Daithi today
> And Fintan surviving.

The narrator also tells us that 'Fintan perceived his own old age and that of the trees.' It becomes clear that no further shape changes will be possible for Fintan: 'He knew that God deemed it time for him to die, without undergoing further changes of form.' The passing of Fintan and the passing of the sacred trees are one and the same thing. Fintan died having received communion and in the presence of the spirit of Patrick, and the sacred trees withered. The newly established Christian ethos has achieved a far more profound assimilation of the pagan energies devoted to the tree than was managed in the story of the praying St Laserian bringing down Eo Rossa. The yew, venerated for its great age and wisdom, becomes a Christian patriarch. The story ends by adding that as the place of his grave is uncertain he may, like Elijah, have ascended physically into heaven.

Allen has found one further source describing the 'tree of the three fruits'. A Welsh legend in *The Mabinogion* tells of St Baglan and how he founded a church. It is also recounted in an eighteenth-century manuscript in the Bodleian Library: 'The Response of Anthony Thomas, Incumbent of Baglan, to Queries by Edward Lloyd, 1700'. It says:

Saint Baglan, a disciple of Saint Illtyd, was one time carrying fire from Saint Cattwg in the skirt of his garment without singeing it in the least, and Saint Illtyd looked upon it to be a miracle that was worthy to prefer the worker;

and gave him a staff ... and bid him that he should let that guide him until he found a tree that bore three sorts of fruite, and there erect a church for himselfe. Arriving at the site where the church now stands he found ye tree that had a litter of pigs nere the roots below; a hive of bees in the body, and a kite's or crow's nest at the top. However he did not like the site, being upon a proclivity, and attempted to build upon the plains below, but what was built there was removed in the night, and at last discouraged he built it where it now stands.

Allen recounts a dream he had about Baglan, Glamorgan, before he first went there, in which he saw a modern church surrounded by many small yews. He knew that the one for which he was looking was not there. Then in the dream he did see an ancient yew, but it was very distant. Later, in 1984, Allen visited Baglan and discovered that, in fact, there were two churches there, one a ruin and one a modern building. In the churchyard a few young-looking yews grew near the new church. The ruined Norman church was some distance away, and near it was an old yew. Allen writes:

When we reached the old yew I had a feeling of something very strange, and it continued to puzzle me long after. The first unusual thing about this yew is that it is so tall. I found remains of female seeds on parts of the old trunk. The yew is decayed a little. It is most definitely a very old tree, but the intriguing thing is that many things about this tree fit in with the original legend; the yew is on top of a steep slope; it is female, therefore it has the three fruits; it is unusually tall, thus a suitable site for a crow's nest. This could be the tree that St Baglan found, known as the Tree of the Three Fruits.

The legend of St Baglan provides one more piece of evidence that points to the 'tree of three fruits', Eo Mugna and Trefuilngid's branch all being the female yew. The story of the pigs, bees and crow, with its echoes of the tree as *axis mundi* existing in three different worlds, may well have been a clumsy attempt by a later scribe to explain the 'three fruits' once the hidden meaning had been lost.

CHAPTER 14

Yew Medicine

The leaves of the tree are for the healing of the nations.

REVELATION 22:2

Discussing a treatment for cancer may seem to be an aside in a book about yew trees. The story of the 'miracle' drug taxol is, however, very much about yews. It could also be said to be a tale of our times.

In the early 1960s cancer researchers were beginning to despair of ever being able to produce a drug which could cure cancer. They turned to nature to try to find new compounds, and the US National Cancer Institute (NCI) launched a campaign to gather samples from as many natural products as possible. The net ranged wide, bringing in flowers, lichens, mosses, trees, even insects. Between 1960 and 1981, 114,045 plant extracts and 16,196 animal extracts were tested. Out of all of those 130,241 samples, just *one* was found to be both effective and safe as a treatment for certain forms of cancer. That was taxol, a substance derived from the yew. (Strangely, Allen seems to have had some kind of premonition of this; in 1980 he wrote to a medical researcher suggesting that fungus growing on the yew might yield an anti-cancer drug.)

Yew has, in fact, been used as a medicine before. John Lowe, who was honorary physician to the Prince of Wales, reported having carried out experiments on himself with taxin: 'The tracings of the pulse show beyond doubt that it is a cardiac tonic of no mean value.'[1] He also said that the leaves were used in India as a stomach medicine, and that in Kussawar, India, a decoction of it was used to treat rheumatism.

Taxol's rise to fame was far from meteoric. For several years it was regarded by drug researchers as just one among many other avenues to explore. The breakthrough came when a biologist discovered that taxol worked in an entirely different way to any other cancer drug. Dr Susan Horwitz of the Albert Einstein College of Medicine in New York was intrigued by the 'strange molecules' of taxol, whose convoluted arrangement she described as 'the kind of molecule no chemist would ever sit down and think of making. It *definitely* comes from a tree.'

Dr Horwitz found that instead of breaking down the internal structure of the cancer cells, as other drugs do, taxol in effect paralyses them. David Bellamy describes the process as 'imprisoning cancerous cells within a cage of microscopic tubules, slowing their growth'. It was taxol's novel and eccentric way of working that meant that its development was taken a stage further.

Taxol went into clinical trial in 1983, but first treatments produced side-effects, and the project was almost shelved by the NCI. However, it was continued thanks to two doctors who believed they could counter the side-effects, and who had noted particularly promising results with ovarian cancer. In subsequent trials carried out with women who had not responded to previous forms of treatment and were regarded as incurable, taxol produced a remarkable 30 per cent response rate. After these results in 1988 rumours of the treatment spread rapidly, and soon taxol was being hailed as a miracle cure.

We now know that taxol is not a 'magic bullet'; only about one out of three cases responds to it. However, with 30,000 women a year suffering from ovarian cancer in the USA alone, even a one-third success rate is highly significant. Taxol also shows promising results with other forms of the disease, such as some cancers of the breast, lung and colon.

It makes a wonderful tale: humanity discovers the cure to a dreaded illness, just waiting to be plucked from a tree. Unfortunately it is in reality far from having a fairytale ending. The demand for taxol is mounting all the time, to the extent that demand far outstrips supply. Taxol is found in yews, but only in small amounts. The best-known source at the moment is the Pacific yew, a native of North America. At least until now, the trees have not been particularly scarce. However, to harvest the taxol the tree's bark has to be removed, which kills the yew in the process. As one year's dose of taxol per patient needs the bark of up to six trees, and in the USA alone around 100,000 people could need it, the Pacific yew is clearly endangered.

The threat to the Pacific yew has its ironic side. Yews produce many compounds to prevent pests and predators from eating them, attacking them or even growing near them. Taxol is just one part of this battalion to repel invaders, but its very success could also be its downfall. A further irony is that until the discovery of taxol the Pacific yew was regarded as a 'trash' tree by loggers and farmers.[2] It grows along the temperate western seaboard of the USA, where an almost uninterrupted stretch of forest once grew between the coast and the Rocky Mountains. These forests were previously regarded as an almost inexhaustible source of timber. Now about 87 per cent of these forests have been felled at least once to make way for farms and timber crops. In the course of this the Pacific yew was usually just slashed and left or burned. Being considered to be of no value, combined with the fact that like other yews it is very slow-growing (it can take 200 years to reach just 40 feet tall), meant that only about 10 per cent of the forests' yews remained.

Curiously, it was not the discovery of taxol that first drew attention to the tree's plight. It was the fight to save the northern spotted owl, an endangered species whose habitat is the Pacific yew. The need for taxol has now made conservation of the tree an even more burning issue. Should more trees be felled to meet the demand for taxol, or should they be saved to protect the northern spotted owl and the trees themselves? When expressed as a choice between the survival of a human being and that of other animals or plants the dilemma is apparent. David Bellamy puts it this way:

One of the most difficult questions I was ever asked came from a fourteen-year-old boy. 'If your children were starving to death, would you kill a rare animal to feed them?' he asked. My answer was very limp: 'Yes, if there were no other way. I hope it never happens.' Well, it has happened – not with a rare animal but with a tree, now under threat even though it could help save human lives.

The dilemma says a lot about our attitude to the natural world. A tree is regarded by many people as worthless, until suddenly we find that we may need it for our survival. The media have often talked about protecting the Pacific yew in terms of 'not killing the goose that lays the golden egg', rather than just protecting it for its own sake. Perhaps we are approaching the question of trees versus human life with the wrong attitude. Photographs of piles of Pacific yews with their bark completely stripped have a horror about them akin to photos of piles of dead human bodies. We seem not even to be honouring the trees for what they give to us, let alone for what they are in their own right. This is in marked contrast to, for instance, the Native American Indians. Before making use of any part of a tree they will attune to it, to ask whether it may be used in this way. They will also give some offering to the earth in order to replace what they are taking. In fact, yews have traditionally been used for medicine by Native Americans, particularly as an anti-inflammatory treatment.

While the argument between conservationists and cancer institutes continues to rage in the USA, scientists are seeking other sources of taxol. Some chemists have tried to make it from only vaguely related but more readily available raw materials, such as the main ingredient found in turpentine, but this requires a lot of chemical engineering. It may also be possible in the future to grow taxol in 'factories'. Two companies in California hope to be able to churn out vat-grown yew cells to produce the drug within the very near future. This again will require a good deal of technical trickery. Meanwhile, vast nurseries of Pacific yews are being planted in the USA. Genetic techniques are being used to speed their growth and increase the amount of taxol, and they should be ready to harvest in four or five years.

In the immediate future the most promising source may be the European yew. A substance found in its needles can be used to produce a material similar to taxol. Work being done by Pierre Potier of the Chemical Institute of Natural Substances in France has produced baccatin, which can be 'engineered' to produce taxotere. This is almost identical to taxol, and may even be more effective and easier to administer than its more natural counterpart. This raises the question of where the needles will come from: is this yet another threat to *Taxus baccata*? Pierre Potier thinks not, as he wrote to Allen:

I know of the old yew trees of the UK and I do not think that the old, respectable (and respected) specimens that you mention will ever be used for collecting their needles ... I know that the needles are collected without any problem just by cutting the leaves as it is sometimes done in gardens. Obviously, there are already studies under way bearing on plantations, nurseries, tissue culture, etc. I have directed research for almost ten years in this field keeping in mind that we have to secure a good balance between the production of sufficient amounts of drug necessary to treat patients and the respect of nature.

Monsieur Potier's words are to be welcomed, and there must indeed be ways of obtaining the drug without decimating the trees which have provided this gift. It is pleasing to think that one day the clippings from garden yew hedges might be put to such a use instead of being consigned to the bonfire. Clippings from the 'Twelve Apostles' yews at Dartington, from the yew hedges at Longleat and from several other places which have large areas of yew hedges have now begun to provide British scientists with thousands of tons of materials for research into baccatin. The leaves of English yew are believed to contain more than twenty promising compounds, and work being undertaken by the Science and Engineering Research Council, and by a Dutch pharmaceutical company, could also come up with a synthetic version of taxol.

A further suggestion gives pause for thought. Dr Lester Mitscher and Dr Rao Gollapudi of the University of Kansas have suggested that it was just a historic accident that the Pacific yew became the predominant source of taxol. Scientists initially never bothered to look elsewhere. They say that the yews found abundantly in the Himalayas also have large amounts of taxol in their needles, and they believe that this might be the most prolific source for the future. The doctors add that a further benefit would be that the harvesters of these needles would not demand the high wages of their North American counterparts. In addition, they say, if the yews provided local people with an income they might be deterred from cutting down their diminishing forests.

Such a suggestion is tantalizing, though certainly open to accusations of colonialism. Is it not, though, time we learned something from the Native Americans' honouring of the tree? Perhaps the yew has taken us a step further towards realizing that a 'worthless' plant may hold many secrets, some of which may one day be vital to our own survival. Cancer could be likened to the way we are treating the world; the illness is growth 'misdirected', as is much of the way we live. It is ironic that in our rush for growth we have almost destroyed the trees which can heal us on many levels. The yew, so long associated with the Tree of Life, not only has yielded to us a life-saving compound but has also shown us how crucial it is to respect all of nature. It could perhaps be said to be a spokesman, or indicator, for the natural world.

CHAPTER 15

Guardian of the Planet

If this tree is gone, then we will no longer exist.

ALLEN MEREDITH

People sometimes ask Allen if he speaks to trees, and he replies that there is no need. To the next question – does the yew tree speak to him? – all he can say is that he doesn't really know, but 'I can say that something does speak to me and that it is connected to the yew tree. When I am given things, shown things, I know they are connected to the yew.' He uses the phrases 'I translate the yew.' There is nothing remotely 'New Age' about Allen, but perhaps the most apt phrase to describe his experiences is one very current in New Age circles: he 'channels' the yew.

Allen now believes that the high number of ancient yews in Britain is not the result of chance or some accidental circumstances. He says that many were deliberately planted in ancient times by 'wise people', whom he regards as the true Druids. They realized the tree was already under threat elsewhere and that Britain, at that time a remote island off the European mainland, offered the best chance for their survival. For this reason he believes Britain has 'the main concentration of sacred trees in the world'. The wise people would have been guided to Britain by visions and dreams: visions of the island Albion, Hesperides, Avalon, 'a place of everlasting life through the sacred tree'.

The intended sanctuary for the sacred trees is now one of the most densely populated places on earth. They were planted for 'some very special reason', by the wise people. Allen knows that time is running out. It has taken courage to speak out, but he feels he has had no choice: 'I've accepted my fate.' Perhaps he could have compromised and become a respectable environmentalist with splendid green credentials as the 'yew tree expert'. Instead he has been impelled to follow a lonely and vulnerable path at the boundaries of what the rational mind will accept. He is as aware as anyone that some things he says 'sound crazy', and he has met his share of incomprehension and indifference. The extraordinary thing is that he has also been listened to, and heard deeply, by a large number of people.

'All over the world,' Allen writes, 'our ancient energy sources have been wounded and destroyed. Life's energy sources are continually under threat from man's greed for more land, and his material wants.' He describes that materialism as 'obsolete', as the number of trees, sacred sites and areas of countryside under threat grows daily. The beautiful Gwenlais valley in Wales, with its ancient yew and sacred well, is wanted by the quarry companies. The site at Wychbury Hill is earmarked to have a bypass through it. Perhaps a few minutes will be saved on vehicle journey time, but that is a poor return for the loss of our birthright. These sites are representatives of countless others where the same process is under way. Ankerwyke is reprieved for the time being, but for how long? Without Allen's effort it would almost certainly already have been lost to the developers, pushed over by heavy plant on caterpillar tracks, to be replaced by the fairway of a golf course or the landscaped car park of a block of flats. That image is itself an appalling summary of our 'progress': the giant caterpillar, blindly unaware of its own power, levelling everything before it, even the Tree of Life itself.

It may be that Allen's wise people understood truths which urgently need to surface at the present time; they were rooted in a deep kinship with rock, tree and the rhythms of the natural world. Around London, a city named after Lugh the Celtic god of light, a motorway extension is proposed. To construct it will require yet more frenzied quarrying into Welsh mountains to cover more acres of the south-east with asphalt. The breathing, undulating form of the goddess, worshipped for thousands of years, will be detonated and desecrated in one place and then suffocated in another.

The process is continual, devastating and increasing in intensity. The modern world has disastrously severed its roots and is adrift. Only a reintegration of our being, a discovery of our roots and our earth, both within ourselves and in the landscape, is likely to halt the process. The yew tree is not a mere symbol of that reintegration; it has witnessed the entire cycle. Neglected and forgotten for centuries in chuchyards, it became a symbol of death. Yet it was planted, revered and honoured as the womb from which humanity had come. The oldest human remains discovered indicate that mankind appeared on the planet 4 million years ago; even at that time the yew tree had been here for 200 million years.

Allen believes that the survival of the ancient yews is interdependent with our own survival. They are guardians in a way we have not yet begun to understand, he says:

The guardians are very few, and we have lost much of the ancient wisdom. We think we are so superior and intelligent: we may be; wise we are not. No wise man would destroy his home. We are destroying the very things that help us to exist. We must live with nature, not go against it. This is our last chance. Now we have to be strong; we have to accept the old ways, the wise ways. We have to listen to the wise men now. They do not speak from books, they speak from the life force of this planet.

Caring for Yews

Many people write to Allen or to the Conservation Foundation to ask how they can best take care of a yew tree in their local church or elsewhere. Guidelines for doing this have been drawn up according to the many years' experience of experts in the care of trees, and these are set out below. The main points of the guidelines are that a yew tree has great potential for regeneration, that the most decrepit-looking tree may be far from dead, and that the least amount of interference is likely to give the tree the best chance of thriving.

First, though, it may be interesting to look briefly at two very different approaches, or attitudes, to how we treat our trees.

In about 1770 the yew tree in the churchyard at Buckland-in-Dover was struck by lightning. It split and shattered, and in so doing demolished the church steeple. Fortunately the yew was not cleared away, despite the fact that half the trunk was lying on the ground, and the whole of the tree including the fallen section carried on living. Just over a hundred years later it was deemed necessary to extend the church, but the yew was in the way. The rector and parishioners were not willing to destroy the tree, even though its aged form was described at the time as 'rude and grotesque'. Instead, they decided to carry out a tremendous feat, and to move the tree 60 feet away from the church:

The operation commenced on the 24th February when a trench was dug on all four sides, four feet wide and five feet deep, and leaving a large block of earth 18 ft by 16 ft broad, and a long cutting was formed from the old position to the new one. Much work with huge planks of timber, chains,

The Buckland-in-Dover yew was successfully moved 60 feet in 1880

rollers and windlasses took place before the whole mass of the tree, estimated at 55 tons, began to move. It arrived within a yard of its destination at dusk on the 4th March.

(Parish magazine, 1880)

This astonishing piece of engineering, without the aid of the mechanical equipment of today, was successful. Nor was it an isolated incident; the man in charge of the work, Mr William Baron, perfected the technique to the extent that he 'built' a much admired garden at Elvaston Castle by planting it with mature trees. The Buckland-in-Dover yew, which is very unusual in being both male and female, still flourishes today. The 1987 hurricane partially damaged it, but extra supports were put in, and the tree continues to be rightly prized.

Compare this with what happened a century later. In 1993 a plan to reconstruct the Privy Gardens at Hampton Court Palace was announced. To go back to the eighteenth-century design would, it was said by the scheme's backers, necessitate cutting down thirty-eight 300-year-old yew trees. Although this was not the palace gardens' original design, it was deemed to be sufficiently important for the yews, which had grown too big to fit the 'correct' pattern, to be destroyed. Conservationists including Allen argued that this was a priority of madness, and that the trees could be moved, or reduced in height and frequently clipped. The idea of relocating the trees was ruled out by the proponents as unlikely to succeed, despite considerable evidence to the contrary such as that the ancient Egyptians are known to have moved large trees around. With some kind of bizarre logic, clippings were taken from the old trees, to be replanted when they have grown in ten years' time. The trees were felled, providing a sad comment on our alleged new-found concern for conserving trees, especially old ones.

For most people wanting to take care of a yew tree it will not be a question of anything as drastic as any of these alternatives; questions of whether to lop branches, whether a hollow tree is dangerous, etc., are more probable. The following guidelines are based on information which the Conservation Foundation sends to people wishing to care for an ancient yew.

Protecting and caring for ancient yews

It is of paramount importance that no *Taxus baccata* yew should be cut down or removed from a churchyard, even when it appears 'dead'. No yew tree can be considered dead. The remains of old trunks should be cared for and protected; they can be several thousand years old and may still come to life again years from now.

A great deal of energy is stored in the tree's branches, particularly with ancient yew, as opposed to being concentrated solely in the ground root system. This means that the tree can regrow by sending an aerial root down inside a hollow trunk or by embedding branches in the ground (details in Chapter 3). Unfortunately many branches which would have eventually reached to the ground and rooted are cut off in the mistaken belief that they are dangerous or take up too much space. If they are allowed to remain they will act as an anchor and support for the main trunk; the cutting of these branches will only result later in very expensive and unnecessary tree surgery. When large branches are cut back, it immediately weakens the tree; it can cause the tree to split; the tree becomes vulnerable to severe storms; and remaining branches are put at risk.

The result of such human interference can be seen in ancient yews around the country, where metal chains and braces have been used to hold the tree together, and wooden props act as crutches to support the tree. Ideally the amputation of large limbs should never be necessary, although support with poles and posts, strapping or binding may sometimes be helpful in order to avoid loss of limbs or splitting of the trunk.

Hollow yews, and cavities in yews, should never be filled with concrete or any other substance, as this not only is unsightly but adds unnecessary weight and stress to the tree and will inhibit the growth of aerial roots. No wood, old or new, should be removed from inside hollow yews, and hollow yews should never be used for storing oil tanks, coal and so on.

Fungus sometimes appears on yew trees. The yellow *Polyporous sulphureus* can be removed or scraped off, but it is not a great danger to the yew unless really out of control. Ivy, however, should be removed, as it can weaken the tree's system, and its weight makes the tree more vulnerable to storm damage. Elder, brambles, etc, should also be removed from around the trunk, as they can hide the beauty of the tree.

The growth of small young shoots surrounding the trunk can be trimmed so that the trunk is visible. Among other benefits of this is that it prevents the tree from taking on the appearance of a bush and hence being regarded as an eyesore and a dumping ground.

To summarize, a yew tree will live longer with the minimal

amount of human interference. Tree surgery should almost never be necessary. Even if a tree falls, resist the temptation to clear it away immediately; as Oliver Rackham points out: 'As a habitat, a fallen tree (alive or dead) is better than any tree planted as a replacement. Tidiness is death to conservation.' He also stresses that trees are hard to kill, and fallen trees very often do regrow. If in doubt, consult a reputable and well-qualified arboriculturalist or get in touch with the Conservation Foundation.

The Conservation Foundation issues certificates recording the ages of ancient yews, signed by David Bellamy, Allen Meredith, Dr Robert Hardy and Sir George Trevelyan. The certificates now hang in churches and village halls throughout the country, hopefully helping to give these ancient trees the protection and respect they deserve. Many known ancient yews are still not protected by Tree Preservation Orders, and even those that are can still be endangered by those willing to flout the law, as the maximum fine is derisory and may even be built into a developer's costs.

It is likely that there are still ancient yew trees to be 'discovered', and registered by the Conservation Foundation. To register a possible ancient yew, send the following information to the Foundation:

1 The girth of the tree, measured at 3 and 4 feet above ground level. If the trunk is fluted or uneven, do not attempt to compensate for the lumps and bumps.
2 Location and grid reference of the tree, if possible.
3 Name of church, if applicable, and position of the tree in relation to the church, i.e. north, south, east or west.
4 Details of ancient burial mounds, barrows or any other archaeological sites within about 200 yards of the tree.
5 Legends, local folk stories or historical facts relating to the tree.
6 Records of the tree including measurements made in the past.
7 Whether the tree is hollow, and its condition.
8 The sex of the tree (the female has berries in early winter).
9 A photograph is helpful if available.

These details are all taken into consideration when estimating the likely age of the tree.

The Conservation Foundation is at 1 Kensington Gore, London SW7 2AR. Tel.: 071–823 8842; fax: 071–823 8791.

The Conservation Foundation has, at the time of writing, no sponsor for the Yew Tree Campaign, unlike many of its other projects. The work is therefore carried out on a very limited budget. However, the Foundation has found that interest in our yew heritage is considerable and it hopes this will help with the campaign's ultimate aim: the protection of all Britain's ancient yew trees.

Recorded Planting Dates and Growth

All planting dates traced by Allen Meredith are recorded here. In several instances the data are at present incomplete, but have been included for their potential research value.

Pre-sixteenth century

Date	Place	Girth	Date measured	Average growth per year
894	Buttington, Powys	25 ft	1989	0.27 in
1060	Hambledon, Hampshire	19 ft 6 in	1988	0.25 in
1100	Chandler's Ford, Hampshire	15 ft	1988	0.20 in
1136	Dryburgh Abbey, Borders	12 ft 7 in	1988	0.17 in
1344	Muckross Abbey, Co. Kerry, Eire	10 ft	1932	0.20 in
1348	Fitzhead St James, Somerset	–	–	–
1348	Wootton Courtenay, Somerset	15 ft	1980	0.28 in
1349	Feniton, Devon	9 ft 5 in	1985	0.17 in
1349	Silchester, Berkshire	12 ft 9 in	–	–

Sixteenth century

Date	Place	Girth	Date measured	Average growth per year
1500	Myddleton House, Middlesex	9 ft 9 in	1976	0.24 in
1500	Myddleton House, Middlesex	8 ft 4 in	1976	0.21 in
1509	Penkridge Hall, Shropshire	8 ft 3 in	1985	0.20 in
1509	Penkridge Hall, Shropshire	10 ft 2 in	1985	0.25 in
1509	Prees, Shropshire	–	–	–
1580	Betteshanger, Kent	–	–	–
1580	Hentland, Hereford and Worcester	13 ft 6 in	1982	0.40 in
1590	Winterslow, Wiltshire	–	–	–
1597	Wateringbury, Kent	11 ft 4 in	1982	0.35 in

Seventeenth century

Date	Place	Girth	Date measured	Average growth per year
1612	Hughendon, Buckinghamshire	10 ft 1 in	1981	0.32 in
1623	Talachddo, Powys	–	–	–
1627	Guilsfield, Powys	10 ft 3 in	1977	0.35 in
1630	Manaton, Devon	–	–	–
1636	Denbury, Devon	12 ft 9 in	1988	0.43 in
1636	Mere, Wiltshire	–	–	–
1638	Carsington, Derbyshire	11 ft 4 in	1983	0.39 in
1640	Farnborough, Kent	–	–	–
1650	Osmaston, Derbyshire	8 ft	1879	0.41 in
1650	Osmaston, Derbyshire	8 ft	1879	0.36 in
1659	Skipton Castle, Yorkshire	7 ft 7 in	1983	0.28 in
1660	Sutton, Sussex	12 ft 10 in	1983	0.47 in
1675	Pitmedden, Grampian	10 ft 8 in	1879	0.62 in
1680	Hampton Court, Middlesex	11 ft	1978	0.44 in
1680	Hampton Court, Middlesex	11 ft 1 in	1978	0.44 in
1680	Hampton Court, Middlesex	12 ft 4 in	1978	0.49 in
1687	Stoke Hammond, Buckinghamshire	11 ft 2 in	1981	0.45 in
1687	Stoke Hammond, Buckinghamshire	10 ft	1981	0.40 in
1693	Hurstbourne Tarrant, Hampshire	{ 8 ft 4 in	1897	0.49 in
		9 ft 5 in	1981	0.39 in
1694	Boughton under Blean, Kent	{ 9 ft 9 in	1895	0.58 in
		13 ft 8 in	1983	0.56 in

Eighteenth century

Date	Place	Girth	Date measured	Average growth per year
1700	Penhow, Gwent	11 ft	1987	0.45 in
1703	Tiverton St Peter, Devon	8 ft 10 in	1983	0.37 in
1708	Aylesford, Kent	8 ft 2 in	1982	0.35 in
1714	Paignton, Devon	–	–	–
1715	Carsington, Derbyshire	5 ft 1 in	1983	0.22 in
1723	Thornton, Leicestershire	10 ft	1937	0.56 in
1724	Axminster, Devon	9 ft 2 in	1983	0.42 in
1725	Winterbourn, Dorset	9 ft	1987	0.62 in
1725	Winterbourn, Dorset	6 ft	1897	0.41 in
1726	Basildon, Berkshire	{ 6 ft 3 in	1780	1.38 in
		{ 10 ft	1981	0.47 in
1728	Matching Tye, Essex	9 ft 3 in	1988	0.42 in
1730	Torbryan, Devon	14 ft	1988	0.65 in
1731	Upton Pyne, Devon	–	–	–
1731	West Dean, Sussex	6 ft 6 in	1983	0.30 in
1731	West Dean, Sussex	7 ft 2 in	1983	0.34 in
1731	Wilmington, Kent	8 ft 3 in	1988	0.38 in
1732	Mugginton, Derbyshire	4 ft 10 in	1983	0.23 in
1740	Beeley, Derbyshire	9 ft 6 in	1983	0.46 in
1741	Hurstbourne Tarrant,	{ 7 ft 3 in	1897	0.55 in
	Hampshire	{ 9 ft 5 in	1981	0.47 in
1759	St Mary Bourne, Hampshire	8 ft 10 in	1982	0.47 in
1760	Honiton, Devon	–	–	–
1770	Monksilver, Somerset	10 ft	1990	0.54 in
c. 1775	Tytherly (Queenswood) Wiltshire	6 ft	1897	0.59 in
1775	Woodbury, Devon	8 ft	1983	0.46 in
1780	Sutton Mandeville, Wiltshire	11 ft 8 in	1982	0.69 in
1789	Dryburgh Abbey, Borders	3 ft 8 in	1987	0.22 in

Date	Place	Girth	Date measured	Average growth per year
1790	Berry Pomeroy, Devon	9 ft	1988	0.54 in
1790	Heightington Rock, Hereford and Worcester	–	–	–
1796	Tiverton St George, Devon	6 ft 3 in	1983	0.40 in

Nineteenth century

Date	Place	Girth	Date measure	Average growth per year
1804	Audley End, Essex	–	–	–
1816	Camperdown, Tayside	3 ft 10 in	1895	0.58 in
1830	Grasmere Church, Cumbria	7 ft 8 in	1987	0.58 in
1832	Mid Woodford Rectory, Wiltshire	10 ft 6 in	1967	0.93 in
1834	Wellow, Somerset	3 ft 7 in	1896	0.69 in
1840	Kentisbeare Poor House, Devon	–	–	–
1854	Betteshanger, Kent	–	–	–
1870	Thorney West, Sussex	–	–	–
1875	Tring, Hertfordshire	–	–	–

Recorded Measurements

In this church-yard is an Yew-Tree, ten yards in compafs, (1650) but not above five foot high.

JOHN AUBREY, *The Natural History and Antiquities of Surrey*, vol. 3, 1718–19

and in the churchyard is a yew-tree 30 feet 9 inches in circumference at 5 feet from the ground; it is hollow, with seats and a table, and ten persons can sit within it.

SAMUEL LEWIS, *Topographical Dictionary of England*, 1845

SELBORNE, HAMPSHIRE

Dates visited	Girth measurements	By
1778	23 ft at breast height	W. S. Scott
1788	23 ft	Gilbert White
1823	23 ft 8 in at 3 ft from the ground	William Cobbett
1859	24 ft at 3 ft from the ground	M. C. Turner
1877	24 ft 6 in at 4 ft from the ground	Dr Bromfield
1897	25 ft 3 in at 3 ft from the ground	John Lowe
1912	25 ft 5 in at narrowest part of trunk	Hugh Boyd Watt
1938	25 ft 4 in at 3 ft from the ground	Revd L. Sunderland
1947	25 ft 7 in at 4 ft from the ground	H. Gardner
1967	25 ft 10 in at 3 ft from the ground	Unknown
1981	25 ft 10 in at 3 ft from the ground	Allen Meredith

In 203 years the tree grew 2 ft 10 in; 0.17 in per year average.

MARSTON ST LAWRENCE, NORTHAMPTONSHIRE

Dates visited	Girth measurements	By
1822	21 ft 9 in at 6 ft from the ground	George Baker
1822	17 ft 10 in at the base	George Baker
1849	22 ft at 6 in from the ground	Unknown
1949	18 ft at the base	*Hist. Gazette and Direc. of Northants*
1975	20 ft 3 in at 3 ft from the ground	H. Gardner
1981	24 ft at 4 ft from the ground	Allen Meredith
1988	17 ft 9 in at the base	P. Jackson
1988	20 ft at 3 ft from the ground	P. Jackson
1988	22 ft 8 in at 4 ft from the ground	P. Jackson

In 166 years the tree grew approx. 11 in; 0.07 in per year average.

CROWHURST, SURREY

Dates visited	Girth measurements	By
1630	30 ft (old parish record)	Unknown
1650	30 ft at 5 ft from the ground	John Aubrey
1664	30 ft	John Evelyn
1833–45	30 ft at 5 ft from the ground	Samuel Lewis
1850	30 ft 9 in at 5 ft from the ground	Brailey's *History of Surrey*
1874	30 ft 9 in at 5 ft from the ground	*Gardener's Chronicle*
1877	31 ft at 5 ft from the ground	Mr Jennings
1984	31 ft 6 in at approx 5 ft from the ground	Allen Meredith

In 354 years the tree grew 1 ft 6 in; 0.06 in per year average.

CROWHURST, SUSSEX

Dates visited	Girth measurements	By
1680	27 ft at 4 ft from the ground	John Aubrey
1680	33 ft at the base	John Aubrey
1835	27 ft 7 in at 4 ft from the ground	Horsfield
1879	26 ft 7 in at 4 ft from the ground	C. S. Greaves
1894	26 ft 9 in at 4 ft from the ground	John Lowe
1954	27 ft 2 in at 3 ft from the ground	E. W. Swanton
1982	28 ft at approx. 4 ft from the ground	Allen Meredith

In 302 years the tree grew 1 ft; 0.04 in per year average.

TOTTERIDGE, HERTFORDSHIRE

Dates visited	Girth measurements	By
1677	26 ft at 3 ft from the ground	Sir John Cullum
1777	26 ft at 3 ft from the ground	Richard Gough
1796	26 ft at 3 ft from the ground	Dr S. Lysons
1877	26 ft at 3 ft from the ground	J. E. Cussons
1982	26 ft at 3 ft from the ground	Allen Meredith
1991	26 ft at 3 ft from the ground	Allen Meredith

No growth in 314 years.

HARLINGTON, MIDDLESEX

Dates visited	Girth measurements	By
1808	15 ft 7 in at 6 ft from the ground	*Gentleman's Magazine*
1833	18 ft 3 in at 4 ft from the ground	Samuel Lewis
1895	19 ft 6 in at 3 ft from the ground	Revd. E. J. Haddon
1921	21 ft at 5 ft from the ground	Herbert Wilson
1981	19 ft 2 in at 3 ft from the ground	Allen Meredith

1989   16 ft at 6 ft from the ground   Allen Meredith

In 181 years the tree grew 11 in; 0.06 in per year average.

FARRINGDON, HAMPSHIRE

Dates visited	Girth measurements	By
1781	30 ft	Gilbert White
1902	30 ft at 5 ft from the ground	W. H. Hudson
1902	30 ft	Cox
1984	30 ft 6 in at approx. 5 ft from the ground	Allen Meredith

In 203 years the tree grew 6 in; 0.03 in per year average.

CUDHAM, KENT (two trees)

Dates visited	Girth measurements	By
1804	Approx. 30 ft	*Gentleman's Magazine*
1804	Approx. 30 ft	*Gentleman's Magazine*
1890	28 ft 4 in at 3 ft from the ground (female)	Revd Nigel Froor
1890	28 ft 4 in at 3 ft from the ground (male)	Revd Nigel Froor
1980	28 ft at 5 ft from the ground (female)	Allen Meredith
1980	27 ft 6 in at 5 ft from the ground (male)	Allen Meredith
1984	28 ft 8 in at 4 ft from the ground (female)	Allen Meredith
1984	27 ft 10 in at 4 ft from the ground (male)	Allen Meredith

Probably no growth in 180 years.

DARLEY DALE, DERBYSHIRE

Dates visited	Girth measurements	By
1792	28 ft at the base	Dr Burgh
1792	32 ft at 4 ft from the ground	Dr Burgh
1836	27 ft 7 in at the base	John E. Bowman

1836	31 ft 8 in at 4 ft from the ground	John E. Bowman
1876	31 ft 8 in at 4 ft from the ground	Dr Cox
1888	32 ft 3 in at 4 ft from the ground	Paget Bowman
1888	27 ft at the base	Paget Bowman
1933	33 ft at 4 ft from the base	A. W. Smith
1933	27 ft at the base	A. W. Smith

Probably no growth in 141 years.

LEEDS, KENT

Dates visited	Girth measurements	By
1831	31 ft 3 in	Robert Mudie
1832	31 ft at its greatest circumference	Robert Mudie
1837	31 ft 2 in at its greatest circumference	J. C. Loudon
1892	28 ft at the base	John Lowe
1892	32 ft at 3 ft 6 in from the ground	John Lowe
1892	25 ft at 5 ft from the ground	John Lowe
1984	The yew is split and separated; any measurement would not be realistic	

Measurement not possible.

ALDWORTH, BERKSHIRE

Dates visited	Girth measurements	By
1644	27 ft at 4 ft from the ground	Capt. Symonds
1760	27 ft at 4 ft from the ground	Rowe Mores
1799	27 ft at 4 ft from the ground	Unknown
1830	27 ft at 4 ft from the ground	Thomas Dugdale
1836	27 ft 3 in at 5 ft from the ground	J. C. Loudon
1857	27 ft at 4 ft from the ground	James A. Hawley
1897	28 ft at 4 ft from the ground	Unknown
1935	28 ft at 4 ft from the ground	William Bradbroke

1972	28 ft at 4 ft from the ground	Unknown
1976	A storm in the night brought tree down	
1980	Remains of tree approx. 13 ft	

In 328 years the tree grew 12 in; 0.04 in per year average.

CHURCH PREEN, SHROPSHIRE

Dates visited	Girth measurements	By
1833	22 ft at 4 ft from the ground	Unknown
1889	21 ft 9 in at 4 ft from the ground	Arthur Sparrow
1946	23 ft at 4 ft from the ground	P. H. B. Gardner
1955	23 ft at 4 ft from the ground	Rev. C. E. Butler
1983	23 ft 1 in at 4 ft from the ground	Allen Meredith

In 150 years the tree grew 1 ft 1 in; 0.09 in per year average.

LLANDDEINIOLEN, GWYNEDD

Dates visited	Girth measurements	By
1769	27 ft	Thomas Pennant
1833–40	28 ft 4 in	Samuel Lewis
1891	28 ft	*Gazetteer of Caernarvonshire*
1984	28 ft 10 in	Reg Wheeler

In 215 years the tree grew 1 ft 10 in; 0.1 in per year average.

TETTENHALL, STAFFORDSHIRE

Dates visited	Girth measurements	By
1874	24 ft	*Gardender's Chronicle*
1984	24 ft	Rev. J. D. Makepeace

No growth in 110 years.

DARTINGTON, DEVON

Dates visited	Girth measurements	By
1787	23 ft	Richard Polwhele
1988	23 ft at under 3 ft from the ground	Allen Meredith

No growth in 201 years.

MUCH MARCLE, HEREFORD AND WORCESTER

Dates visited	Girth measurements	By
1882	28 ft 6 in at 5 ft from the ground	John Duncumb
1989	29 ft at 5 ft from the ground	Allen Meredith

In 107 years the tree grew 6 in; 0.06 in per year average.

LLANFAREDD, POWYS

Dates visited	Girth measurements	By
1811	36 ft	Revd Jonathon Williams
1891	36 ft	Gazetteer of British Isles
1905	36 ft	E. Davies, History of Radnor
1945	35–36 ft	Revd D. Stedman Davies
1982	35 ft 8 in at 3 ft from the ground	Allen Meredith

No growth in 171 years; the tree may even have shrunk.

EASTLING, KENT

Dates visited	Girth measurements	By
1874	30 ft at approx. 4 ft from the ground	John Taylor
1982	30 ft 4 in at approx. 4 ft from the ground	Allen Meredith

In 108 years the tree grew 4 in; 0.04 in per year average.

DRYBURGH ABBEY, BORDERS

Dates visited	Girth measurements	By
1837	12 ft 1 in	J. C. Loudon
1890	11 ft 4 in	John Lowe
1988	12 ft 7 in	Alan Mitchell

Gazetteer of Ancient Yews

This Gazetteer lists all known yews in mainland Britain, and a few of note elsewhere, aged over 1,000 years. There are gaps in the data for a variety of reasons. Sometimes the information available is simply incomplete; it is difficult, for example, to determine the sex of trees at some periods of the year. Not all yews are in churchyards, and in such instances no orientation is given. Allen has only assessed the age of those yews he has actually seen, and occasionally he has decided that because of the condition of the tree it is impossible to give an accurate estimate.

Site	Girth	Sex	Orientation from church	Estimated age
Abbots Leigh, Somerset	25 ft	F	NE	1,600
Aberedwy, Powys	22 ft	F	NW	1,400
It is recorded sixty couples danced beneath the tree				
Aberglasney, Carmarthen				1,000
A remarkable yew tunnel				
Abergwesyn, Powys	28 ft	M	NW	
Near ruins of church	21 ft	F	E	
Acton Beauchamp, Hereford and Worcester	18 ft	F	S	1,400
Tree measured 22 ft in 1856; now broken and ivy-covered				
Acton Burnell Park, Shropshire	25 ft			
Tree not in churchyard				

Acton Scott, Shropshire	24 ft	M	W	2,000

Hollow with internal stem; other old yews on site

Addington, Middlesex	18 ft	F	S	1,400

Alderbury, Wiltshire	21 ft	F	S	1,500

Subject of controversy over how to care for it

Alderley Edge, Cheshire	18 ft	M	SE	

New trees have layered from original trunk

Aldingbourne, Sussex	26 ft	M	SW	1,300

Aldworth, Berkshire	27 ft (1970)	E	E	2,000

Badly damaged in 1976 storm

Alfold, Surrey	22 ft	M	S	1,300

Allestree, Derbyshire	17 ft 8 in	M	S	1,400 +

Over 20 ft in girth a hundred years ago

Alltmawr, Powys	30 ft	M	W	3,000

Alton Priors, Wiltshire	28 ft	F	S	1,700

Saxon church in field; Green Man on site

Alveston (Rudgeway), Gloucestershire	25 ft	F	E	1,800

Near ruins of an old church; hollow, with many shoots

Ankerwyke, Buckinghamshire	31 ft	M	N	2,500

North of ruins of convent; other old yews on site

Ashampstead, Berkshire			NW	

Details unobtainable as trunk incorporated into church wall in Norman period; only part now showing

Ashbrittle, Somerset	38 ft	M	SE	3,000

On pre-Christian mound

Ashford Carbonnel, Shropshire   27 ft   M   1,500
Many yews all around church; one aged 1,300, two aged 1,000

Ashill, Somerset   21 ft   F   NW   1,400
                                 17 ft   M   W

Ashstead, Surrey   23 ft   F   S   1,400

Astbury, Cheshire   14 ft   M   N   2,000
Ancient shell left leaning over path; possible neolithic site

Awre, Gloucestershire   22 ft   M   N   2,000
Broken but healthy; overlooking the river Severn

Bacton, Hereford and Worcester   24 ft   M   E   1,500

Baglan, Glamorgan   19 ft   F   W   1,500
Near ruins of old church

Bampton, Devon   29 ft   S   1,500
More than one old yew

Barlavington, Sussex   26 ft   M   1,800
Yew on farm

Barlow, West Yorkshire   19 ft   F   1,500
Yew on farm

Baschurch, Shropshire   17 ft   M   E

Bedhampton, Hampshire   20 ft   M   S   1,200
                                 20 ft   F   S   1,200

Beeley, Derbyshire   20 ft   M   SW

Benington, Hertfordshire   23 ft   M   SW   1,400
Castle ruins opposite

Bersted, Sussex

Bettws Newydd, Gwent   33 ft   F   W   4,000
Internal stem; more than one old yew

Bicknoller, Somerset	24 ft	F	S	1,500
Bidborough, Kent	26 ft		NE	1,700
Bignor, West Sussex	22 ft 2 in	F	SE	1,400
Billingsley, Shropshire	20 ft	M	S	

More than one old yew

Boarhunt, Hampshire	26 ft	M	E	1,800
	27 ft		NW	
Bockleton, Hereford and Worcester	21 ft	F	S	1,200

More than one old yew

Borrowdale, Cumbria	24 ft	F	

On mountain side in Lake District; impossible to estimate age due to exposed site and severe climate; Wordsworth's 'Fraternal Four', only three remain

Brailsford, Derbyshire	21 ft 10 in	F	SW	1,000
Breamore, Hampshire	30 ft	F	SW	2,000

Green Man in church; tree shattered

Breinton, Hereford and Worcester	20 ft		NW	1,100
More than one old yew	17 ft 6 in		NE	1,700
Britwell Salome, Oxfordshire	23 ft	F	E	1,400
Broad Windsor, Dorset	33 ft	M	SE	

Impossible to estimate age; many new stems obliterating original trunk

Broadwell, Gloucestershire	25 ft	F	S	1,300

Tree of Life on stone in porch

Brockenhurst, Hampshire	20 ft	F	S	1,000
Brockhampton, Gloucestershire	21 ft	M	E	

Near hotel and roofless church

Broomfield, Somerset	23 ft	F	S	1,500

25 ft in 1880

Broxbourne, Hertfordshire	20 ft	F	N	1,100
Buckland-in-Dover, Kent	23 ft	M/F	W	2,000
Tree moved in 1880; is both male and female				
Bulley, Gloucestershire	18 ft	F	S	1,000
Damaged by storms				
Bunbury, Cheshire	20 ft	M	SE	1,000
Burcott Farm, Hereford and Worcester	23 ft	F		1,500
In a hedgerow on an old trackway				
Burghill, Hereford and Worcester	25 ft		E	
Burrington, Somerset	23 ft	M	NW	1,300
Buttington, Powys	26 ft	M	SW	1,100
Buxted, Sussex	30 ft		E	2,000
Arrows made from tree for Battle of Hastings				
Bystock, Devon	24 ft	M	SW	1,400
(St John in the Wilderness)				
Caerhun, Clwyd	18 ft 6 in	M	S	1,200
	18 ft	F	SW	1,200
On an ancient site of Roman fortress				
Capel, Kent	27 ft	F	E	2,000
Capel, Surrey	17 ft	F	E	1,700
Capel-y-iffin, Gwent	20 ft	M	SE	1,500
Several yews on site				
Carno, Powys	21 ft			
Cascob, Powys	25 ft	F	W	1,500
Church on ancient mound				

Castle Frome, Hereford and Worcester	21 ft	M	SE	1,000

Cathedine, Brecon	23 ft	M	S	1,100
Several yews

Cefnllys, Powys	19 ft	M	ESE	1,200

Chailey, Sussex	28 ft	M	S	1,500

Challock, Kent	18 ft	F	W	

Charlwood, Surrey	21 ft		SE	1,200

Cherkley Court, Surrey	23 ft 4 in			
	19 ft 11 in			
On private estate

Chevening, Kent	20 ft	F	NNW	
600 yards NNW of church, on Pilgrim's Way

Chewton Mendip, Somerset			S	1,200
More than one old yew

Chilcompton, Somerset	28 ft	M	SW	1,600

Chilham, Kent	22 ft	F	SW	1,300
Storm-damaged in 1987

Church Preen, Shropshire	22 ft	F	N	1,536
Planted AD 457

Cilycwm, Dyfed	25 ft	M	SE	1,500

Claverley, Shropshire	28 ft	M	N	2,500
Church on ancient burial mound

Clifton on Teme, Hereford and
    Worcester
Effigy of knight in church, found dead under the yew

Clun, Shropshire	33 ft	M	N	3,000
Cold Waltham, Sussex Hollow	33 ft	F	N	3,000
Colva, Powys				
Combe Flore, Somerset	28 ft	F	SW	1,500
Compton Dundon, Somerset	23 ft	M	S	1,400
Congresbury, Somerset Impossible to measure, inside beech tree			E	1,400
Corhampton, Hampshire Green Man on site	24 ft	F	S	1,400
Cradley, Hereford and Worcester More than one old yew	21 ft	M	ESE	1,200
Creech St Michael, Somerset	17 ft	F	W	1,600
Crowcombe, Somerset Described by Mee in 1948 as split, now appears solid; Green Man in church	17 ft	F	S	1,000
Crowhurst, Surrey Door in tree; once had table inside hollow trunk	32 ft	M	ENE	4,000
Crowhurst, Sussex	28 ft	F	S	2,000
Cudham, Kent	28 ft 8 in	F	S	1,800
	27 ft 10 in	M	SW	1,700
Culmstock, Devon Growing from the tower				
Cusop, Hereford and Worcester More than one old yew	30 ft	M	SW	1,800
Cwmcarfan, Gwent	21 ft 6 in			

Darley Dale, Derbyshire	33 ft	F	S	2,000
Green Man on site				
Dartington, Devon	25 ft	F	W	1,500
Near remains of church				
Defynnog, Brecon	40 ft	F	N	3,500

More than one yew; may all be part of one original one; all female; pre-Christian stone in porch

Didcot, Oxfordshire	22 ft		SW	1,200
Dinder, Somerset	32 ft	M	SE	1,800
Dinmore Chapel, Hereford and	21 ft		SW	1,200
Worcester				
Dinton, Wiltshire	22 ft 5 in	M	SSE	
Many yews in churchyard				
Discoed, Powys	37 ft	M	N	5,000
	22 ft	F	SW	1,400
Discoed, Powys	24 ft			

Yew on Offa's Dyke, near spring; a boundary marker

Doveridge, Derbyshire	22 ft	F	E	1,600

Maid Marian and Robin Hood said to have wed beneath the tree; Green Man on site

Downe, Kent	25 ft		S	1,400
Very hollow				
Druid's Grove, Surrey	24 ft approx. (many trees)			2,000
Remains of ancient yew wood				
Duddleston, Shropshire	19 ft		W	1,200 +
Hollow tree; bell once hung inside				
Dundonnell, West Ross	23 ft			

Dunsfold, Surrey	24 ft	F	S	1,500
Holy well near church; Green Man on site				
Dunster, Somerset			W	
A ruined wreck of a yew				
Durley, Hampshire	23 ft		S	1,400
Eardisley, Hereford and Worcester	19 ft		SW	1,000
East Chiltington, Sussex	21 ft	F	S	1,200
East Chinnock, Somerset	21 ft	M	S	1,100
Eastham, Cheshire	21 ft	F	E	1,600
Mentioned in charter				
Easthope, Shropshire	22 ft			
Ancient site, said to be haunted				
Eastling, Kent	31 ft	F	W	2,000
Edington, Wiltshire	21 ft	M	E	
Site of monastery destroyed in Dissolution				
Egerton, Kent	23 ft		NE	
Hollow				
Elmsted, Kent	19 ft	F	NW	
	17 ft	F	NE	
	19 ft 6 in	M	S	
	22 ft	M	SW	
All are hollow				
Elworthy, Somerset	29 ft	F	NNE	2,000
Redundant church				
Enmore, Somerset	19 ft	M	SW	
More than one yew in churchyard				
Estry, Normandy	38 ft			

Etchingham, Sussex	20 ft	M		
Farringdon, Hampshire	30 ft	M	W	3,000 +

Huge hollow shell; other yews in churchyard

Farway, Devon	25 ft	F	SE	1,400
Ffynnon bedr, Gwynedd	24 ft	F		1,500

Over holy well

Forthampton, Gloucestershire	8 ft		S	

27 ft girth in 1820; storm-damaged in 1860s

Fortingall, Tayside	56 ft approx.	M	NW	5,000

Separated ruin of a tree

Fountains Abbey, Yorkshire	22 ft	F	W	1,500

Several yews; Green Man in abbey ruins

Fulbrook, Oxfordshire	19 ft	F	S	1,000 +

Trimmed in 1988

Funtington, Sussex	21 ft			
Garth Brengy, Brecon	21 ft			
Garthbeibio, Brecon	23 ft	F	N	1,400
Glasbury, Powys	24 ft		S	
	22 ft		E	
Glyncorrwg, Glamorgan	24 ft	F	S	1,500

Many yews in decayed state

Godmersham, Kent	24 ft		N	

Several old yews

Goostrey, Cheshire	23 ft	M	S	1,200
Goytrey, Gwent	23 ft	F	S	1,500

Several old yews, and a very large stump south-west of church

Great Burstead, Essex	17 ft	F	S	1,000
Gresford, Clwyd	29 ft	M	SE	1,600 +
Over thirty yews in churchyard; Green Man on site				
Gwenlais, Dyfed	14 ft	F		1,000 +
Over a holy well at head of valley; not in churchyard				
Gwytherin, Clwyd	28 ft 7 in	F	W	2,000
	28 ft 8 in	F	E	
Several old yews; on ancient burial mound with pre-Christian stones				
Hambledon, Hampshire	19 ft 6 in	F	S	940
Reputed to have been planted in 1060				
Hambledon, Surrey	35 ft	M	SE	2,000
	20 ft	M	S	
Hanchurch, Staffordshire	20 ft			1,500
Line of ancient yews; possible site of monastery				
Harlington, Middlesex	19 ft	F	S	1,000
Harrietsham, Kent	31 ft	M	S	
	19 ft	F	NW	
Several old yews				
Hawkley, Hampshire	22 ft	F	SW	1,200
Hayes, Kent	23 ft	F	S	1,300
	24 ft	F		
Hayling South, Hampshire	33 ft	F	S	2,000
Hedsor, Buckinghamshire	23 ft		SE	1,400
More than one old yew				
Helmdon, Northamptonshire	28 ft		E	1,700
Hemyock, Somerset	30 ft 6 in approx.	M	SW	1,400
Split into three sections				

cutting from this tree planted OLDSTOCK St. Mary's 1.1.2000

Hewelsfield, Gloucestershire	21 ft	M	S	1,300
Holcombe, Somerset				
Holne, Devon	13 ft	F	S	1,000
Hoo St Werburgh, Kent	21 ft			1,400
Hope Bagot, Shropshire	23 ft	F	N	1,600
Holy well beneath tree				
Horton, Staffordshire	21 ft	F	S	
Partly hollow				
Huntley, Gloucestershire	21 ft	F	NW	1,500
Hurstbourne Priors, Hampshire	21 ft		S	1,400
Hurstmonceux, Sussex	16 ft	F	SE	
22 ft in 1882; greatly damaged over the years				
Icklesham, Sussex	20 ft	F	N	
Iffley, Oxfordshire	25 ft	F	S	1,500
Ilston, West Glamorgan	17 ft	F	S	1,000
Tall yew on mound				
Itchen Abbas, Hampshire	26 ft	M	E	1,700
Charter boundary yew				
Keffolds Farm, Surrey	29 ft	F		2,000
Opposite farmhouse				
Kemble, Gloucestershire	16 ft	F	W	1,600
Internal stem in tree				
Kemsing, Kent	23 ft	M		1,300
On Pilgrims' Way, 300 yards north of St Clere House				
Kenley, Shropshire	28 ft	F	W	1,400
A broken tree				

Kenn, Devon	40 ft	M	SE	2,000

Hard to measure; part of trunk missing

Kennington, Kent	31 ft	F	W	2,000

Large burial mound opposite church; large portion of tree missing; several old yews on site

Kentchurch Court, Hereford and Worcester	31 ft	F		2,000

Many large yews in deer park

Kilmington, Wiltshire	22 ft	M	S	

Kingstone, Somerset	25 ft 6 in	M	E	

Kinsham, Powys

Knighton on Teme, Hereford and Worcester	22 ft	M	S	1,300

Knowle Park, Kent	20 ft			1,000

In park grounds on steep bank

Knowlton, Dorset	25 ft	M		2,500–3,000

Ancient yews on pre-Christian site with henge monument

La Haye de Routot, Normandy	37 ft	M	N	

Small chapel inside hollow yew

Lamberhurst, Kent	26 ft	M	SW	1,500

Langley, Buckinghamshire	28 ft	M	SSW	1,400

Green Man in church

Langley Park, Buckinghamshire	23 ft	F		1,500

Surrounded by younger yews layered from parent; no church; moat around site.

Lea, Gloucestershire	22 ft			

Leamington Hastings, Warwickshire	23 ft			1,000

Not in churchyard

Leeds, Kent	30 ft	F	W	2,000
Lessingham House, Norfolk				1,000
Not in churchyard				
Linton, Hereford and Worcester	33 ft	F	NW	4,000
Internal stem in tree; several old yews on site				
Little Bookham, Surrey	19 ft		SW	1,300
Very decayed				
Little Chart, Kent			S	
Church wrecked by flying bomb in war; more than one old yew				
Little Hereford, Hereford and Worcester	15 ft 1 in		S	
Split and burnt but with green shoots				
Llanafan-Fawr, Powys	32 ft	F	E	2,000
Green Man on site				
Llanarmon Dyffryn Ceiriog, Clwyd	25 ft	M		
More than one old yew				
Llanarth, Gwent	26 ft	F	S	2,000
Internal stem in tree				
Llanbadarn Fawr, Powys	20 ft	M	SSW	1,300
Llanddeiniolen, Gwynedd	28 ft	F	E	2,000
Llande Faelog Fach, Brecon	20 ft		W	1,200
Llandeilo Graban, Powys	25 ft	M	SSE	1,500
Llandewi cwm, Brecon	25 ft			
Llandinabo, Hereford and Worcester	28 ft	F	S	1,600
Several old yews on site				
Llandre, Dyfed		F	N	1,800
Split and separated; impossible to measure				

Llandybie, Dyfed	21 ft	M		
Llandyfeisant, Dyfed	21 ft	M		1,300
Llanedeyrn, Gwent	27 ft	F	S	1,600
Little more than shell; now in two pieces				
Llanelltyd, Gwynedd	21 ft	F	S	1,500
More than one old yew				
Llanelly, Gwent	20 ft		E	
More than one old yew; circle of yews around church				
Llanerfyl, Powys	35 ft	F	S	1,600
Girth cannot be measured accurately; pre-Christian stone found on site				
Llanfair Discoed, Gwent	22 ft	F	S	1,500
Llanfair Kilgeddin, Gwent	28 ft	F	S	1,500
More than one old yew on site				
Llanfair Clydoga, Dyfed	22 ft			
Llanfaredd, Powys	36 ft	F	W	3,000
Llanfeugan, Brecon	32 ft	F	E	2,000
Llanfihangel Crucorney, Gwent	25 ft			
Llanfihangel-nant-melan, Powys	30 ft		SW	1,800
Circle of ancient yews				
Llanfihangel Talglyn, Brecon	28 ft		S	
Llanfoist, Gwent	25 ft	F	S	1,500
Llangadwaladr, Clwyd	25 ft		N	1,600
Avenue of old yews				
Llangathen, Dyfed	20 ft	M	N	1,500
Llangeithio, Dyfed	21 ft	M	W	1,300
More than one old yew; door on hollow yew				

Llangernyw, Clwyd		M N	5,000

Impossible to measure; circle of yews on prehistoric site; oil tank inside old yew

Llangollen, Clwyd	21 ft	M W	1,000
	25 ft	M W	
Llangovan, Gwent	22 ft	E	1,500
Llangower, Gwynedd	24 ft	F E	1,600
Llangunnor, Carmarthen			1,000
Llangwm, Clwyd	30 ft		
Llangwm St Jeromes, Gwent	20 ft	F N	1,200

Green Man on site

Llanhilleth, Gwent	24 ft		

Circle of yews in churchyard, by ruined church

Llanllowel, Gwent	26 ft	SE	1,500
Llanfihangel Place, Glamorgan	22 ft largest		

Sixty-three old yews

Llanrhidian, Gwent	22 ft	F S	1,400
Llansantffraed in Elvel, Powys	28ft	M SW	

Several yews growing on mound

Llansilin, Clwyd	25 ft		1,600

Avenue of yews

Llansoy, Gwent	30 ft	M W	
Llanspyddid, Brecon	27 ft	F W	1,800
Llanthewy Rytherch, Gwent	20 ft	F E	1,300

Large internal stem

Llantrithyd Park, Glamorgan	17 ft		N	1,100
In a churchyard which is in a park				
Llanwarne, Gwent				
Llanwenarth Citra, Gwent	26 ft	F	SW	1,800
Llanwnog, Powys	25 ft		E	
Llanwrda, Dyfed	18 ft		S	1,200
Church given to Talley Abbey in 1192				
Llanycil, Gwynedd	21 ft	F		
Circle of yews				
Llanymawddy, Gwynedd	27 ft	F	NNE	1,800
Llanyre, Powys	25 ft	M	N	
Old yews on burial mound				
Llywel, Brecon	20 ft	M	SW	1,200
More than one old yew				
Lockerley, Hampshire	25 ft	F	S	1,500
Long Sutton, Hampshire	32 ft 3 in	M	N	
	19 ft 7 in		SE	
	18 ft		SW	
Longbridge Deverill, Wiltshire	29 ft		SW	1,600
Loose, Kent	33 ft	M	SW	2,000
Lorton, Cumbria	19 ft	F		

Measured 27 ft in 1806; only half trunk remains; in a field near a stream; the Quaker Fox preached beneath the tree; Wordsworth refers to the yew as 'Pride of Lorton Vale'

Loughton, Shropshire	33 ft	F	E	2,000

Lydney, Gloucestershire	20 ft	M	NE	1,500

Hollow; much of tree recently removed by tree surgeons

Lyneham, Wiltshire	25 ft	F	S	1,500

Lytchett Matravers, Dorset	23 ft		N	1,600

Internal stem

Maentwrog, Gwynedd	19 ft	F	S	1,300

Three yews, each at least 1,300 years

Mallwyd, Gwynedd	31 ft	M	E	1,800

Mamhead, Devon	31 ft	M	W	2,000

Crown removed but sprouting; very sound for such a large girth

Mamhilad, Gwent	31 ft	F	S	2,000

Split yew with internal stem

Maple Beck, Nottinghamshire	20 ft

Marbury, Cheshire		1,200

Marston Bigot, Somerset	30 ft 3 in

On private estate but on site of church now gone

Marston Montgomery, Derbyshire

Marston St Lawrence, Northamptonshire	21 ft	M	N	1,500

Martindale, Cumbria	22 ft	M	E	2,000

Merdon Castle, Hampshire	23 ft		2,000

Several trees on ancient British camp near the castle

Merthyr Cynog, Brecon	26 ft		S

Only ruins of church remain

Mid Lavant, Sussex	24 ft	M	N	2,000

Internal stem

Middleton Scriven, Shropshire	29 ft	F	S	1,600

Two large yews in field opposite church

Minsterworth, Gloucestershire	20 ft 6 in	M	E	
Next to river Severn				
Molash, Kent	29 ft		N	2,000
Much Marcle, Hereford and Worcester	30 ft	F	S	1,500
Round seat inside hollow yew				
Muckross Abbey, Ireland	12 ft			
Abbey founded 1440; tree may be older				
Muggington, Derbyshire	24 ft	F	S	1,400
Munsley, Hereford and Worcester	22 ft	F	NE	1,100
Mynddislwyn, Gwent	27 ft		S	2,000
More than one old yew; possibly originally a circular churchyard				
Nant Glyn, Clwyd	26 ft	M	S	1,600
Pulpit in yew				
Nantmel, Powys	30 ft	F	S	2,000
Old yews on mound				
Newlands Corner, Surrey	24 ft largest			2,000
Remains of ancient yew grove				
Newton Valence, Hampshire	19 ft	F	W	1,000
Ninfield, Sussex	21 ft	M	SE	
A mere skeleton				
Norbury, Shropshire	33 ft	M	S	
Impossible to age				
North Perrott, Somerset	23 ft 6 in	F	NW	
Northiam, Sussex	21 ft	F	S	1,200 +
Nurstead, Kent				

Odstock, Wiltshire   17–18 ft   2,000
Ancient woodland on private estate

Old Church, Cumbria   22 ft   F   1,500
No church remains; tree is on banks of Ullswater, near hotel

Old Enton, Surrey   25 ft   F
Impossible to estimate age; two trees in field on site of possible hill fort

Orchard Portman, Somerset   21 ft   F   SE   1,000

Overton on Dee, Clwyd   20 ft   M   NW   2,000
One of the 'seven wonders of Wales'

Panillydw, Dyfed   20 ft   M   1,200
Not in a churchyard; branches grow to the ground; very isolated

Pauntley, Gloucestershire   24 ft   M   NE   1,500

Payhembury, Devon   46 ft 6in   M   NE
Impossible to age; old trunk split and separated

Peaslake, Surrey   21 ft   M   1,000
Tree is due north of a house near Franksfield, Peaslake

Penalt, Gwent   24 ft   F   E   1,600

Pennant Melangell, Gwynedd   27 ft   M   E   2,000
                                  F   SE   1,200
More than one old yew on site

Penpergwm, Gwent   24 ft   M   W   1,800
Growing in outer church wall

Penpont, Brecon   26 ft   E
Church surrounded by circle of yews, now broken by main road; thirty-
eight trees left

Peperharrow, Surrey   27 ft   M   SE   1,500

Peterchurch, Hereford and Worcester	28 ft	F	W	1,700
Pilton, Somerset	18 ft 10 in	M	NE	
Plymtree, Devon	21 ft			1,100
Portbury, Somerset	17 ft	M	SW	1,400

Internal stem; more than one old yew on site

Priors Dean, Hampshire				25 ft	F
Priston, Somerset	20 ft	M	SW	1,000	

21 ft girth in 1790 (Collinson, *History of Somerset*)

Puddlestown, Hereford and
   Worcester
'A fine old yew near porch' (*King's England*, 1938)

Purton St Mary's Wiltshire	15 ft	F	S	1,000

Outside south porch; very hollow and decrepit

Ratby, Leicestershire
'A venerable yew all gnarled and worn' (1937)

Ringwould, Kent	24 ft	M	N	1,300
	23 ft	M	NW	

More than one old yew on site

Rotherfield, Sussex	23 ft 8 in	F	E	1,600
Ruyton-XI-Towns, Shropshire	26 ft	F	SE	1,700

Broken

Rycote Manor, Oxfordshire	25 ft	M	SW	1,000

Said to have been brought from Garden of Gethsemane by returning crusader

St Brides Super Ely, Glamorgan	26 ft	M	E	1,600

Broken

St Dogmaels, Dyfed		F	S	1,000

Impossible to measure; cemented in

St Mary Bourne, Hampshire	20 ft 7 in	M	SW	
Sandford Orcas, Dorset	17 ft	F	S	
Sarnesfield, Hereford and Worcester	21 ft		S	
Seavington St Mary, Somerset	21 ft	F	S	1,000
Selborne, Hampshire	26 ft	M	SW	1,400

Came down in storm in January 1990; re-erected three weeks later

Sellindge, Kent	20 ft		S	1,200
Selling, Kent	26 ft		SW	1,400

More than one old yew on site; stump covered by ivy (1983)

Shenley, Hertfordshire	17 ft	F	S	1,000
Shirwell, Devon	24 ft	M	S	1,500

More than one old yew

Sidbury, Shropshire	22 ft	M	N	

Badgers' set beneath tree

Silverton, Devon	23 ft	M	S	1,300

More than one old yew on site

Slaugham, Sussex	24 ft	F	S	1,500
Snoddington Manor, Hampshire	26 ft	M		2,000

Internal stem; in a field

South Moreton, Oxfordshire	23 ft 2 in	F	E	1,600

Ancient burial mound nearby

Stanford Bishop, Hereford and Worcester	23 ft	M	NW	1,100

St Augustine's chair is in church

Stanmer, Sussex	21 ft	F	N	1,100
Internal stem				
Stanstead, Kent	28 ft	M	NW	
Staunton, Gloucestershire	31 ft	M	W	2,000 +
Staverton, Devon	24 ft	F	S	1,500
Stedham, Sussex	30 ft	M	W	2,000
Steep, Hampshire	23 ft	F	S	1,500
Stelling, Kent	24 ft		W	1,600
Stelling Minnis, Kent	25 ft 2 in	F	SSW	1,500
Steventon, Hampshire	23 ft	F	NW	1,000
Jane Austen worshipped at this church				
Steventon, Oxfordshire	22 ft 11 in	F	W	1,100
Stockbury, Kent	28 ft	F	W	
Stoke Gabriel, Devon	17 ft	F	NW	850
Ston Easton, Somerset	22 ft	M	SW	1,400
Stoodleigh, Devon	21 ft		S	1,000
Cemented in concrete which has restricted growth of tree				
Stopham, Sussex	25 ft	F	S	1,300
Stourton Caundle, Dorset	15 ft 6 in	M	W	
Stowting, Kent	20 ft	F	S	1,200
More than one old yew on site				
Strata Florida, Dyfed	22 ft	F	N	1,400
Daffyed ap Gwilym buried under the yew				
Stue an t-Iobart, Inverbeg	20 ft			
On the banks of Loch Lomond; Robert the Bruce's tree				

Sullington, Sussex	20 ft			
More than one old yew on site				
Sunninghill, Berkshire	18 ft		NW	1,100
Very hollow				
Sydling St Nicholas, Dorset	14 ft	M	N	1,000
Tandridge, Surrey	36 ft	F	W	2,500
Bees occupy a hollow in tree				
Tangley, Hampshire	19 ft	M	N	1,500
Previously measured 24 ft; three sarsen stones in churchyard				
Tangmere, Sussex	24 ft	F	S	1,500
Temple Farm, Wiltshire	30 ft			2,000
Not in churchyard				
Tettenhall, West Midlands	24 ft	M		
Thorley, Hertfordshire	20 ft	M	S	1,000
Burnt out; associated with witchcraft				
Thorpe Mandeville, Northamptonshire	20 ft 2 in	M	E	1,000
Oliver Cromwell is said to have cut bows from tree				
Three Cocks, Powys	18 ft 6 in		S	
Church fell into ruin; could have been Capel y Yewen				
Thurnham, Kent	24 ft		S	1,500
Tilmanstone, Kent	30 ft	F	SW	1,600
Badly damaged in 1987 storm				
Tisbury, Wiltshire	31 ft	M	N	4,000
Hollow and cemented in				
Titsey Place, Surrey	21			1,000
Church no longer occupies site				

Totteridge, Hertfordshire	26 ft	F	W	2,000
Tredunnock, Gwent	25 ft	F	S	
Tunstall, Kent	27 ft	M	NNE	

Almost destroyed by fire in 1989, caused by birds dropping burning straw

Ulcombe, Kent	35 ft	M	SW	
	26 ft	F	S	1,700
Ullingswick, Hereford and Worcester	21 ft		SW	1,200
Uppington, Shropshire	29 ft	F	SE	1,700

Roman altar found in churchyard

Walberton, Sussex	20 ft	M	NNE	1,000
Waldershare Park, Kent	30 ft	F	S	1,500
	25 ft 7 in	F	S	1,300
Walmer, Kent	22 ft 5 in	F	S	1,400
Warblington, Hampshire	26 ft	F	S	1,500

St Thomas à Becket's churchyard

Warburton, Lancashire	10 ft	M	NE	

Very hollow

Warlingham, Surrey	23 ft		S	1,200

More than one old yew

Waverley Abbey, Surrey	21 ft	F	E	1,000
West Kingsdown, Kent	25 ft 4 in	M	W	1,500
West Liss, Hampshire	18 ft 1 in	M	N	1,000
West Monkton, Somerset	20 ft	F	S	1,500

24 ft in 1970

West Tisted, Hampshire	20 ft	M	S	1,300

Internal stem

Westbury Sub Mendip, Somerset	26 ft		SE	

Whatley, Somerset   1,000
Yew grove of about 100 trees; pollarded to 3 ft from ground about 600 years ago; threatened by nearby quarrying

White Waltham, Berkshire	26 ft	F	NE	1,600

Whittington, Hereford and   15 ft   F   N
   Worcester
Hollow, was once much bigger; impossible to estimate age

Whitton, Powys	27 ft	M	SW	1,400
Wilmington, Sussex	30 ft	F	N	1,500
Winscombe, Somerset	21 ft	M		1,000

Not in churchyard

Wintershall, Surrey	29 ft	F		2,000

On edge of wood; cut down hundreds of years ago, but sprung up again; a boundary tree

Wivelsfield, Sussex	16 ft	F	N	

Hollow and ancient

Woldingham, Surrey	21 ft	F	S	1,200
Woodcott, Hampshire	27 ft	M	W	1,700
Woolland, Dorset	32 ft	F	S	2,000

Wychbury Hill, West Midlands   1,500
Several trees on site of ancient hill fort

Yarkhill, Hereford and Worcester	19 ft	F	SE	1,000
Yazor, Hereford and Worcester	29 ft		W	1,800

Yew near ruined church

Yewdale, Westmorland
More than one old yew; one tree 26 ft in girth in 1870

Ysbyty Ifan, Clwyd   F

A strange site; three hollow yews growing very close together with a combined girth of 50 ft

Ystrad Fellte, Powys	23 ft	NW	1,200

Possible pagan origins; caves nearby; more than one old yew

Ystradgynlais, Brecon	24 ft	F	SE	1,600
Zeal Monachorum, Devon	18 ft		S	1,200

Lost yews

Ancient yews once existed, mostly until very recently, on the following sites.

Asthall Leigh, Oxfordshire	19 ft	Cut down in 1985
Bignor, Sussex	20 ft	Cut down in 1982
Bishopston, Gower	20 ft	Removed recently
Bolton Abbey, Yorkshire		Removed in nineteenth century
Bowdon, Cheshire		
Brabourne, Kent	57 ft	
Bucklebury, Berkshire	27 ft	Removed around 1954
Chilham, Kent	30 ft	Cut down pre-1790
Condover, Shropshire		
Dibden, Hampshire	30 ft	Cut down in nineteenth century after storm damage
Durfield, Derbyshire		Cut down after storm damage
East Lavant, Sussex	28 ft	Cut down in 1982
Fountains Abbey, Yorkshire	26 ft	Removed in 1975
Gartheli, Dyfed		Cut down in 1985
Goytre, Gwent	21 ft	Cut down in 1973
Goudhurst, Kent	27 ft	
Hampstead Marshall, Berkshire		

Llanafan, Dyfed		Cut down in 1970
Llandderfel, Gwynedd		Cut down in 1993
Llandewi Fach, Gwent	30 ft	Cut down and burnt in 1975
Llanfarnain, Gwent		
Llanfihangel Abercywyn, Dyfed		Cut down near restored church in 1980
Llanhamlach, Brecon		Many cut down in 1985
Llanhilleth, Gwent		
Llanwrin, Powys	28 ft	Cut down in 1984
Manest Court Farm, St Illtyd, Brecon		Removed around 1830
Marden, Herefordshire	30 ft	
Mathern, Gwent		
Old Colwyn, Clwyd		
Penpont, Brecon	24 ft	Cut down in 1970
Rhdderch, Gwent		
Rhulen, Powys		Partially blown down; cut up in 1987
Sedbery, Yorkshire		Two very large trees gone
Stanford Bishop, Herefordshire	30 ft	Cut down around 1880
Stone, Kent	28 ft	Removed in 1980
Tankersley Park, Yorkshire		
Taplow Court, Buckinghamshire	21 ft	Removed during excavations in 1880s
Wilcrick, Gwent		
Wormelow Tump, Herefordshire		Was on the tump

Notes and References

1 The Tree of Life

1 Cornish, V., *The Churchyard Yew and Immortality*, London, Muller, 1946.
2 Pope, A., *Selected Prose*, ed. P. Hammond, Cambridge, Cambridge University Press, 1987.

3 Regeneration

1 Morton, A., *The Trees of Shropshire*, Shrewsbury, Airlife, 1986.

4 'The life of a yew, the length of an age'

1 Lowe, J., *The Yew-Trees of Great Britain and Ireland*, London, Macmillan, 1897, p. 49.
2 Mitchell, A., in *The Field*, August 1991.
3 Lowe, op. cit., p. 81.
4 Rackham, O., *The History of the Countryside*, London, Dent, 1990.
5 Allcroft, H., *The Circle and the Cross*, 1927.
6 Mee, A., *The King's England*, rev. E.T. Long, London, Hodder & Stoughton, 1968.

5 Why are yews in churchyards?

1 Chandler, J., 'Old men's fancies: the case of the churchyard yew', *Newsletter of the Folklore Society*, 15, July 1992.

2 Collected in British Library, 11645g 53.

3 Pliny, *Natural History*, Book 13, ch. 4.

4 Graves, R., *The White Goddess*, Faber, 1961, p. 412.

5 Bryant, J., *A New System or an Analysis of Ancient Mythology*, London, 1774, vol. 1, pp. 319–29.

6 Puhvel, J., *Hittite Etymological Dictionary*, Publishers (Berlin, New York and Amsterdam, Mouton), 1984.

7 Bates, B., in the *Sunday Times*, 20.12.92.

8 Lowe, op. cit., p. 149.

6 Hidden clues – the name of the yew

1 Rackham, op. cit.

2 Lowe, op. cit., p. 22.

3 *The Bloomsbury Dictionary of Place Names in the British Isles*, ed. A. Room, London, Bloomsbury, 1989.

4 Mills, A.D., *English Place Names*, Oxford, Oxford University Press, 1991.

5 Tittensor, R., 'Ecological history of yew *Taxus baccata l.*, in southern England', *Biological Conservation*, 1980.

6 Strutt, J. G., *Sylva Britannica*, 1822.

7 Watson, W. J., *Celtic Place Names of Scotland*, 1927, p. 89.

7 Ankerwyke

1 Lowe, op. cit.

2 Sheahen, J. J., *History and Topography of Buckinghamshire*, 1862, p. 876.

3 Quoted in Lowe, op. cit., p. 181.

4 Strutt, op. cit.

8 The World Tree

1 Turville-Petrie, *Myth and Religion of the North*, New York, Holt, Rinehart & Winston, 1964.

2 Long, B., *The Origins of Man and the Universe*, London, Routledge & Kegan Paul, 1984.

3 Eliade, M., *Shamanism*, London, Arkana, 1989.

4 Eliade, M., *Encyclopaedia of Religion*, vol. 13, London and New York, Macmillan, 1987, pp. 201–2.

5 Thorsson, E., *Futhark*, Maine, USA, Weiser, 1992.

6 Pennick, N., *Rune Magic*, London, Aquarian, 1992.

7 Sturluson, S., *The Prose Edda*, trans. A.G. Brodeur, New York, American Scandinavian Foundation, 1970.

8 *The Book: An Introduction to the Teachings of Osho*, Poona, India, Osho Commune, 1984, p. 498.

9 Jung, C.G., Foreword, *I Ching*, London, Routledge & Kegan Paul, 1973.

10 Quoted in Elliott, R., 'Runes, yews and magic', *Speculum*, 32, 1957.

9 The yew and the goddess

1 Renfrew, C., *Archaeology and Language – the Puzzle of Indo-European Origins*, London, Penguin, 1989.

2 Lowe, op. cit., p. 98.

3 Henslow, G., *The Plants of the Bible*, 1906, pp. 48–53.

4 For a fuller discussion of the role of the goddess in Jewish history, see Baring, A. and Cashford, J., *The Myth of the Goddess*, London, Viking, 1991, ch. 12.

5 Eliade, M., *Studies in Comparative Religions*, London and New York, 1958.

6 Quoted in Bennett, M.R., 'Legend of the green tree and the dry', *Archaeological Journal*, LXXXIII, 1926, p. 25.

10 The yew in Celtic tradition

1 Roses, A. *Pagan Celtic Britain*, London, Sphere, 1974.

2 Quoted in Rutherford, W., *The Druids*, London, Aquarian, 1978, p. 67.

3 Rutherford, op. cit.

4 Carr Gomm, P., *The Elements of the Druid Tradition*, Shaftesbury, Elements, 1991, p. 27.

5 Dames, M., *The Silbury Treasure*, London, Thames & Hudson, 1976, p. 58.

11 Groves and lone trees

1 Tittensor, op. cit.

2 *Wordsworth: The Poems*, vol. 1, London, Penguin 1977, p. 662.

3 Ashe, O., 1890

4 Lowe, op. cit., p. 187.

5 Ibid., p. 32.

6 Ibid., p. 238.

7 Tittensor, op. cit.

8 Blomfield, Sir R., *The Formal Garden in England*, London, Macmillan, 1892.

9 Marks, J., *The Hanchurch Yews*, North Staffs Field Club, 1934.

10 Quoted in Allardice, P., *Myths, Gods and Fantasy*, Prism Unity, 1990.

11 Watkins, A., *The Old Straight Track*, London, Methuen, 1925, pp. 61, 63.

12 Quoted in Ashe, G., *Mythology of the British Isles*, London Methuen, 1990.

12 Under the greenwood tree

1 Holt, J. C., *Robin Hoos*, London, Thames & Hudson, 1982.

2 Quoted ibid.

3 Wilks, J. H., *Trees of the British Isles in History and Legend*, London, Muller, 1972.

4 Anderson, W. and Hicks, C., *Green Man*, London HarperCollins, 1990, p. 29.

5 Quoted ibid., p. 18.

6 Mooney, B., *Bel Mooney's Somerset*, London, Weidenfeld & Nicolson, 1989, p. 31.

7 Green, M., *Dictionary of Celtic Myth and Legend*, London Thames & Hudson, 1992.

8 Graves, R., *The White Goddess*, London, Faber, 1961, p. 396.

9 Stephens, Prof., *Studies on Professor Bugge's 'On Northern Mythology'*, 1884.

10 Quoted in Holt, op. cit., p. 32.

11 Ibid.

13 *The sacred trees of Ireland*

1 Gerald of Wales, *The History and Topography of Ireland*, trans. J. O'Meara, London, Penguin, 1982; and *Historical Works of Gerald Cambrensis*, trans. Forester, 1891.

2 Lucas, A. T., 'The sacred trees of Ireland', *Journal of the Cork Historical and Archaeological Society*, LXVIII, 1963.

3 Dames, M., *Mythic Ireland*, London, Thames & Hudson, 1992.

4 MacCulloch, J. A., *The Religion of the Ancient Celts*, Edinburgh, T. & T. Clark, 1918.

5 *The Settling of the Manor of Tara*,' trans. Best, *Eriu*, 4, 1910.

14 *Yew medicine*

1 Lowe, op. cit., p. 145.

2 Hartzell, H., *The Yew Tree*, Oregon, USA, Hulogosi, 1991.

Select Bibliography

Allcroft, H., *The Circle and the Cross*, 1927.

Anderson, W. and Hicks, C., *Green Man*, London HarperCollins, 1990.

Ashe, G., Mythology of the British Isles, London, Methuen, 1990.

Aubrey, J., *History of Surrey*, 1673–1719.

Baring, A. and Cashford, J., *The Myth of the Goddess*, London, Arkana, 1993.

Bauschatz, P. C., *The Well and the Tree*, Amherst University of Massachusetts Press, 1902.

Cobbett, W., *Rural Rides*, London, Penguin, 1967.

Collingson, Revd J., *History and Antiquities of Somerset*, 1789–91.

Cook, R., *The Tree of Life*, London, Thames & Hudson, 1974.

Cornish, V., *The Churchyard Yew and Immortality*, London, Muller, 1946.

Dames, M., *The Silbury Treasure*, London, Thames & Hudson, 1976.

Eliade, M., *Shamanism*, London, Arkana, 1989.

Davidson, H. R. (Ellis), *Gods and Myths of Northern Europe*, London, Penguin, 1964.

Evans, J. D., *The Churchyard Yews of Gwent*, Pontypool, Archangel, 1980.

Evelyn, J., *Sylva – a Discourse on Trees*, 1664.

Gerald of Wales, *The History and Topography of Ireland*, trans. J. O'Meara, London, Penguin, 1982.

Graves, R., *The White Goddess*, London, Faber, 1961.

Hartzell, H., *The Yew Tree*, Oregon, USA, Hulogosi, 1991.

Hubert, H., *The Greatness and Decline of the Celts*, 1934.

Jones-Davies, Revd J., 'Yews in Brecon, unpublished papers, Brecknock Museum, Brecon.

Kendrick, T. D., *The Druids*, London, Methuen, 1927.

Long, B., *The Origins of Man and the Universe*, London Routledge & Kegan Paul, 1984.

Lowe, J., *The Yew-Trees of Great Britain and Ireland*, London, Macmillan, 1897.

Lucas, A. T., 'The sacred trees of Ireland', *Journal of the Cork Historical and Archaeological Society*, LXVIII, 1963.

MacCulloch, J. A., *The Religion of the Ancient Celts*, Edinburgh, T. & T. Clark, 1911.

Mee, A., *The King's England*, rev. E. T. Long, London, Hodder & Stoughton, 1968.

Mitchell, A., *The Complete Guide to Trees of Britain and Northern Europe*, London, Dragon's World, 1985.

Morgan, M. D., *The Mabin of the Mabinogion* and *The Light of Britainnia*, Research into Last Knowledge Organization, 1901 and 1902; Wellingborough, Thorsons, 1984.

Morris, R., *Churches in the Landscape*, London, Dent, 1989.

Morton, A., *The Trees of Shropshire*, Shrewsbury, Airlife, 1986.

Nash Williams, V. E., *Early Christian Monuments of Wales*, 1950.

Neihardt, J. G., *Black Elk Speaks*, Lincoln, Neb., and London, University of Nebraska Press, 1979.

Nichols, R., *The Book of Druidry*, London, Aquarian/Thorsons, 1990.

Pennick, N., *Rune Magic*, London, Aquarian, 1992.

Philpot, J. H., *The Sacred Tree*, London, Macmillan, 1897.

Rackham, O., *The History of the Countryside*, London, Dent, 1990.

Raglan, Lady, 'The Green Man in church architecture', *Folklore*, 50, 1, 1939.

Renfew, C., *Archaeology and Language*, London, Penguin, 1989.

Rock, Dr D., *Church of Our Fathers*, 1840.

Ross, A., *Pagan Celtic Britain*, London, Sphere, 1974.

Ross, A., *The Pagan Celts*, London Batsford, 1986.

Ruspoli, M., *Cave of Lascaux*, London, Thames & Hudson, 1987.

Rutherford, W., *The Druids*, London, Aquarian, 1978.

Stubbs, P., *The Anatomy of Abuses*, 1583.

Swanton, E. W., *The Yew Trees of England*, Farnham, Farnham Herald, 1958.

Thorsson, E., *Futhark*, Maine, USA, Weiser, 1982.

Vallencey, C., *Collectanea*, 1802.

Watkins, A., *The Old Straight Track*, London, Methuen, 1925.

SELECT BIBLIOGRAPHY

Watson, Prof. W. J., *Celtic Place Names of Scotland*, 1927.

White, G., *Natural History and Antiquities of Selborne*, 1789.

Wilks, J. H., *Trees of the British Isles in History and Legend*, London, Muller, 1972.

JOURNALS

Eriu (all volumes), *Gardener's Chronicle* (all volumes), *Gentleman's Magazine*.

Index

References to illustrations are in *italic* type.